POLICY ISSUES IN THE EARLY YEARS

The Critical Issues in the Early Years Series

This series provides both national (UK wide) and international perspectives on critical issues within the field of early years education and care.

The quality of early childhood education and care (ECEC) has remained a high priority on government agendas in recent years (OECD, 2006). This series reflects this developing early childhood context which includes professionalising, and up skilling, the early childhood workforce. In particular, the series brings a critical perspective to the developing knowledge and understanding of early years practitioners at various stages of their professional development, to encourage reflection on practice and to bring to their attention key themes and issues in field of early childhood.

Series Editor

Linda Miller is Professor Emeritus of Early Years at the Open University. Since 2005 Linda has been co-director of an international project the 'Day in the Life of an Early Years Practitioner' based within the European Early Childhood Research Association (EECERA). In 2010–11 she was a member of the Expert Advisory Group for an EU study on Competencies in ECE and was co-lead researcher for the England case study. She has been a member of government stakeholder reference groups and working parties concerned with workforce development in the Early Years. Linda has written and co-edited a wide range of books for early years practitioners, and has published in national and international journals.

Titles in the series

Miller and Cable, *Professionalization, Leadership and Management in the Early Years*
Miller and Hevey, *Policy Issues in the Early Years*
Miller and Pound, *Theories and Approaches to Learning in the Early Years*

Reference

Organisation for Economic Co-operation and Development (OECD) (2006) *Starting Strong II: Early Childhood Education and Care*. Paris: OECD.

POLICY ISSUES IN THE EARLY YEARS

Edited by Linda Miller and Denise Hevey

Los Angeles | London | New Delhi
Singapore | Washington DC

First published 2012

SAGE Publications Ltd
1 Oliver's Yard
55 City Road
London EC1Y 1SP

SAGE Publications Inc.
2455 Teller Road
Thousand Oaks, California 91320

SAGE Publications India Pvt Ltd
B 1/I 1 Mohan Cooperative Industrial Area
Mathura Road
New Delhi 110 044

SAGE Publications Asia-Pacific Pte Ltd
3 Church Street
#10–04 Samsung Hub
Singapore 049483

Library of Congress Control Number: 2011931090

British Library Cataloguing in Publication data

A catalogue record for this book is available from the British Library

ISBN 978-0-85702-962-1
ISBN 978-0-85702-963-8 (pbk)

Typeset by C&M Digitals (P) Ltd, Chennai, India
Printed in Great Britain by CPI Group (UK) Ltd, Croydon, CR0 4YY
Printed on paper from sustainable resources

Education at SAGE

SAGE is a leading international publisher of journals, books, and electronic media for academic, educational, and professional markets.

Our education publishing includes:

- accessible and comprehensive texts for aspiring education professionals and practitioners looking to further their careers through continuing professional development

- inspirational advice and guidance for the classroom

- authoritative state of the art reference from the leading authors in the field.

Find out more at: **www.sagepub.co.uk/education**

CONTENTS

ABOUT THE EDITORS AND CONTRIBUTORS

Editors

Linda Miller was Professor of Early Years at The Open University until 2008, when she became Emeritus Professor, Early Years. She has been involved in national consultations and working groups on the Children's Workforce Strategy at the DfES, National Children's Bureau and Teacher Development Agency. From 2003 to 2008, Linda was Chair of the Sector Endorsed Foundation Degrees in Early Years (SEFDEY) national network and is now an honorary life member. From 2010 to 2011, she was a member of the Expert Advisory Team for a European Commission study on the competence requirements of staff in Early Childhood Education and Care and co-author of the England case study. In 2011, she co-authored an expert report on early years teacher education in England for the University of Bremen, Germany. Linda has published widely in co-edited and single authored books and in national and international journals.

Denise Hevey joined the School of Education at The University of Northampton in November 2005 as their first Professor of Early Years. She had previously spent 18 years at the Open University where she produced the first training pack for childminders and courses such as *Working with Children and Young People*, before establishing the Vocational Qualifications Centre to promote vocational and professional training across the University. She joined Ofsted in 2001 as Head of Policy in the Early Years Directorate and two years later was seconded to the DfES. Her experience of public policy making includes the consultation and development of the Childcare Approval Scheme and the government response to the Bichard Inquiry, and subsequent policy and legislative changes related to the vetting and barring of those unsuitable to work with children. She now teaches on the BA (Hons) Early Childhood Studies and is Director of the Early Years Professional Status programme.

Contributors

Jane Barlow is Professor of Public Health in the Early Years at the University of Warwick. She is an international expert on the role of early parenting in the aetiology of mental health problems and in particular the evaluation of early interventions aimed at improving parenting practices during infancy. She is Director of the Warwick Infant and Family Wellbeing Unit, which provides training in innovative evidence-based methods of supporting parenting during pregnancy and the early years to a wide range of early years and primary care practitioners. She authored a highly acclaimed research review for Research in Practice on safeguarding (2010), and jointly authored a book (with Schrader-MacMillan) entitled *Safeguarding Children from Emotional Abuse* (DCSF, 2009).

Mary Crowley is President of the International Federation for Parenting Education, a worldwide organisation which promotes and supports education for parents around the parent–child relationship (www.fiep-ifpe.fr). She was first Chief Executive of Parenting UK, the UK national umbrella body. She led the development of the National Occupational Standards for Work with Parents which were approved for the UK in April 2005 and revised in 2010. In 2008, she was awarded the OBE for services to children and families.

Roger Downer is a professor, author, co-author/editor of five books and 164 scientific papers and has been awarded the honorary degrees of LL.D (Queens University Belfast) and D.Sc. (University of Waterloo). He has been elected to the Fellowship of the Royal Society of Canada and Membership of the Royal Irish Academy. He has held senior academic positions in Canada, Asia and Europe and, upon his retirement, was appointed President Emeritus of the University of Limerick, having served as President from 1998 to 2006. He serves on the boards of a number of corporate and not-for-profit organisations, including Chair of the Advisory Board of MEHRI.

Naomi Eisenstadt CB is currently a senior research fellow in the Department of Education, University of Oxford. Naomi's early career was in front-line delivery, working in nurseries and then establishing a Children's Centre in Milton Keynes. In 1999, Naomi joined the UK civil service to become director of the Sure Start Unit at the Department of Education. In this role, she had responsibility for all early years, childcare and family policy for the UK government. From 2006 to 2009, she was Director of the Social Exclusion Task Force in the Cabinet Office. She led the Families at Risk Review, which resulted in policy development on the relationship between adults' and children's services. In 2002, she was awarded an Honorary Doctorate from the Open University and in 2005 was made a Companion of the Bath (CB).

Eva Lloyd is Reader in Early Childhood at the Cass School of Education, University of East London, where she is co-director of the International Centre for the Study of the Mixed Economy of Childcare (ICMEC). She is a Visiting Fellow at Bristol University's School for Policy Studies, where she previously held a Senior Lectureship. Her research focuses on UK and international early childhood policies and child poverty strategies. As part of her career, she also spent 15 years working for children's NGOs.

Ulviyya Mikailova PhD is Executive Director of the Centre for Innovations in Education in Baku, Azerbaijan, which is a member of the International Step by Step Association (ISSA). Her experience in public service started in 1998 when she became the Step by Step Program Director at the Open Society Institute – Azerbaijan National Foundation. She has also taught courses on gender and politics and education policy at a leading national university in Azerbaijan. In 2006, she was awarded a Fulbright Scholarship Award and spent three months researching at the International and Comparative Education Department at Columbia University, New York. She is a member of the Azerbaijani National Society of Physiologists, and of the Child Protection Network in Azerbaijan. In 2002–2006, she was an ISSA Board Member, and in 2008–2011 was a member of the ISSA Program Committee.

Peter Moss is Professor of Early Childhood Provision at the Institute of Education, University of London. He is a coordinator of the international network on leave policies and research, and co-editor of the book series Contesting Early Childhood. His latest book is *Radical Education and the Common School: A Democratic Alternative*, written with Michael Fielding (Routledge, 2010).

Sue Owen PhD is currently Director of Practice Improvement at the National Children's Bureau and a member of the Senior Management Team; prior to that, she was Director of the Early Childhood Unit there. In the past, Sue has held a number of posts in the early childhood field, including Early Years Lead Officer for Humberside County Council, Information Officer for the National Childminding Association, Playgroup Adviser for Manchester City Council, and Deputy Director of the Early Years National Training Organisation. Sue's latest book is *Authentic Relationships in Group Care for Infants and Toddlers – RIE Principles into Practice* (co-edited with Stephanie Petrie, Jessica Kingsley, 2005). Her doctoral dissertation was on the development of professionalism in childminding.

Wendy Rose was a Senior Research Fellow at The Open University from 1999 until 2010. Previously, for 11 years she was a senior civil servant in England advising on children's policy. Recently, with Professor Jane Aldgate, she has been a professional adviser to the Scottish Government for five years on the development of its policy, *Getting it right for every child*. She works on national and international child welfare research and development projects, has published widely on policy and practice issues concerned with improving outcomes for children and families, and has been closely associated for many years with the voluntary organisation, Home-Start UK. She is currently contributing to the Welsh government's programme of child protection improvement and reform, including the development of a new approach to multi-agency learning and reviewing. She was awarded the OBE in 2009 for services to children and families.

Caroline Sharp BSc is an experienced researcher and research manager and is a Research Director at the National Foundation for Educational Research. Caroline has worked on a wide range of educational research projects, but has specialised in the early years and primary education. Her research into early childhood includes studies of children starting school, season of birth and transition from the Foundation Stage to Key Stage 1. She is currently directing a study of Children's Centres targeting services for the most needy families. Caroline was Reviews Coordinator for the Early Years theme at the Centre for Excellence and Outcomes (C4EO).

Stuart Shanker is Research Professor of Philosophy and Psychology at York University and Director of the Milton and Ethel Harris Research Initiative at York University, Canada. Among his awards are the Walter L. Gordon Fellowship at York University and his research grants include, most recently, a $7,000,000 grant from the Harris Steel Foundation to establish MEHRI, a state-of-the-art cognitive and social neuroscience centre. Dr Shanker is Director of EPIC: an international initiative created to promote the educational potential in children by enhancing their self-regulation. Over the past decade, he has served as Director of the Council of Human Development and Director of the Canada–Cuba Research Alliance; he was the first President of the Council of Early Child Development in Canada. He has served as an advisor on early child development to government organisations across Canada and the USA and countries around the world. Recent publications include *Human Development in the Twenty-first Century* (co-edited with Alan Fogel and Barbara King, Cambridge University Press, 2008).

Gerda Sula is the Executive Director of Qendra Hap pas Hapi (the Step by Step Center) in Tirana, Albania, a member of the International Step by Step Association (ISSA). Her main interest is in applying child-centered philosophy in Albania's traditional teaching environment in early childhood. She is involved as a lecturer in teacher preparation programmes at the Faculty of Social Sciences, University of Tirana. Gerda has served as a consultant for several government and international organisations, including UNICEF Kosovo, UNICEF Albania, the World Bank, the Ministry of Education and Sciences in Albania and Plan International. She has published articles in national and international professional journals and is editor-in-chief of *Femija ne Qender*. She has been involved in training at local, national, regional and international levels and has presented at national and international conferences. She has served as a member of national and international organisations, committees and scientific conferences.

Jenny Spratt is Head of Early Years Foundation Stage (EYFS) and Children's Centre Services in an English Local Authority where she has led the Early Years and Childcare Strategy since 1998. She has a background in Early Childhood Education and was head teacher of a nursery school for nine years. Jenny represents the Local Authority Early Years Network on the Early Childhood Forum, which is co-ordinated through the National Children's Bureau, and is an early years sector specialist for the Centre for Excellence and Outcomes (C4EO). She co-authored *Essentials of Literacy from 0–7* with Tina Bruce (Sage, 2011).

Lesley Staggs has worked as an early childhood consultant since 2006, acting as strategic adviser to a number of local authorities. She is an external examiner at two higher education institutions, trustee for a national early years charity and vice chair of the Board of the Learning Trust, which runs education in Hackney. Lesley has worked in early years education as a teacher, head teacher and early years inspector. She led the work on developing the Early Learning Goals and Curriculum Guidance for the Foundation Stage in England, was a senior adviser within the DfES and the first National Director for the Foundation Stage.

Dawn Tankersley has worked as a Program Specialist for the International Step by Step Association (ISSA) and the Open Society Institute since 1999. She has worked on several international Roma early childhood education initiatives as the lead pedagogical expert and has been the lead author of those ISSA publications connected with ISSA's Principles of Quality Pedagogy. In addition, she is the author of ISSA's *Educating for Diversity: Education for Social Justice Activities for Children* programme and *Teacher Guidebook, Speaking for Diversity: Effective Teaching and Learning of Minority-Language Children in Pre-school* and *Opening Magic Doors: Reading and Learning Together with Children* (2009).

Angela Underdown PhD is an Associate Professor of Public Health in Early Years at the University of Warwick Medical School. She is also deputy director of the Warwick Infant and Family Wellbeing Unit (WIFWU) which brings together expertise with the goal of providing research, training and innovation in effective evidence-based ways of supporting parenting during pregnancy and the first two years of life. Angela's research interests are in the effectiveness of early interventions to promote infant and family well-being. She is particularly interested in the evaluation of interventions that are directed at promoting early infant–parent relationships. She has evaluated the processes and effects of infant massage and is currently exploring community support for parents with infants born pre-term. Angela teaches on a wide range of post-graduate courses aimed at promoting healthy development within early relationships.

CHAPTER 1

CRITICAL PERSPECTIVES ON EARLY YEARS POLICY

Linda Miller and Denise Hevey

Overview

The aim of this book is to explore early years policy and the ways in which policy is formulated and in turn impacts on services, practitioners and their practice, from predominantly an England perspective but informed, where relevant, by wider international perspectives. In this, the first chapter, we describe the structure and rationale of the book and we signal some of the key themes and issues that are developed in the ensuing chapters.

We begin by considering what policy is and why it should matter to early years practitioners. We then introduce the four parts of the book which link to key overarching themes: Part 1: Poverty and social disadvantage; Part 2: The evidence

(Continued)

(Continued)

base for early intervention; Part 3: Marketisation and democracy; and Part 4: Frameworks, regulations and guidelines. Some chapters give an account of how policy is conceived, developed and implemented; others review the evidence base for current policy directions and initiatives. Some chapters are written by academics and researchers and others by those directly involved in policy development and implementation.

In this book, and in all the books in this series, we use the terms early years and early childhood education and care (ECEC) interchangeably. 'Early years' is a term more commonly used in the United Kingdom (UK) to reflect the bringing together of both care and education under one policy umbrella. However, both terms embrace the view that it is impossible to educate without caring, nor care without developing and promoting children's learning (Owen and Haynes, 2008). We also use the term *she* when referring to individuals to reflect the feminised nature of the early years workforce.

What is policy and why does it matter?

The study of early childhood is quintessentially multi- and inter-disciplinary, because young children's lives and experience can't easily be partitioned into health, education and care; therefore, any study of early years policy will contain elements of health, education and social care/social welfare policy, which themselves have different traditions and exponents and have been linked historically with different departmental responsibilities at national government level in the UK.

National policy often seems remote to early years practitioners and other professionals working directly with children and families; it is not always recognised as affecting our services and lives. At most, it provides a framework that we are required to work within and is often considered uncontestable because both the public and practitioners feel powerless to challenge. Policy initiatives are increasingly supported by guidelines and training through which ideas are communicated and legitimized as the best way forward. In this book, we take the view that it is essential for all practitioners and others committed to early years services to achieve not just an awareness of policy and its implications for practice, but what Simpson and Connor have termed 'policy literacy': 'Policy literacy aims to make recipients and practitioners of social welfare more critical and discriminating readers, performers and producers of policies' (2011: 2).

They describe three phases in the achievement of policy literacy:

1   Understanding policies and their impact on the lives of children and families.

2   Learning to analyse and question the basis, construction and coverage of policies, including what is missed out.

3 Exploring underlying issues and principles behind policy formation, including: whose interests a particular policy ultimately serves? Whose viewpoints are represented (or ignored)? What are the alternatives? And, how can existing policy be challenged?

Through consideration of the development and implementation of recent policies across the education, health and social care/social welfare spectrum, in England and elsewhere, this book attempts to lead readers through phase 1 and phase 2 above and to start to raise some of the questions that constitute phase 3. In other words, it highlights the relevance of policy and policy making to all those involved with early years and supports the trajectory of thinking from the personal to the political.

Part 1: Poverty and social disadvantage

A key aim of most governments is to reduce and preferably eliminate poverty and social disadvantage in young children and to ensure their well-being. In 1997–2010, under the Labour government in the UK, early years became the target of widespread reform aimed at supporting families in combining work and caring responsibilities and thus addressing the high level of child poverty (OECD, 2011). Before the current financial crisis, child poverty fell in the UK more than in any other OECD country but this is now predicted to increase because of cuts to, for example, child and family benefits – regardless of the fact that the OECD (2011) report *Doing Better for Families* argues for social spending as a long-term solution to poverty issues. In Chapter 2, Naomi Eisenstadt describes the policy background in Britain and explores the challenges of establishing a new model of service provision for young children and families, aimed at reducing child poverty through 'progressive universalism'; that is, designing public services to ensure maximum support for the most disadvantaged, while avoiding stigma and ensuring a minimum service base for all. Sure Start was targeted at poor areas in the UK and aimed to ameliorate the negative impact of living in poverty for very young children and their families. Eisenstadt discusses the origins and development of the programme as grounded in local communities and designed to respond to local needs. The chapter considers the lessons learned as Sure Start moved towards a more standardised universal model based on Children's Centres and considers implications for future policy.

Sue Owen, Caroline Sharp and Jenny Spratt continue the theme of universal versus targeted provision in Chapter 3, when they focus on policies and practice change aimed at: (a) improving developmental outcomes for all young children entering school; and (b) narrowing the gap between the poorest, most disadvantaged children and the rest (see also Chapter 10). Through an illustrative case study, they explore the issues and problems which can arise when policy objectives such as these appear in practice to be difficult to achieve simultaneously. They argue for specific, targeted interventions, within a universal framework, in order to address the challenge of narrowing the gap of disadvantage.

Part 2: The evidence base for early intervention

The chapters in this section contribute to our understanding of the evidence that can be used to support and justify early years policies and practice initiatives, particularly by exploring the more scientific/medical aspects around brain development and psycho-physiological regulation with which many early years practitioners are less familiar. This evidence complements and adds to the now considerable weight of evidence to emerge from a series of important reviews commissioned by successive governments and undertaken in England between February 2010 and May 2011. These include: Frank Field's (November 2010) review of poverty and life chances, *The Foundation Years: Preventing Poor Children Becoming Poor Adults*; Graham Allen's (2011) review *Early Intervention: The Next Steps*; Michael Marmot's review of health inequalities, *Fair Society, Healthy Lives*, originally published in February 2010 and updated on its anniversary in 2011; Dame Claire Tickell's review of the Early Years Foundation Stage framework, *The Early Years: Foundations for Life, Health and Learning* (March 2011); *The Munro Review of Child Protection Report: A Child-centred System* (May 2011). All of these reviews have emphasised the critical importance of the early years for development and well-being throughout the life span and called for greater investment in early years services and better training of personnel. At the time of writing, the government has yet to publish a definitive response to all of the above. A revised Workforce Strategy for the early years sector is also anticipated in order to meet the challenges of implementing any recommendations arising from the reviews.

The main purpose of such reviews has been to create the evidence base on which future government policy can be formulated. This follows on from a decade or more in which 'evidence-based practice' has been espoused for the development of professional areas such as nursing, teaching and social work. Adopting an evidence-based approach implies that policy making is a rational process of evaluating the evidence and applying that knowledge to formulate policy within budgetary constraints. However, as we shall see through this book, fundamentally policy making is as much about values, moral and political judgements as it is about evidence. Core values and political ideologies underpin the direction of travel in policy because they determine the end point in terms of what sort of society we want to live in, what sort of childhood we want for our children and what sort of people we want those children to become.

Angela Underdown and Jane Barlow in Chapter 4 argue that evidence from brain research and observational data demonstrates the particular importance of the first and second years of life, in terms of infants' brain development and emotional attachments as the foundation for good developmental outcomes and later mental health. They make a strong case for intervening at the earliest stages of life through a partnership approach to working with parents, as enshrined in the Healthy Child Programme (HCP). Based on a model of progressive universalism (see above), the HCP promotes services that begin during pregnancy through to the first year of life to help parents to provide sensitive, responsive parenting and so to promote brain growth and strong, positive attachments. They conclude that early years practitioners have a key role in promoting infant mental health, by working alongside other practitioners in the delivery of the HCP.

Evidence, evaluated rigorously and applied rationally, is rarely the sole basis on which policy choices are made. However, in Chapter 5, Stuart Shanker and Roger Downer describe the origins and impact of the Enhancing Potential In Children (EPIC) project – a research-based programme investigating the neurobiological and social basis of children's ability to 'self-regulate' – that may prove to be an exception. They identify the challenge of applying lessons learned from the laboratory into clinical practice and later up-scaling into workable curricula and environments for early years settings, while at the same time working to persuade policy makers of their value. In translating the scientific evidence into policy and practice, they describe the policy response in one state of Canada (Ontario) that in April 2010 agreed to start rolling out pre-school programmes based on EPIC principles, in order to increase the ability of children to achieve their full educational potential.

In Chapter 6, Mary Crowley returns to the theme of working in partnership with parents where she documents the gradual expansion of services and support for parents in England from the early 1990s until 2010, and the evidence base to support these developments. She discusses the important role of Parenting UK in developing training for work with parents, leading to the development of National Occupational Standards in this area. She notes the accumulating evidence for, and growth in awareness of, the importance of supporting parents amongst policy makers, including, increasingly, recognition of the role of fathers. The variety and scope of new services for parents have developed significantly over the last decade or so. However, not all parents are aware that support and help may be available. Crowley argues for investment in raising awareness and in training those who deliver parent support.

Part 3: Marketisation and democracy

National, international and global forces demand a well-qualified workforce with appropriate remuneration and working conditions, universal access to early childhood education and care, and substantial public investment in services and infrastructure (OECD, 2006). However, as Dahlberg and Moss (2005) discuss, global forces and international organisations may offer a blueprint of how things might be, but how institutions and services are conceptualised and viewed and how policy is determined remain the business of nation states. Such decisions will incorporate a notion of how societies should be and how children are viewed and valued. Dahlberg and Moss (2005) (and Moss in Chapter 7) offer the Swedish pre-school system as an example of pre-school education viewed as a public good and where a national pre-school curriculum makes a clear commitment to democracy as a fundamental value. In contrast, some economies, including England, have developed a trend towards a 'market' in early childhood provision which critics such as Woodrow (2011) believe leads to economics, rather than factors such as learning and well-being, being the driving factors for investing in early years services. Within this approach to early childhood provision and services, education is seen as a commodity, with practitioners accountable for effective delivery.

Peter Moss in Chapter 7 argues for democracy as a fundamental value in early childhood education and care (ECEC) and makes a case for alternative discourses to those of the market place. He argues for more ethical and democratic practices and considers the possibility of democracy as a fundamental value in early childhood centres. He considers what democracy might mean in the early childhood centre and offers examples of how it might be practised by adults and children alike. He considers factors and conditions that might either stifle democracy or enable democratic practice to flourish in early childhood education (ECE).

In Chapter 8, Eva Lloyd considers the marketisation of early childhood services and provision. She explains that different models of state support for early years education and childcare provision are employed across Europe and globally, but that most early years systems include a mix of both private (for-profit and not-for-profit) and publicly funded provision, often referred to as a mixed economy of childcare or the childcare market. In her chapter, she explores the rationale for, and the problems associated with, adopting a market-based approach. She focuses primarily on childcare market policy developments in England but also reviews national and international evidence of the impact of such an approach.

As Dahlberg and Moss (2005) note, institutionalisation of childhood can be a force for good, but it is imperative that practitioners are informed and vigilant and can maintain a critical stance in relation to both policy and practice (2005: vi). The role that professional development can play in enabling practitioners to become critical and aware is clearly articulated in Chapter 9. In this chapter, Dawn Tankersley, Gerda Sula and Ulviyya Mikailova tell the fascinating story of the work of the International Step by Step Association (ISSA) and its member Non-Governmental Organisations (NGOs). They describe the role these organisations have played in working together to introduce a new paradigm of democratisation in the form of a child-centered approach to early childhood education, through professional training in the former communist bloc region. They describe how ISSA has brought new values and principles into the ECEC sector in the region and discuss how this work has positively influenced the behaviours and practice of many practitioners and contributed to the growth of democratic approaches in the wider society.

Part 4: Frameworks, regulations and guidelines

Policy frameworks, regulations and guidelines can be both enabling and restrictive as we see in Chapters 10 and 11. They can empower children and families and those who work with them and ensure their entitlement to services and provision, but can also, as we note above, be a means of legitimising questionable policy initiatives as being for the common good. As we discuss above, the period in which the Labour government was in power was a period of considerable policy change for early years in

England, which included the centralisation of regulation and inspection under Ofsted with national standards for early years provision, development of new professional roles and statuses (DfES, 2006), new qualification frameworks (CWDC, 2010) and new curriculum initiatives (DCSF, 2008).

Increased public investment requires greater accountability and brings with it greater monitoring and regulation of both people and public services which, it has been argued, reduces the professional autonomy of those working in the early years (see Miller and Cable, 2011 for critiques). In such a policy context, there is a danger that both practitioners' daily practice and children's progress and well-being are only measured and valued as 'outcomes' against externally prescribed standards and benchmarks to ensure that services are worth the investment.

In Chapter 10, Lesley Staggs returns to the theme of Chapter 2, of a universal framework for young children, but takes a different perspective. Drawing upon her personal and professional experience of policy development and implementation, she documents the trend towards a national and centralised form of curriculum and assessment strategy for young children in England, and describes how external and competing policies influenced its development and implementation. In particular, she notes the lack of government appetite for taking a long-term view of policy in favour of quick results.

Differences in curricular approaches stem from different conceptions of children and childhood, and as Bennett (2001) argues, developing and implementing curricula for young children involves making important decisions and choices about what and how they learn. The national education and assessment strategies Staggs describes, encompassing key learning areas, learning goals and a sequential approach to achievement, have been criticised as the 'schoolification' of early childhood with an over-emphasis on 'academic' provision for young children (OECD, 2006: 62), and for encouraging practitioners to focus on 'strategic compliance' with national requirements rather than playful learning (Goouch, 2008: 93).

Safeguarding is the theme of Chapter 11, where Wendy Rose explores the development and implementation of a policy framework as a mechanism for bringing about change in Scotland. She discusses part of a national programme which aims to improve outcomes for all children and young people and which emphasises the need for a deep change in culture, systems and practice rather than 'bolt-on' policies and superficial consultations, through a whole system change. She introduces the notion of 'proportionate universalism' as a means of reducing disadvantage in children's lives and the need for a unified and coordinated approach to intervention through multi-agency services and universal services to deliver prevention and early intervention.

Final thoughts

In this chapter, we have argued that policy matters for those who work with young children and families, and have introduced chapters from a range of perspectives that illustrate this point. However, we argue that to be aware of policy agendas and developments is not enough. Practitioners need to develop their skills of analysis and critical evaluation, to question the link between evidence and the dominant discourse, and to consider and reflect on the values and assumptions on which each policy is based.

Summary

In this chapter, we have:

- introduced the four overarching themes which frame the chapters in this book: poverty and social disadvantage; the evidence base for early intervention; marketisation and democracy; and frameworks, regulations and guidelines
- encouraged you to begin to think about how and why policy matters in the early years
- introduced the notion of 'policy literacy' as a means of enabling practitioners working with young children and families to become more critical and reflective in relation to policies and related practices.

 Questions for discussion

1 Can you think of a recent policy change that has impacted on you or your practice? Can you say how and why?
2 Why is it important for education, health and social welfare/care professionals to work together?
3 What do you think are the benefits of a common framework encompassing skills, knowledge and competence for those working in early years services? *(Higher-level question)*

Further reading

Levels 5 and 6

Baldock, P., Fitzgerald, D. and Kay, J. (2009) *Understanding Early Years Policy*, 2nd edition. London: Sage.
The authors provide an accessible introduction to early years policy and explore how policy is made, implemented and developed.

Frost, N. and Parton, N. (2009) *Understanding Children's Social Care: Politics, Policy and Practice*. London: Sage.

This book describes and analyses the nature of social care in the UK, including its location in an historical and political context, an analysis of key areas of children's social care and an overview of social care in England at the time of writing.

Levels 6 and 7

Jones, P. and Walker, G. (eds) (2011) *Children's Rights in Practice*. London: Sage.
In this book, conventions and legislation relating to children's rights and their implications from a range of professional perspectives are explored. The chapters include implications for child-centred policy, services and practice across education, health and health promotion, safeguarding and social care and a specific chapter on early years.

Miller, L. (2008) Developing professionalism within a regulatory framework in England: challenges and possibilities. *European Early Childhood Education Research Journal*, 16(2): 255–68.
This article provides a critical review of policy developments leading to the creation of a new workforce role in England, the Early Years Professional, within the context of externally prescribed standards and regulatory frameworks.

Pugh, G. and Duffy, B. (eds) (2010) *Contemporary Issues in the Early Years*, 5th edition. London: Sage.
The fifth edition of this book offers wide-ranging coverage of early years issues including a focus on health issues, multi-agency working, policy, research and practice.

Websites

www.cwdcouncil.org.uk
This website provides information, links to policy initiatives, publications and reports relating to early years workforce reform.

www.oecd.org
The stated mission of the Organisation for Economic Cooperation and Development (OECD) is to promote policies that will improve the economic and social well-being of people around the world.
    The OECD website for the Directorate for Employment, Labour and Social Affairs (www. oecd.org/department/0,3355,en_2649_34819_1_1_1_1_1,00.html) provides information, reports and publications relating to family policies in OECD countries.

References

Allen, G. (2011) *Early Intervention: The Next Steps*. Available at: www.dwp.gov.uk/docs/early-intervention-next-steps.pdf (accessed 30 May 2011).
Bennett, J. (2001) Goals and curricula in early childhood. In: S. Kamerman (ed.) *Early Childhood Education and Care: International Perspectives*. Columbia, OH: The Institute for Child and Family Policy at Columbia University.
Children's Workforce Development Council (CWDC) (2010) *Refreshing the Common Core of Skills and Knowledge for the Children's Workforce*. Leeds: CWDC.
Dahlberg, G. and Moss, P. (2005) *Ethics and Politics in Early Childhood Education*. Abingdon: Routledge and Falmer.

Department for Children, Schools and Families (DCSF) (2008) *Statutory Framework for the Early Years Foundation Stage*. Nottingham: DCSF Publications.

Department for Education and Skills (DfES) (2006) *Children's Workforce Strategy: Building a World-class Workforce for Children and Young People.* Nottingham: DfES Publications.

Field, F. (2010) *The Foundation Years: Preventing Poor Children Becoming Poor Adults*. Available at: http://webarchive.nationalarchives.gov.uk/20110120090128/; http://povertyreview.independent.gov.uk/news/101203-review-poverty-life-chances.aspx (accessed 30 May 2011).

Goouch, K. (2008) Understanding playful pedagogies, play narratives and play spaces. *Early Years: An International Journal of Research and Development*, 28(1): 93–102.

Marmot, M. (2011) *Fair Society, Healthy Lives*. Available at: www.marmotreview.org (accessed 25 May 2011).

Miller, L. and Cable, C. (eds) (2011) *Professionalization, Leadership and Management in the Early Years*. London: Sage.

Munro, E. (2011) *The Munro Review of Child Protection Report: A Child-centred System*. Available at: www.education.gov.uk/munroreview/downloads/8875_DfE_Munro_Report_TAGGED.pdf (accessed 30 May 2011).

Organisation for Economic Cooperation and Development (OECD) (2006) *Starting Strong II: Early Childhood Education and Care*. Paris: OECD.

Organisation for Economic Cooperation and Development OECD (2011) *Doing Better for Families*. Available at: www.oecd.org/document/49/0,3746,en_2649_34819_47654961_1_1_1_1,00.html (accessed 30 May 2011).

Owen, S. and Haynes, P. (2008) Developing professionalism in the early years: from policy to practice. In: L. Miller and C. Cable (eds) *Professionalism in the Leadership Early Years*. London: Hodder Education.

Simpson, G. and Connor, S. (2011) *Social Policy for Social Welfare Professionals: Tools for Understanding, Analysis and Engagement.* Bristol: The Policy Press.

Tickell, C. (2011) *The Early Years: Foundations for Life, Health and Learning*. Available at: http://media.education.gov.uk/MediaFiles/B/1/5/%7BB15EFF0D-A4DF-4294-93A1-1E1B88C13F68%7DTickell%20review.pdf (accessed 30 May 2011).

Woodrow, C. (2011) Challenging identities: a case for leadership. In: L. Miller and C. Cable (eds) *Professionalization, Leadership and Management in the Early Years*. London: Sage.

PART 1

POVERTY AND SOCIAL DISADVANTAGE

CHAPTER 2

POVERTY, SOCIAL DISADVANTAGE AND YOUNG CHILDREN

Naomi Eisenstadt

Overview

This chapter provides a brief overview of the policy context in Britain in 1997 that led to the development of a range of early years services, including Sure Start, the programme aimed specifically at poor children under the age of 4. It describes the initial design of Sure Start and how the programme evolved over 10 years from the early ambition of establishing 250 local Sure Start programmes, to a comprehensive service across England of 3500 Sure Start Children's Centres. It also provides detail of the evaluation of Sure Start, and how the results from the evaluation, as well as other United Kingdom (UK) studies, influenced the development from local programmes to children's centres. Finally, the chapter explores the key lessons from Sure Start about the challenges of establishing a new model of service provision for young children and families.

The policy context: New Labour, poverty and young children

Before 1997, early years' provision in Britain was very patchy. The delivery of early education was left to local authorities to decide, with some areas investing in considerable levels of provision, and others with barely any nursery schools or classes at all. Childcare for working parents was also variable both in availability and quality. Indeed, by 1997, there was still considerable debate on whether mothers with children should work before their children were in full-time education. The Labour Manifesto for the 1997 election had two key commitments on early years: the promise of a National Childcare Strategy to increase the quantity and accessibility of childcare for working mothers and the promise of universal free nursery education for all 4-year-olds, with a further commitment to extend the free offer to 3-year-olds before the next election (Labour Party, 1997).

Furthermore, when the Labour government came to power in 1997, Britain had some of the highest levels of child poverty in Europe (Stewart, 2009). The British measure of poverty has traditionally been a relative measure. Poverty is not measured by absolute income of a family, but by income in comparison with other families in the UK. A family is considered poor if its income is below 60 per cent of the median income of similar-sized families in the UK. As the country becomes more prosperous, the median income goes up; hence the actual income that defines the poverty level goes up. The importance of this relative measure is that it assumes a commitment to sharing increasing prosperity across the income spectrum. What had been happening during the 1990s was an increase in income at the very top of the spectrum with very little change at the bottom; hence child poverty levels were increasing. Unemployment was found to be a key factor in poverty, so a government wanting to address child poverty needed to help workless families into jobs, while at the same time developing services that would mitigate the impact of poverty during childhood (Waldfogel, 2010).

Not long after the election, a third strand in the policy debate about what should be provided for under-5s began to emerge. While the main anti-poverty agenda of the New Labour government was through welfare to work policies, and particularly getting lone mothers into work, the Treasury became increasingly interested in a more community-based response to child poverty. In 1998, the Chancellor, Gordon Brown, asked Tessa Jowell, then the Minister for Public Health, to chair a review of services for children under 8. The review was one of several cross-cutting reviews, that is reviews that examined spending and activity by several departments concerning one issue, in this case services for young children. There were also cross-cutting reviews on youth crime and illegal drugs. The *Comprehensive Spending Review: Cross Departmental Review on Provision for Young Children* (HM Treasury, 1998) looked at three key issues: what services for young children looked like in England in 1998, the impact of poverty on young children, and what kinds of services seemed to deliver the best outcomes for young children. The results of the review would change the landscape of early years' services in England for many years to come.

First, the review found that several different government departments were funding services for young children, but there was no overall strategy or clear aims across government. Most of the funding went on services for children over 5, that is, school-aged children. The only universal provision for under-5s was delivered through health: midwifery and health visiting. Nursery education and childcare was delivered by local authorities, the voluntary sector or the private sector. Local authorities decided for themselves whether to fund services, provide them directly or indeed leave funding and provision to the market and voluntary sector. This meant that some areas had considerable provision, other areas very little, and across the country services were of mixed quality.

Second, the review found that poverty was bad for children, and particularly for very young children. The impact of poverty on the first few years of life was long-lasting, with poor children more likely to do less well when they got to school, more likely to work in lower-paid jobs or not work at all as adults, and more likely to experience poorer health than their better-off peers. They were also more likely to have their own children in the teen years, and, particularly if male, more likely to be involved in criminal activities as young adults (Duncan and Brooks-Gunn, 1997; Duncan et al., 1998).

Finally, the review reported a set of key features that seemed to make a difference. Services needed to work with both adults and children, to work across the disciplines of health, social care and education, and to be rooted in local communities, responding to the needs of local people.

Considering all the issues together, the Treasury team recommended to ministers the establishment of a new programme, Sure Start. From the very beginning, there was a particular emphasis on two key features: bringing services together and working with local parents. Sure Start would be an area-based initiative providing services for children under 4, designed in collaboration with local voluntary sector organisations, statutory agencies and local parents, with the aim of improving long-term outcomes for poor children.

Sure Start: a new way of supporting children in poverty

By 1999, two years into the New Labour government, three strands of policy were in play for young children: nursery education for all children, expansion of childcare for working parents and Sure Start for poor children. The head of the Sure Start Unit was based in the Department for Education and Employment (DfEE), but reported to the Minister for Public Health. A Sure Start steering group was chaired by the Minister for Public Health and included ministers from six departments. David Blunkett, then Secretary of State at the DfEE, spoke for Sure Start at Cabinet. These arrangements for the governance of Sure Start were an important part of the innovative nature of the programme. They represented much of how the New Labour government wanted to develop and deliver policy across government, rather than individual departments acting on their own. They demonstrated the government's desire to develop new policies in new ways.

Over the following 10 years, four themes would continue to shape early years policy:

- *reducing child poverty*, set out with the historic aim to end child poverty, announced by the Prime Minister in 1999 in a speech to the Fabian Society (Waldfogel, 2010)
- *evidenced-based policy*, that is, ensuring new policies were based on strong data establishing the need for the policy and its mode of implementation
- *supporting parents and supporting parenting*: policies to reduce pressures on families and policies to improve outcomes for children by encouraging better parenting styles
- *progressive universalism*: designing public services to ensure maximum support for the most disadvantaged, while avoiding stigma and ensuring a minimum service base for all.

Sure Start represented all four of the above themes. It was carefully targeted at poor areas and aimed to ameliorate the negative impact of living in poverty for very young children and their families. Within two or three years of initiating the programme, it aimed not only to ameliorate the impact of poverty, but to reduce the numbers of children living in poverty by adopting a strong employment focus. The employment agenda ensured Sure Start was aligned with the other government welfare to work efforts. Certainly, the need for Sure Start was based on the solid evidence mentioned above, that children growing up in poverty do less well as adults than their better-off peers. However, the actual design of the programme had less to do with research evidence and much more to do with what key stakeholders, particularly in the voluntary sector, thought would work the best. These views were very much in line with government views on how the programme should be set up. Hence, the views of those delivering early years' services at the front line prevailed against the views of many academics at the time, who believed that fundamental aspects of the design were flawed. Most prominent of the critics of the design was Sir Michael Rutter, who wrote:

> The ways in which the details of SSLP (Sure Start Local Programmes) implementation were organised were completely out of keeping with the research evidence ... and served to undermine its efficacy ... It was really poor and it is to be regretted that more attention was not paid to the advice of academics who knew about prevention. (Rutter, 2007: 207)

There continues to be a debate on whether the programme was or was not evidence-based. However, there is no debate on the strength of the evidence used to support the case for helping young children living in poverty.

The theme of supporting parents was also a very strong part of the Sure Start story. However, the nature of parental engagement changed over the years. The emphasis to start with was empowerment, involving parents in the design of local programmes and in the management and governance of programmes. This changed over the years to a more focused approach. The evaluation results described later in this chapter explain the thinking behind the changes. Finally, the principles of progressive universalism can be seen in the area-based design of Sure Start. The approach was to establish programmes in areas of deep poverty where there would be a very high likelihood that users of Sure Start would be poor. But once a Sure Start area was established, it was for all in the catchment area with young children. There was a strong emphasis on avoiding the stigma often associated with highly targeted social programmes, while at the same time, ensuring generous resources were aimed at the poorest areas.

Programme design

Sure Start began as an area-based initiative. Very poor areas were chosen, usually with an under-4s population of about 800 children. Once an area was chosen, a partnership was formed, made up of local parents and the key providers of services for young children. Each programme was required to ensure the delivery of a set of core services: outreach and home visiting, good quality play, learning and childcare, support for parents, advice on health, and support for children with special needs (DfEE, 1999). Given the evidence from the Comprehensive Spending Review that services were extremely patchy, Sure Start funding was meant to fill the gaps in existing services and additionally provide other services that would contribute to a set of outcomes. These outcomes were articulated as the Sure Start Public Service Agreement (PSA). They included specific targets on improvements in child language, fewer hospital admissions, parent satisfaction with services and a reduction in the number of low birthweight babies. Given the variety of existing provision locally, it would be up to the local partnerships, in close collaboration with local parents, to decide the precise set of services that would achieve the outcomes defined by the PSA. Each of the programmes were asked to set out a plan identifying local needs, what they would offer with the funding to meet the needs and how these services would deliver the outcomes. The initial resource of £450 million was announced in Parliament in July 1998. It would fund 250 local programmes over three years, 1999–2002. In summary, the fundamental logic to Sure Start can be described through the three principles below:

- Bringing services together in poor areas will improve outcomes for poor children.
- Local areas vary enormously in their current provision, so central government will define a set of core services, and local areas will decide how to bring their current services together to work more effectively, and what new services would be needed to meet the core offer.
- The PSA defines the desired outcomes in terms of improved health, well-being and development for young children; the inputs needed to achieve the outcomes should be defined locally.

Programme evaluation

The programme design was in line with key features that the Labour government wanted reflected in public policy making: user- not provider-led, evidence-based, defining outcomes not inputs. However, the design made evaluation incredibly challenging. Sure Start was not one intervention, but 250 different interventions. Moreover, before the evaluation even started, ministers decided to double the number of local programmes to 500. While doing the research for the Comprehensive Spending Review, the Treasury had found many examples of services that did improve the life chances of children growing up in poverty. However, they were largely American interventions that had been subjected over many years to the gold standard of evaluation, the randomised control trial. Such an evaluation methodology requires a standard set of inputs assigned randomly to a similar group of individuals, some who receive the intervention, and others who do not. Both groups are then tested after the intervention to see if there is a difference between those who experienced the intervention and those who did not. The most famous of these interventions was High Scope, which was claiming a return on investment of $7 for every $1 spent on the programme. The children from the High Scope study were followed up well into adulthood, and much of the savings accrued over the years were for the criminal justice system. Fewer of the High Scope children wound up in prison as adults. There were also fewer teen pregnancies and higher levels of employment among the children who attended the High Scope programme. High Scope was highly targeted at very poor children and had a clearly prescribed and consistently delivered curriculum (Schweinhart and Weikart, 1993).

Government ministers had already ruled out a design for Sure Start that would be predetermined from the centre. The emphasis on local design ruled out a standard set of inputs. They believed strongly in the power of local communities to design their own solutions. Most of the academics advising ministers and the Treasury, including Michael Rutter, argued against the level of local diversity inevitable in the proposed model, mainly because it would make it almost impossible to evaluate, but also because it was not consistent with the High Scope features that were found to be successful, i.e. clear targeting and a standardised curriculum. Ministers were also firmly against a randomised control trial design for the evaluation. In the case of Sure Start, ministers were so convinced that it would work, that they considered random allocation almost immoral. Why would you deny a random set of families a service that you were absolutely sure would help them? Finally, Sure Start was meant to improve a number of key areas: health, social development, cognitive development, parenting skills. With a variety of inputs, it would be virtually impossible to establish causal relationships between any particular activity and any outcome.

What worked and what did not

The evaluation design was very complex, and over the 10-plus years since 2000 there has been a very large number of reports produced by the National Evaluation of Sure

Start (NESS) team. These can all be found on the NESS website (www.ness.bbk.ac.uk). The rest of this chapter provides a summary of some of the key findings, and what they meant for the development of Sure Start. Clearly, the most important findings related to the actual impact of Sure Start on children and parents. Three impact reports have been published (National Evaluation of Sure Start Team, 2005, 2008, 2010).

Case study 1: Impact study 1

The first impact study was a cross-sectional study of randomly chosen families in the Sure Start areas, comparing them with randomly chosen children from comparably poor areas, which did not yet have Sure Start. Children of 9 months and 3 years of age were in this first group. This first impact study was mixed in its results. Overall, there were few detectable positive results. However, when broken down into sub-groups, there were both positive and negative results. For non-teen mothers, the vast majority of the sample, both children and parents, seemed to be benefiting from Sure Start: greater child social competence, fewer child behaviour problems and less negative parenting. However, the children of teen mothers, 14 per cent of the sample, were doing less well in Sure Start areas than in non-Sure Start areas. The children of teen mothers had less social competence, more behaviour problems and poorer child verbal ability. Poorer child verbal ability was also the case for children in lone-parent families and children in workless households. These findings became interpreted by the press as Sure Start failing the poor, and being taken over by middle-class mothers. In fact, the average income of the whole sample was very near the poverty line, but the teen mothers were, as a group, significantly poorer. Sure Start was succeeding for the poor, but failing the very poorest (Belsky and Melhuish, 2007).

Case study 2: Impact study 2

The second impact study followed the same group of 9-month-old children, now aged 3, and compared them with a similar group of children from the Millennium Cohort Study (MCS). The MCS is a multi-disciplinary research project following the lives of around 19,000 children born in the UK in 2000/1 (www.cls.ioe.ac.uk). Given that ministers had ruled out a randomised trial, matching children from Sure Start areas with children with similar social and economic characteristics from this large-scale study seemed the best way forward. The results from the

(Continued)

(Continued)

second impact study were both more consistent and more positive. Importantly, there were *no* differences between sub-groups. The poor and the poorest were benefiting from Sure Start. Children in the Sure Start sample exhibited more positive social behaviour, child independence and self-regulation, improved child–parent interaction, improved home learning environment and increased use of services. The Sure Start children also had higher rates of immunisation and fewer child accidents. However, these last two findings could not be safely attributed to Sure Start, in that the data for the millennium cohort children were collected earlier, which could account for the differences (Melhuish et al., 2008). Nevertheless, the overall results were encouraging.

From local programmes to Children's Centres

So what changed between the first and second impact studies that can explain the big differences in results? Sure Start was never a static programme; as ministers changed in both the Departments of Health and the DfEE, the direction of the programme changed as well. As early as 2002, as a result of the Childcare Review carried out by the Prime Minister's Strategy Unit, the model of the local programme was being transformed into Children's Centres (The Strategy Unit, 2002). In part, this was because the concept of a local programme was more difficult to explain than the concrete notion of a centre. But it was also recognised in the review that the separation of Sure Start from the rest of early years and childcare policy was weakening the government's overall strategy on young children. In short, more of the Sure Start money should be supporting the childcare agenda and, in particular, the welfare to work policies. Moreover, the very popularity of Sure Start local programmes was causing problems. It became increasingly unfair for children living very near to but not within the local programme areas to be denied Sure Start local programme services. By the end of 2004, the direction of travel was firmly fixed with the publication of *Choice for Parents: The Best Start for Children – A Ten Year Childcare Strategy* (HM Treasury, 2004). This document moved Sure Start from an area-based initiative to a national plan for Sure Start Children's Centres in every community. Sure Start Children's Centres would no longer be funded directly by central government but through funding to local authorities, who would then decide how much of the dedicated early years resources they received would go to each of the centres. This naturally meant that the initial 500 local programmes would be less generously funded. Although funding continued to increase, the increase in funding was not enough to maintain the initial level of local programme funding when the money had to spread over a significantly larger number of Children's Centres. What would be included in those centres was strongly influenced by both the first NESS impact study that raised concern about missing the poorest children, and by the *Effective Provision of Pre-school Education* (EPPE) study that found that early years settings with more highly qualified staff achieved better outcomes for children (Siraj-Blatchford, 2010).

The first NESS impact results described above were published at the end of 2005. There was huge concern within government concerning these mixed results. While no impact would have been disappointing, the finding that a small group of children in Sure Start areas were doing less well than their counterparts in non-Sure Start areas was causing consternation. Ahead of publishing the results, the government asked the NESS team to investigate the possible reasons for the differences between the results for the sub-groups. The Programme Variability Study looked at a range of factors that made programmes more or less effective. It became clear that good programmes tended to do well over most of the features. The key elements of good programmes were: effective governance and management, informal but professional ethos, and empowerment of service providers and users. It was also found that the health-led programmes tended to do better than those led by local authorities or voluntary organisations (Belsky et al., 2006). Critically, the conclusions from the programme variability study were not that the basic design of Sure Start was flawed, but that implementation of the design was incredibly difficult (Anning et al., 2007). What was asked of local programme managers was significantly more challenging than had been anticipated. Bringing services together, working with local people, reaching the hardest to reach, and delivering the PSA targets was a complex set of requirements. Some programme managers were very good at it, but others were clearly struggling.

There was also a failure to anticipate how long it would take to get programmes started. Most took at least three years to get the full range of services up and running. The delays in becoming fully functional were also exacerbated by the generous capital funding. Many programme managers spent considerable energy and effort in their first year or two just getting buildings commissioned. The lack of proper premises and the months, and sometimes years, it took to get buildings built considerably delayed full functioning for many programmes. Hence, the differences in the two studies were in part about timing. It is likely that some of the families selected for the first impact study had no contact with Sure Start at all, as many programmes were not yet fully operational. Moreover, many programmes were having difficulty getting data from statutory agencies about where pregnant women and mothers with very small children were living. Without this data, initial home visiting was very difficult. This may be why health-led programmes were doing better, as they had the data. There was much to learn about how to bring this new service together, how to work with local partners, and particularly how to establish good data systems so that staff knew who were the hard-to-reach families. Many of the civil servants who devised the design of Sure Start had been on visits to local centres, usually run by voluntary agencies that seemed to be doing exemplary work. But replicating that style of working across 500 local areas was harder than anyone had imagined.

While the analysis above explains why some programmes were doing better than others, it does not explain the particular difference in the sub-groups. Why were teen parents doing less well than most others? To some extent, the very success of the early programmes may contribute to understanding this difference. The programmes were immensely popular with local people. For many areas, it was the first dedicated provision for families with young children. It was almost always mothers using the services and they were delighted and appreciative. For staff working in these very difficult areas, having users that are willing and grateful is very reinforcing. They had no incentives to find new customers, in part because their efforts at finding them were often hampered by lack of data, but also because the customers they had were very skilled at taking up huge amounts of time, and making staff feel good. Such a group of apparently confident women would be very off-putting for younger, less confident teen parents. Work with fathers was similarly challenging. For men, or indeed very young women, entering Sure Start community facilities would have been difficult. The importance of the evaluation was that it identified these problems. Consequently, programmes were encouraged to strengthen their efforts at outreach, and at working with fathers as well as mothers. Why the teen mothers were doing less well than in non-Sure Start areas is harder to understand. It seems possible that in areas that had Sure Start, some of the universal statutory services were withdrawing, assuming that Sure Start services would fill in the gaps. Hence, the teen parents in non-Sure Start areas may have been getting a more intense service from health visitors than teen parents in Sure Start areas, where the health visitors would assume they would be getting the support they needed from Sure Start. This hypothesis could also explain why it seemed from the evaluation that health-led local programmes were doing better than local authority or voluntary agency led programmes (Belsky et al., 2006).

At the same time, results from the EPPE study were also coming out and proved to be influential in changes to Sure Start. Particularly important was the EPPE finding that quality in early years settings made a difference to child outcomes and that quality correlated with better qualified staff, as noted above. EPPE also found that the most important factor in determining child outcomes was the home learning environment (Sammons, 2010). The impact of both of these on Sure Start was profound. Sure Start had no requirements on staff qualifications, and while there was considerable activity with parents, much of the activity did not seem to be clearly focused on what we were learning actually makes the greatest positive impact on children. The key conclusions looking at the NESS and EPPE results together, were that the significant investment in Sure Start needed to be focused more clearly on those activities with parents and children that were most likely to make a measurable difference: high quality early education for young children and interventions with parents that were more structured and clearly aimed at improving parenting, not just empowering parents. Empowerment was an important first step to getting engagement, but on its own it was not likely to deliver for children; parents liking the service was essential but not sufficient to deliver better outcomes for their children.

Hence, the move from Sure Start Local Programmes to Children's Centres changed three key features of the original Sure Start model:

- *Governance arrangements*: no longer neighbourhood programmes with a light touch from government, now centres would be directly provided or commissioned by the local authority.

- *Funding arrangements*: no longer a specified pot of money from government to the programme, now a specified pot of money would be allocated to the local authority to spend on early years' services, but to be distributed as the local authority saw fit.
- *Service mix*: there would be a much stronger emphasis on childcare for working parents, a stronger emphasis on the quality of the childcare, and a stronger emphasis on outreach to those not accessing services, presumed to be the most disadvantaged. There was, consequently, a weakening of local control and parental engagement in service design.

These changes to Sure Start need to be seen within the much wider radical reform of all children's services. The Every Child Matters agenda was taking hold across all of England. It encompassed many of the early Sure Start principles of joining up a variety of services at the local level, intervening early to prevent serious problems later in life and working with parents as well as children to improve outcomes. It also required every local authority to have a Director of Children's Services responsible for outcomes for *all* the children living in the area. It would have been unworkable to have these new posts and continue to fund and manage Sure Start from a central government unit. Sure Start needed to be an integral part of the new landscape of children's services including childcare, early education, schools, child health and youth justice.

The third impact study was published in autumn 2010 (National Evaluation of Sure Start [NESS] Team, 2010) and used the same children from the second impact study, now aged 5. The same group will be followed up again at age 7. The report was published after the change of government in May 2010, and attracted virtually no press comment. The findings from the study showed a small number of mainly positive effects on 5-year-olds and parents. Child positive impacts were better physical health and lower body mass index among children in Sure Start areas compared to children in non-Sure Start areas. There were also a number of positive effects on parents. Home environments were less chaotic and more cognitively stimulating among the families of Sure Start 5-year-olds compared to the non-Sure Start families. Mothers in the Sure Start group also reported greater life satisfaction and engaged in less harsh discipline than the non-Sure Start group. However, the Sure Start mothers reported more depressive symptoms and were less likely to visit their child's school than the non-Sure Start mothers (NESS, 2010). The failure to find any impacts related to cognitive development was disappointing. However, it may be explained by the availability of pre-school education in both Sure Start and non-Sure Start areas. The children in the non-Sure Start areas would have been as likely to have had pre-school education as those in the Sure Start areas, and therefore benefited in the ways suggested by the Effective Provision of Pre-School Education research (Sylva, 2010). Moreover, the expansion of Children's Centres meant that wide differences in the availability of family support services between what were the original Sure Start programme areas and the non-Sure Start areas in 1999 were rapidly closing by the time the third impact study data was being collected. A near universal service was being established.

Final thoughts: what have we learned?

The experience of developing and changing Sure Start over the last 10 years has been exhilarating and challenging: a new government wanting to invest serious funding in young children. Much has been learned from the experience that should be used to inform future policy and practice. First, we learned how difficult it is to integrate services to deliver better outcomes. Joining up services is challenging, and unless coupled with shared goals and good information systems will not deliver better quality services for children and families.

The NESS evaluation demonstrated that community development methods on their own do not result in better outcomes for children. They need to be linked with focused, well-delivered services that are clear in their purpose. We learned that working with adults who happen to be parents does not improve their parenting skills. Parenting skills are improved by structured interventions delivered by highly skilled staff to parents who are motivated to change their behaviour. Furthermore, we learned that too strong an emphasis on community development can result in the most disadvantaged missing out. Highly targeted efforts need to be made to ensure that those who have the greatest needs are not excluded by their own community. We learned from EPPE that early education does deliver better outcomes, but again, the best outcomes are delivered by graduate leaders (predominantly trained teachers) in high quality settings. Most importantly, we learned that the factor that makes the most difference for children, the home learning environment, is the most difficult to change.

The coalition government, formed after the May 2010 election, has so far been supportive of early years services, with clear commitments to maintaining a network of Sure Start Children's Centres, continuing universal free early education for all 3- and 4-year-olds, and expanding provision for disadvantaged 2-year-olds. However, while early years services have not been subject to the savage cuts of some public services, much more has been left to local authorities to determine, with ring fencing on children's services removed. Local authorities will now need to be convinced of the importance of early years provision. The new government has also reaffirmed the commitment to ending child poverty. However, it has put a much greater emphasis on stopping the transmission of poverty from one generation to the next through improved services for disadvantaged families, rather than reducing current levels of child poverty, through increasing family income. All the lessons above will be critically important as we face a future in Britain with less money to spend on early years. Spending it wisely will be our responsibility for this generation of children, and the nation's future.

▣ Summary

- This chapter has described the policy context which surrounded Sure Start, its relationship to other early years policy areas, and the significant changes that have taken place in children's services more widely since 1997.

(Continued)

(Continued)

- It has explained the original arguments that led to the establishment of Sure Start, the key findings in the evaluation of Sure Start and changes to the programme as it matured from its inception in 1999 to the present day.
- The context for Sure Start was a new government wanting to make its mark, not just in developing new policies, but in implementing policy in new ways: working across government, using outside experts and creating services influenced as much by the users of services as by the providers.
- The landscape of early years provision is unrecognisable from 10 years ago. Maintaining the infrastructure of Children's Centres and universal pre-school provision is the challenge for a new coalition government that has expressed strong commitment to addressing issues of child poverty through better quality and more targeted programmes.

Questions for discussion

1 What do you see as the advantages and disadvantages of universal compared with targeted provision for young children and families?
2 What are some of the key problems in offering a service to all children in particular areas of poverty?
3 How can services best ensure the full participation of the most vulnerable or 'hard-to-reach' families?
4 The new coalition government in the UK has espoused 'targeted universalism' and 'localism' as policy principles. Drawing on the experience of Sure Start, what might be the implications for services for young children and families? *(Higher-level question)*

Further reading

Levels 5 and 6

Lochrie, M. (2007) *Children's Centres: Ensuring that Families Most in Need Benefit.* Teddington: Beechgrove Press.
This Esmee Fairburn Foundation funded report is based on four detailed case studies of 'exemplar' Sure Start Children's Centres and critically evaluates their effectiveness in terms of reaching out to the most vulnerable and hard-to-reach families.

Sylva, K., Melhuish, E., Sammons, P., Siraj-Blatchford, I. and Taggart, B. (2010) *Early Childhood Matters: Evidence from the Effective Pre-school and Primary Education Project.* Abingdon: Routledge.

This book provides an overview of the main findings of the original EPPE project and its extension into primary schools and into Researching Effective Pedagogy in the Early Years (REPEY). Separate chapters relate to each of the main components of the wider EPPE project, and an overview of the evidence base supporting future policy is provided.

Levels 6 and 7

Eisenstadt, N. (2011) *Providing a Sure Start: How Government Discovered Early Childhood.* Bristol: Policy Press.
This book tells the story of how Sure Start was set up, the numerous changes it went through, and how it has influenced the landscape of services for young children in England. It offers keen insight into the policy-making process, as well as the key debates on services for young children, and concludes with both the things that policy makers got wrong and the legacy of Sure Start.

Field, F. (2010) *The Foundation Year: Preventing Poor Children Becoming Poor Adults.* London: HM Government.
This is the report of the Independent Review on Poverty and Life Chances that overviews research evidence, including that relating to EPPE and Sure Start, and makes a clear case for increased investment in the early years in order to break the cycle of poverty and disadvantage leading to poor outcomes for children who in turn become less employable and more disadvantaged as future parents. It provides 24 recommendations for public policy, including better measurement and monitoring of life chances.

Waldfogel, J. (2010) *Britain's War on Poverty.* New York: Russell Sage Foundation.
This book describes the three-pronged approach to tackling child poverty in the UK, welfare to work programmes, improved benefits for working parents, and investment in the childcare infrastructure to ensure parents wanting to work have access to affordable childcare. Jane Waldfogel contrasts this with the much more limited approach adopted in the USA.

Websites

www.cls@ ioe.ac.uk
This is the home page for a range of large-scale longitudinal studies, including the Millennium Cohort Study of 19,000 children born in the millennium. The ESRC-funded database created by the surveys is accessible to all researchers and includes a range of publications.

www.direct.gov.uk/en/Dl1/Directories/DG_10010859
Sure Start is a government programme which provides services for pre-school children and their families. It works to bring together early education, childcare, health and family support. Services provided include advice on health care and child development, play schemes, parenting classes, family outreach support and adult education and advice.

www.ness.bbk.ac.uk
A large number of reports produced by the National Evaluation of Sure Start (NESS) team can be found on this website.

References

Anning, A. and the National Evaluation of Sure Start Research Team (2007) *National Evaluation Summary, Understanding Variations in Effectiveness amongst Sure Start Local Programmes: Lessons for Sure Start Children's Centres.* Nottingham: DfES.

Belsky, J. and Melhuish, E. (2007) The impact of Sure Start local programmes on children and families. In: J. Belsky, J. Barnes and E. Melhuish (eds) *The National Evaluation of Sure Start: Does Area-based Early Intervention Work?* Bristol: The Policy Press.

Belsky, J., Melhuish, E., Barnes, J., Leyland, A., Romaniuk, H. and the NESS Team (2006) Effects of Sure Start local programmes on children and families: early findings from a quasi-experimental, cross-sectional study. *British Medical Journal*, 332(7556). Also available at: www.bmj.com/cgi/content/full/332/7556/1476

Department for Education and Employment (DfEE) (1999) *Sure Start: Making a Difference for Children and Families*. Suffolk: DfEE.

Duncan, G. and Brooks-Gunn, J. (1997) *Consequences of Growing up Poor*. New York: Russell Sage Foundation.

Duncan, G., Yeung, J., Brooks-Gunn, J. and Smith, J. (1998) How much does childhood poverty affect the life chances of children? *American Sociological Review*, 63: 406–23.

HM Treasury (1998) *Comprehensive Spending Review: Cross Departmental Review of Provision for Young Children*. London: HMSO.

HM Treasury (2004) *Choice for Parents: The Best Start for Children – A Ten Year Strategy for Childcare*. Norwich: HMSO.

Labour Party (1997) *New Labour Because Britain Deserves Better*. London: Labour Party Publications.

Melhuish, E., Belsky, J., Leyland, A., Barnes, J. and the National Evaluation of Sure Start (NESS) Team (2008) Effects of fully-established Sure Start Local Programmes on 3-year-old children and their families living in England: a quasi-experimental observational study. *The Lancet*, 372: 1641–7.

National Evaluation of Sure Start (NESS) Team (2005) Early impacts of Sure Start Local Programmes on children and families. Research Report No. NESS/2005/FR/013. London: HMSO.

National Evaluation of Sure Start (NESS) Team (2008) The impact of Sure Start Local Programmes on three year olds and their families. Research Report No. NESS/2008/FR/027. London: HMSO.

National Evaluation of Sure Start (NESS) Team (2010) The impact of Sure Start Local Programmes on five year olds and their families. Research Report No. DFE-RR067. London: Department for Education.

Rutter, M. (2007) Sure Start Local Programmes: an outsider's perspective. In J. Belsky, J. Barnes and E. Melhuish (eds) *The National Evaluation of Sure Start: Does Area-based Early Intervention Work?* Bristol: The Policy Press.

Sammons, P. (2010) Does pre-school make a difference? Identifying the impact of pre-school on children's cognitive and social behavioural development at different ages. In: K. Sylva, E. Melhuish, P. Sammons, I. Siraj-Blatchford and B. Taggart (eds) *Early Childhood Matters: Evidence from the Effective Pre-school and Primary Education Project*. Abingdon: Routledge. pp. 92–113.

Schweinhart, L. and Weikart, D. (1993) *The High Scope Perry Pre-school Study through Age 27*. Ypsilanti, MI: High Scope Press.

Siraj-Blatchford, I. (2010) A focus on pedagogy. In: K. Sylva, E. Melhuish, P. Sammons, I. Siraj-Blatchford and B. Taggart (eds) *Early Childhood Matters: Evidence from the Effective Pre-school and Primary Education Project*. Abingdon: Routledge. pp. 149–65.

Stewart, K. (2009) A scar on the soul of Britain: child poverty and disadvantage under New Labour. In J. Hills, T. Sefton and K. Stewart (eds) *Towards a More Equal Society? Poverty, Inequality and Policy Since 1997*. Bristol: The Policy Press. pp. 47–69.

Sylva, K. (2010) Re-thinking the evidence base for early years policy and practice. In K. Sylva, E. Melhuish, P. Sammons, I. Siraj-Blatchford and B. Taggart (eds) *Early Childhood Matters: Evidence from the Effective Pre-school and Primary Education Project*. Abingdon: Routledge. pp. 223–35.

The Strategy Unit (2002) *Delivering for Children and Families: The Inter-departmental Childcare Review*. Norwich: HMSO.

Waldfogel, J. (2010) *Britain's War on Poverty*. New York: Russell Sage Foundation.

CHAPTER 3

CLOSING THE GAP: POLICY INTO ACTION

Sue Owen, Caroline Sharp and Jenny Spratt

Overview

In this chapter, we use the Labour government's 2008 policy developments in England of a universal early years framework for practitioners (the Early Years Foundation Stage [DCSF, 2008a; DfES, 2007]), its assessment tool (the Early Years Foundation Stage Profile [DCSF, 2008b]) and related national targets for attainment, to indicate some practical problems in putting policy into practice. In this example, it will be seen that two perfectly reasonable aspirations: to improve the overall progress of young children entering school in a local authority area, and to narrow the gap between children from advantaged and disadvantaged backgrounds, can be difficult to achieve simultaneously. Specific and planned interventions need to be put in place by local authority managers and practitioners if this challenge is to be addressed. We demonstrate this process through a case study based on the work of the Centre for Excellence and Outcomes in Children's and Young People's Services (C4EO). The coalition government which came into power in 2010 has commissioned a review of the EYFS and removed much of the national framework of targets, but the aspiration to narrow the gap of disadvantage is still being maintained and interventions such as those described in this case are being funded to support local authorities.[1]

The Labour government (1997–2010) put in place a large number of policy initiatives directed at improving services for young children and leading to a higher level of attainment by those children on entry to school. This was often described in policy documents as making children 'ready for school', a phrase which has been criticised by many early years experts who argue that high quality and enjoyable experiences for young children are important for this vital stage in children's development, rather than simply because they make it easier for children to take advantage of later, more formal, schooling (OECD, 2006).

Nevertheless, there is evidence of a considerable achievement gap among young children in England. For instance, Feinstein (2003) showed that differences in cognitive and non-cognitive skill levels of young children can be observed as early as 22 months and then widen by the age of 5. The government's policy was to ensure that, as far as possible, publicly funded early years services should be supported, and expected, to address this imbalance in the achievement of children from different social and cultural groups. Policy initiatives designed to address this included financial and regulatory support to enable a higher qualified workforce in early years settings, with the aim that all settings should be led by a graduate, and a range of specific programmes directed at improving young children's language and literacy, such as the Every Child a Talker (ECaT) programme (DCSF, 2008c). However, one of the most fundamental changes was the creation of a universal early years framework for practitioners to follow from birth to age 5 (the Early Years Foundation Stage), together with its assessment tool (the Early Years Foundation Stage Profile) and related national targets for attainment (see Chapter 10).

Meeting the targets

Consequently, since 2008, English local authorities have been able to measure children's attainment, and track the local authority's year-on-year progress in improving this, through use of the Early Years Foundation Stage Profile (EYFSP). The EYFSP records each child's progress and learning needs at the end of the Early Years Foundation Stage. It is based on early childhood practitioners' observations and assessments in six areas of learning: personal, social and emotional development; communication, language and literacy; mathematical development; knowledge and understanding of the world; physical development; and creative development. Staff must complete summary profiles for each child at the end of the Foundation Stage (four weeks before the end of the summer term when children are 4 to 5 years old and at the end of their Reception year).[2]

Also, since 2008, local authorities have had a duty to make progress in relation to a set of National Indicators, two of which are specific to the early years[3]:

- NI 72 Achievement of at least 78 points across the 13 scales of the Early Years Foundation Stage with at least 6 in each of the scales in Personal, Social and Emotional Development and Communication, Language and Literacy (the definition of a 'good level of development'); and
- NI 92 Narrowing the gap between the lowest achieving 20 per cent in the Early Years Foundation Stage Profile and the rest.[4]

The official figures indicate that there has been progress in relation to these targets. In 2010, 56 per cent of children achieved a good level of development (as defined in NI 72 above) compared with 52 per cent in 2009. The gap between the lowest achieving 20 per cent and the rest has closed somewhat in recent years – it was 35.6 per cent in 2008, 33.9 per cent in 2009 and 32.7 per cent in 2010 (DfE, 2010), but results for individual local authorities don't always show a positive trend.

For local authorities and early years education providers, the requirement to both raise achievement and simultaneously narrow the gap can be difficult to deliver, as raising the achievement of all children can result in widening the gap between the lowest achieving children and the rest. To some extent, this is the result of the use of a continuous measure (EYFSP scores), combined with a 'threshold' outcome measure (per cent achieving at least 78 points) set above the mean. It is possible for a local authority to record improved results from year to year, but for fewer children in the disadvantaged group to cross the threshold than for other children. This is illustrated in Figure 3.1.

EYFSP scores in Year 1

Figure 3.1 shows a hypothetical distribution of scores in two years, where the scores are divided into six categories, each representing 20 points. We have assumed that 20 per cent of the children in this sample are from disadvantaged backgrounds, and that those children tend to achieve lower scores. The distribution of scores is the same in both years, except for the fact that the scores have shifted up a category in Year 2 (i.e. children are scoring up to 20 points higher in Year 2).[5] However, in the second year, the gap between children from disadvantaged backgrounds and the rest has increased from 15 to 40 per cent because a higher proportion of children from non-disadvantaged backgrounds has achieved the threshold.

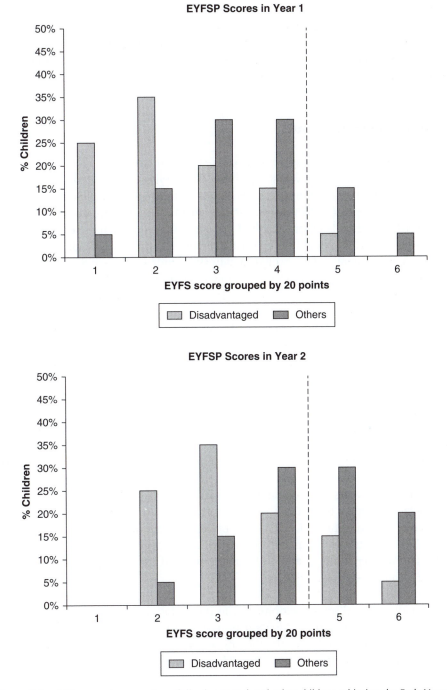

Figure 3.1 Differences in proportion of disadvantaged and other children achieving the Early Years Foundation Stage Profile threshold in two years.

Source: NFER

Another reason for difficulties in closing the achievement gap could be that children from more advantaged backgrounds have a greater capacity to take advantage of improvements in provision, as a result of their early learning and family support. For these reasons, the twin policy imperatives of raising overall achievement and closing the gap can be quite challenging to achieve in practice.

Influences on outcomes

Research has shown that deprivation has a strong influence on children's achievement throughout the early years (Feinstein, 2003; Sylva et al., 2004). These studies show that a mother's education, as measured by her highest qualification, is a very powerful predictor of achievement for her children (Sammons et al., 2004; Siraj-Blatchford and Siraj-Blatchford, 2009). One of the ways in which maternal education and poverty both influence children's achievement is through the quality of the home learning environment (HLE). A high quality HLE tends to be associated with higher socio-economic backgrounds and better qualified mothers. Children who experience a high quality HLE are more likely to achieve well at school and children from disadvantaged backgrounds who experience a high quality HLE achieve better results (Sammons et al., 2004). This finding led the researchers to conclude that what parents do with their children is more important than who they are.

So what factors make a difference to children's outcomes and contribute to narrowing the achievement gap? Relevant studies have recently been brought together as 'knowledge reviews' produced by the Centre for Excellence and Outcomes in children's and young people's services (C4EO), funded by central government for an initial three-year period beginning in 2008, with the aim of identifying 'what works' to improve outcomes for children and families. It takes a 'sector-led' approach which assumes that practitioners and managers best understand local needs and can contribute to improving practice.

The first early years review undertaken by C4EO looked at the factors associated with achievement in the EYFSP (Coghlan et al., 2010). In addition, the National Foundation for Educational Research (NFER) carried out multi-level modelling of the 2008 EYFSP results in relation to children's age, sex, Special Educational Needs (SEN) status and ethnicity, and a variety of background and environmental characteristics. The NFER analysis revealed that:

- A child's age and sex were dominant in predicting the probability of achieving a good level of development (defined as in NI 72, above) with, as would be expected, older children doing better than younger ones or those with Special Educational Needs (SEN). Girls also outperformed boys in every measure.
- Poverty and deprivation were associated with lower levels of development. Children receiving free school meals[6] were only half as likely as their classmates to achieve the threshold and the differences were greatest for communication, language and literacy; mathematical development; and personal, social and emotional development.

- Children in poverty have poorer health and safety; they do worse academically and make less progress in learning throughout the early years; and child poverty affects certain ethnic groups in particular. In 2006/7, the majority of Pakistani, Bangladeshi and Black non-Caribbean children were living in poverty, compared with around a quarter of White children.
- A relationship between EYFSP results and ethnic background remained even after accounting for the effects of poverty. Children from Gypsy Roma, Irish traveller, Bangladeshi and Pakistani ethnic groups, in particular, achieved lower scores than children from other cultural backgrounds.
- Children with English as an additional language (EAL) (and also predominantly from ethnic minority groups) have poorer academic and social outcomes in the early years. Despite this, the evidence shows that they catch up as their English language skills improve so that there are few remaining differences in attainment between ethnic groups at age 5 and none at age 7.

So although poverty has the greatest influence on children's outcomes, other factors including ethnic background, EAL, health and safety (including freedom from abuse), parental education and the home learning environment were all found to be signifi- cant in children's attainment, particularly in the early years.

The impact of early years provision

The C4EO review showed that early learning environments can have a specific impact on children's sense of identity. Transitions to pre-school and school pose particular challenges for young children from minority ethnic backgrounds and those with EAL (Melhuish et al., 2001). Children from minority ethnic groups can find cultural activi- ties in early childhood provision challenging. A lack of shared experiences between children and staff can lead to marginalisation of these children and some may then adopt different identities in order to fit into the dominant culture (Barron, 2007; Rich and Davis, 2007).

Children with EAL face particular communication challenges. Staff can misinterpret their needs and children can find group sessions in English alienating. Children's com- munication difficulties can have a negative impact on relationships with teachers and other children, lead to frustration and undermine their confidence (Barron, 2007; Chang et al., 2007; Fumoto et al., 2007; Melhuish et al., 2001). On the other hand, best practice in early childhood learning environments helps children from all back- grounds to settle in and make good progress. Awareness of potential difficulties and use of culturally appropriate materials are helpful, as are strategies to improve interac- tion for children with EAL (Siraj-Blatchford et al., 2003, 2004). Bilingual staff have a valuable role in providing support for children with EAL, given appropriate leadership and training (Barron, 2007; Conteh, 2007; Sims and Hutchins, 2001). Children from diverse cultural backgrounds and children with EAL need support to ensure positive experiences in their early years. Initiatives to support children's language and literacy development can improve learning for children at risk of poorer outcomes, including those from poor families (D'Anguilli, 2005; McIntosh et al., 2007; Silverman, 2007; Stuart, 2004).

Strategies for improvement

The review also highlighted factors which help children to access the curriculum and make good progress. Attending pre-school benefits children from all backgrounds, especially those living in poverty, but high quality is vital if good outcomes are to be realised (Siraj-Blatchford et al., 2003; Sylva et al., 2004, 2008). The features of high quality pre-schools include the following:

* Effective pre-schools are characterised by a focus on individual children's needs, both in terms of learning and social development.
* Free play is important because it enables children to explore their own interests and take responsibility for their own learning. In effective pre-schools, children spend two-thirds of their time in child-initiated activities.
* 'Sustained shared thinking' is a key educational technique in helping young children to learn. This involves adults interacting with children and extending their thinking, for example by asking open-ended questions.
* Strong leadership in curriculum and planning, high staff qualifications, low turnover and opportunities for professional development are all characteristics of effective pre-schools.
* An important factor is the ability to intervene to target literacy and language in ways which can improve outcomes for children at risk of low attainment, such as those living in poverty and children with EAL.
* Supporting the home learning environment through regular communication with parents and outreach programmes tailored to the needs of particular individuals and groups, is essential.

If the home learning environment can ameliorate the effects of disadvantage and is, ultimately, the most important factor in determining children's academic and social outcomes, then initiatives to improve parents' involvement in learning activities with their children at home are essential (Anning et al., 2007; Kazimirski et al., 2008; Siraj-Blatchford et al., 2003; Toroyan et al., 2004). This can be achieved either directly through working with parents, or indirectly through improving mothers' level of education. This was the thinking behind two consecutive programmes funded by central government to support practitioners to improve their work with parents: the Parents, Early Years and Learning programme (PEAL) and the Early Learning Partnership Programme (ELPP) between 2005 and 2008 (Wheeler and Connor, 2009). In order to deliver high quality provision, early childhood providers need adequate resources, good leadership, highly qualified staff and access to high quality staff training and development opportunities. The skills, qualities and professionalism that practitioners bring to their work are central to effective practice and can be enhanced by training (Adams et al., 2002). The longitudinal study Effective Provision of Pre-School Education (EPPE) (Siraj-Blatchford et al., 2003; Sylva et al., 2004) showed that strong leadership in curriculum and planning, together with low staff turnover, a supportive and clear philosophy and opportunities for professional development, are all characteristics of effectiveness.

In the context of local authorities, planning is needed to ensure that high quality provision is available where and when it is needed to support children at particular risk of poor outcomes, and to ensure that those children and their families who need help most are enabled and empowered to use those services.

Making sense of policies and targets

C4EO was established to provide not only information on 'what works' but also practical support to local authority managers in putting this into practice in their particular situations. So, for instance, one of the Centre's strategies has been to develop and train a cadre of 'sector specialists', drawn from experienced practitioners within local authorities, so that they are able to support colleagues in other areas. Using an Outcomes Based Accountability (OBA) model, these sector specialists support other practitioners to identify and deal with problems based on the outcomes that they wish to achieve (Chamberlain et al., 2010).

Initially, this tailored support from a sector peer was only provided in response to requests for assistance from a Director of Children's Services (DCS) to focus on system-level, strategic change (rather than improving front-line practice). Since April 2011, however, there has been funding from the Department for Education to provide this type of peer-to-peer support at both strategic and practice levels.

The 'menu' of typical 'hands-on' support that sector specialists provide, might include:

- help to spread knowledge of 'what works' for a particular issue, for example by running a local workshop
- support to use evidence-based audit tools to assess performance and practice
- providing an external perspective to challenge local policy, processes and practice, in light of the knowledge base acquired from the knowledge reviews
- assistance in 'translating' C4EO outputs into an appropriate local improvement plan
- facilitating the use of performance improvement or change management approaches, such as Outcomes Based Accountability (OBA) methodology
- facilitating local 'learning sets' to explore and apply the evidence base to a priority issue
- arranging and hosting events to showcase examples of effective practice from within a local area.

The following case study explains how some of these methods have been used by one sector specialist to improve outcomes.

Case study: Improving outcomes in one local authority

A local authority requested sector specialist support based on analysis of their Early Years Foundation Stage Profile data, showing that after two years of targeted work on early communication, overall outcomes had improved 5 per cent on the previous year but achievements of the most disadvantaged 20 per cent had only increased by 2 per cent; so instead of narrowing the attainment gap, it had widened.

The early years team was hence faced with the prospect that continuing efforts at improvement could make the gap worse. Data analysis enabled the sector specialist and the early years team leader to plan a system-level strategic change to their service delivery. It was decided that for this to become embedded, the work should start with Children's Centres, which were the first point of contact for many families. A workshop with all Children's Centre managers was held, at which the data showing five-year improvement trends for their postcode-reach areas identified that the priority for improvement was around narrowing the gap.

The sector specialist used the evidence from the C4EO review concerning the factors associated with achievement in the EYFSP (Coghlan et al., 2010) and identified poverty, health, parental education and the Home Learning Environment (HLE) as being significant. This led to informed discussions around the 'causes and forces' at work and the team discussed how they could use the Outcomes Based Accountability methodology to 'turn the curve' in the right direction. They identified 'Families have healthy lifestyles' as the outcome to consider for the 'turning the curve' exercise, and an action plan of what they planned to do, how and when, was written up as a 'report card' (Figure 3.2) in the Outcomes Based Accountability format, to provide a document that would be easy to review against progress.

The next stage was to meet with one of the Children's Centre staff teams to consider how they might focus their work more on 'narrowing the gap' and how they might measure the impact of this work.

The workshop with the Children's Centre team involved consideration of the issues around NI 92 that had been discussed by the senior managers, and the 'report card' around 'Families have healthy lifestyles' was explained. Each team was then asked to think about the effort that they put into their work with families – considering specifically 'how much did we do?' (the quantity) and 'how well did we do it?' (the quality). This needed them to populate the top two quadrants of an OBA service performance measures pro forma with criteria that they identified (Figure 3.3). Having completed this part of the task, the team was then asked to judge the effect of the actions they had identified, asking the questions – What difference did it make? (or How much change did we produce?) And, in the bottom right quadrant, what quality of change did we produce?

(Continued)

(Continued)

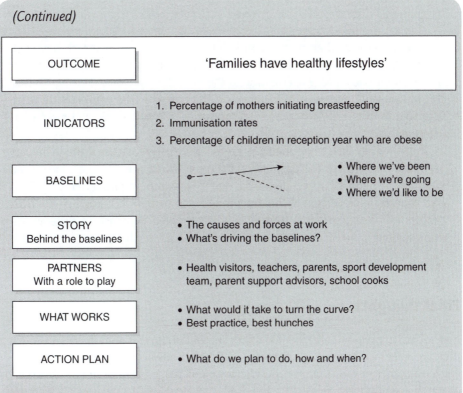

| OUTCOME | 'Families have healthy lifestyles' |

| INDICATORS |
1. Percentage of mothers initiating breastfeeding
2. Immunisation rates
3. Percentage of children in reception year who are obese

BASELINES
- Where we've been
- Where we're going
- Where we'd like to be

STORY
Behind the baselines
- The causes and forces at work
- What's driving the baselines?

PARTNERS
With a role to play
- Health visitors, teachers, parents, sport development team, parent support advisors, school cooks

WHAT WORKS
- What would it take to turn the curve?
- Best practice, best hunches

ACTION PLAN
- What do we plan to do, how and when?

Figure 3.2   'Families have healthy lifestyles' report card

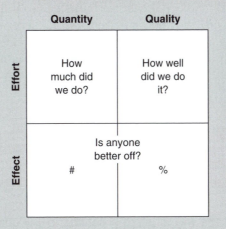

	Quantity	Quality
Effort	How much did we do?	How well did we do it?
Effect	#	Is anyone better off? %

Figure 3.3   A sample OBA service performance measures pro forma

Once the percentage responses were recorded, the team was able to identify one action that they would work on for the following year, repeating the exercise

(Continued)

(Continued)

each term to review their progress and identify whether the impact of their work was improving the outcome of narrowing the gap. They would do this by working on a 'turning the curve' exercise around the identified outcome. Having devised this system-wide approach to focusing on the outcome, the whole centre team was able to work together to address the issues in a systematic and more cost-effective way.

The following July, when the EYFS Profile results were released, the team was very eager to analyse the data around the narrowing the gap outcome to see whether the gap had in fact narrowed, and it was encouraging to see that there had been an improvement in the data. In order to sustain this progress, the OBA process was repeated again to give another targeted approach to system-wide improvement.

Final thoughts

Policies put in place by central or local government politicians and officials, even when they are informed by research findings and expert advice, can sometimes have perverse outcomes or can contain contradictory elements. It is important to use available research and specialist support to drill down at a local level to the issues which might be affecting the successful delivery of policy goals, and to use the information gleaned from such exercises to modify policy in the future and to help practitioners in other areas. For this to be effective, policy makers and funders need to understand the importance of putting in place ongoing programmes of evidence collection and dissemination at a national level so that practitioners can learn from each other and, ultimately, achieve better outcomes for children more quickly and effectively.

Summary

In this chapter, we have covered the following:

- an explanation of the policy context within which our chosen case study was delivered
- a description of the way in which a national policy goal can have perverse outcomes
- a case study of a local authority in which this happened and how this was tackled through in-depth support from a sector specialist working with a team of practitioners to identify and change their own practice.

Questions for discussion

1 From what you have learned about the work of 'sector specialists', how do you think they can provide help to a team of practitioners; could this be more effective than if they worked alone or with one of their own managers?

2 In what ways might practitioners be able to network with each other to disseminate their successes and their problems in the way that is suggested in the chapter, and what would managers need to put in place to make this possible?

3 How can statistics and other forms of data support local authority managers to improve children's outcomes: is it better to crunch numbers or observe the children?

4 The coalition government moved speedily to devolve policy making to the local level: what advantages and disadvantages do you think this might have? *(Higher-level question)*

Further reading

Levels 5 and 6

Chamberlain, T., Golden, S. and Walker, F. (2010) *Implementing Outcomes Based Accountability in Children's Services: An Overview of the Process and Impact (LG Group Research Report)*. Slough: NFER. Available online only at: www.nfer.ac.uk/nfer/publications/OBA02/OBA02.pdf

This report from the National Foundation for Educational Research (NFER) explains the origins and current usage of the OBA approach and also looks at its impact on LA practice in children's services. It provides more case studies of how the approach has been used in differing local authorities and also of barriers to its use and how these were overcome.

Wheeler, H. and Connor, J. (2009) *Parents, Early Years and Learning: Parents as Partners in the Early Years Foundation Stage*. London: National Children's Bureau.

This book describes the evidence base and practical strategies for improving relationships with parents in early years settings in order to support children's learning. It thus provides a specific example of the relationship between research, policy and practice.

Levels 6 and 7

Feinstein, L. (2003) Inequality in the early cognitive development of British children in the 1970 cohort. *Economica*, 70: 73–97.

This journal article describes the data analysis used to identify the outcomes gap which has been the subject of continuing government policy initiatives.

Sylva, K., Melhuish, E., Sammons, P., Siraj-Blatchford, I. and Taggart, B. (2004) *The Effective Provision of Pre-School Education (EPPE) Project: Final Report. A Longitudinal Study Funded by the DfES 1997–2004*. London: DfES. Available at: www.dcsf.gov.uk/research/data/uploadfiles/SSU_FR_2004_01.pdf

This is the final report of the EPPE study, evidence from which has underpinned much government policy on early years over the past 10 years.

Websites

www.c4eo.org.uk/themes/earlyyears/default.aspx
The C4EO website's early years pages include the in-depth reviews which were undertaken to inform the work illustrated in this chapter. The three themes reviewed were:

- narrowing the gap in outcomes for young children through effective practices in the early years
- improving children's attainment through a better quality of family-based support for early learning
- improving development outcomes for children through effective practice in integrating early years services.

www.education.gov.uk/tickellreview
The DfE website can be searched for a variety of sources of information and data on early years policies and for the publications which result from reviews such as the Tickell Review of the Early Years Foundation Stage which is the subject of the above link (accessed in May 2011). The Tickell Review includes a helpful discussion of the early years policy context which resulted in the policy goals described in the chapter.

Notes

1   Voluntary sector grant funding made available from April 2011 includes support for national early years organisations to provide peer-to-peer sector improvement (see www.education. gov.uk/inthenews/pressnotices/a0074906/voluntary-and-community-organisations-awarded-60-million-grant).

2   The review of the EYFS by Dame Clare Tickell was published in March 2011 and contained recommendations for simplification of the learning goals and the EYFSP (see www.education. gov.uk/tickellreview).

3   The coalition government has announced that from 2011/12, there will be no statutory early years targets but the Department for Education would expect LAs to continue to improve quality and narrow the gap. This chapter uses the original NI targets as examples of the issues related to transforming policy into practice.

4   Percentage inequality gap in achievement is calculated as follows:

(Median score for the whole population – Mean score for lowest 20 per cent of performers)/ Median score *100

5   An improvement in scores of 20 points within two years is not a realistic scenario; it is merely presented for illustration purposes.

6   FSM is only a partial measure of poverty in Key Stage 1. This is because young children are more likely than older children to have packed lunches and take-up of free school meals is not even across all ethnic groups.

References

Adams, S., Moyles, J. and Musgrove, A. (2002) *SPEEL Study of Pedagogical Effectiveness in Early Learning* (DfES Research Report No. 363). London: DfES. Available at: www.dfes.gov.uk/research/ data/uploadfiles/RR363.pdf (accessed 20 November 2009).

Anning, A., Stuart, J., Nicholls, M., Goldthorpe, J. and Morley, A. (2007) *Understanding Variations in Effectiveness amongst Sure Start Local Programmes* (Sure Start report no. 024). London: DCSF. Available at www.dfes.gov.uk/research/data/uploadfiles/NESS2007FR024.pdf (accessed 20 November 2009).

Barron, I. (2007) An exploration of young children's ethnic identities as communities of practice. *British Journal of Sociology of Education*, 28(6): 739–52.

Chamberlain, T., Golden, S. and Walker, F. (2010) *Implementing Outcomes Based Accountability in Children's Services: An Overview of the Process and Impact (LG Group Research Report)*. Slough: NFER. Available online only at: www.nfer.ac.uk/nfer/publications/OBA02/OBA02.pdf

Chang, F., Crawford, G., Early, D., Bryant, D., Howes, C., Burchinal, M. et al. (2007) Spanish-speaking children's social and language development in pre-kindergarten classrooms. *Early Education and Development*, 18(2): 243–69.

Coghlan, M., Bergeron, C., White, K., Sharp, C., Morris, M. and Wilson, R. (2010) *Narrowing the Gap in Outcomes for Young Children through Effective Practices in the Early Years* (C4EO Early Years Knowledge Review 1). London: Centre for Excellence and Outcomes in Children and Young People's Services. Available at: www.c4eo.org.uk/themes/earlyyears/ntg/files/c4eo_narrowing_the_gap_full_knowledge_review.pdf.

Conteh, J. (2007) Opening doors to success in multilingual classrooms: bilingualism, codeswitching and the professional identities of ethnic minority primary teachers. *Language and Education*, 21(6): 457–72.

D'Anguilli, A. (2005) Benefits of early literacy-intensive teaching. *Literacy Today*, 43: 1–21.

Department for Children, Schools and Families (DCSF) (2008a) *The Early Years Foundation Stage*. London: DCSF.

Department for Children, Schools and Families (DCSF) (2008b) *Early Years Foundation Stage Profile Handbook*. London: DCSF.

Department for Children, Schools and Families (DCSF) (2008c) *Every Child a Talker: Guidance for Early Language Lead Practitioners*. Available at: http://nationalstrategies.standards.dcsf.gov.uk/downloader/ca717c417ac6555a980ba002bfd758e0.pdf (accessed 11 March 2011).

Department for Education (DfE) (2010) *Early Years Foundation Stage Profile Results in England, 2009/10* (statistical first release 28/2010). London: DfE.

Department for Education and Skills (DfES) (2007) *Statutory Framework for the Early Years Foundation Stage*. Nottingham: DfES.

Feinstein, L. (2003) Inequality in the early cognitive development of British children in the 1970 cohort. *Economica*, 70: 73–97.

Fumoto, H., Hargreaves, D. and Maxwell, S. (2007) Teachers' perceptions of their relationships with children who speak English as an additional language in early childhood settings. *Journal of Early Childhood Research*, 5(2): 135–53.

Kazimirski, A., Dickens, S. and White, C. (2008) *Pilot Scheme for Two Year Old Children: Evaluation of Outreach Approaches* (DCSF Research Report No. 21). London: DCSF. Available at: www.dfes.gov.uk/research/data/uploadfiles/DCSF-RR021.pdf (accessed 20 November 2009).

McIntosh, B., Crosbie, S., Holm, A., Dodd, B. and Thomas, S. (2007) Enhancing the phonological awareness and language skills of socially disadvantaged pre-schoolers: an interdisciplinary programme. *Child Language Teaching and Therapy*, 23(3): 267–86.

Melhuish, E., Sylva, K., Sammons, P., Siraj-Blatchford, I. and Taggart, B. (2001) *Technical Paper 7: Social/behavioural and Cognitive Development at 3–4 Years in Relation to Family Background* (The Effective Provision of Pre-School Education [EPPE] project). London: DfEE/Institute of Education, University of London.

Organisation for Economic Cooperation and Development OECD (2006) *Starting Strong II: Early Childhood Education and Care*. Available at: www.oecd.org/dataoecd/14/32/37425999.pdf (accessed 11 March 2011).

Rich, S. and Davis, L. (2007) Insights into the strategic ways in which two bilingual children in the early years seek to negotiate the competing demands on their identity in their home and school worlds. *International Journal of Early Years Education*, 15(1): 35–47.

Sammons, P., Sylva, K., Melhuish, E., Siraj-Blatchford, I., Taggart, B., Elliot, K. and Marsh, A. (2004) *Technical Paper 11: Report on the Continuing Effects of Pre-school Education at Age 7* (The Effective Provision of Pre-School Education [EPPE] Project). London: DfES/Institute of Education, University of London.

Silverman, R.D. (2007) Vocabulary development of English-language and English-only learners in kindergarten. *Elementary School Journal*, 107(4): 365–83.

Sims, M. and Hutchins, T. (2001) Transition to child care for children from culturally and linguistically diverse backgrounds. *Australian Journal of Early Childhood*, 26(3): 7–11.

Siraj-Blatchford, I. and Siraj-Blatchford, J. (2009) *Improving Children's Attainment through a Better Quality of Family-based Support for Early Learning* (C4EO Early Years Knowledge Review 2). London: Centre for Excellence and Outcomes in Children and Young People's Services. Available at: www.c4eo.org.uk/themes/earlyyears/familybasedsupport/files/c4eo_family_based_support_kr_1.pdf

Siraj-Blatchford, I., Sylva, K., Taggart, B., Melhuish, E., Sammons, P. and Elliot, K. (2003) *Technical Paper 10: Intensive Case Studies of Practice across the Foundation Stage* (The Effective Provision of Pre-School Education [EPPE] Project). London: DfES/Institute of Education, University of London.

Siraj-Blatchford, I., Sylva, K., Taggart, B., Melhuish, E., Sammons, P. and Elliot, K. (2004) Technical paper 10: intensive case studies of practice across the foundation stage. Paper presented at the 5th Annual Conference of the Teaching and Learning Research Programme, Cardiff, 22–24 November.

Stuart, M. (2004) Getting ready for reading: a follow-up study of inner city second language learners at the end of Key Stage 1. *British Journal of Educational Psychology*, 74(1): 15–36.

Sylva, K., Melhuish, E., Sammons, P., Siraj-Blatchford, I. and Taggart, B. (2004) *The Effective Provision of Pre-School Education (EPPE) Project: Final Report. A Longitudinal Study Funded by the DfES 1997–2004*. London: DfES. Available at: www.dcsf.gov.uk/research/data/uploadfiles/SSU_FR_2004_01.pdf

Sylva, K., Melhuish, E., Sammons, P., Siraj-Blatchford, I. and Taggart, B. (2008) *Final Report from the Primary Phase: Pre-school, School, and Family Influences on Children's Development during Key Stage 2 (Age 7–11)* (DCSF Research Report No. 61). London: DCSF. Available at: http://publications.dcsf.gov.uk/eOrderingDownload/DCSF-RR061.pdf (accessed 13 January 2010).

Tickell, C. (2011) *The Early Years: Foundations for Life, Health and Learning*. Available at: http://media.education.gov.uk/MediaFiles/B/1/5/%7BB15EFF0D-A4DF-4294-93A1-1E1B88C13F68%7DTickell%20review.pdf (accessed 30 May 2011).

Toroyan, T., Oakley, A., Laing, G., Roberts, I., Mugford, M. and Turner, J. (2004) The impact of day care on socially disadvantaged families: an example of the use of process evaluation within a randomized controlled trial. *Child: Care, Health and Development*, 30(6): 691–8.

Wheeler, H. and Connor, J. (2009) *Parents, Early Years and Learning: Parents as Partners in the Early Years Foundation Stage*. London: National Children's Bureau.

PART 2

THE EVIDENCE BASE FOR EARLY INTERVENTION

CHAPTER 4

PROMOTING INFANT MENTAL HEALTH: A PUBLIC HEALTH PRIORITY AND APPROACH

Angela Underdown and Jane Barlow

Overview

During the past decade, there has been increasing recognition of the importance of infants receiving early sensitive care as a foundation for optimal development. Infants' brains develop rapidly in response to early interactions and evidence from disciplines such as neuroscience, psychology, biology and psychoanalysis indicates that early care-giving relationships have a long-term influence on the way individuals regulate their emotions and behaviour, and form relationships (Belsky, 2001; Fonagy et al., 2004; Panksepp, 1998; Schore, 1994; Sroufe, 1995; Stern, 1998). The sensitivity of care is influenced by a range of factors, including parents' own experiences of care giving, their mental and physical health and their broader social well-being.

(Continued)

(Continued)

Over the past decade, the UK government has prioritised early development including emotional well-being, and the Sure Start initiative (Home Office, 1998) reflected this increased recognition of the importance of the family environment, and parenting in particular, in influencing key outcomes for children (see Chapter 2). The last decade has witnessed a raft of policies that have placed early support for families with young children high on the agenda, and initiatives such as the Healthy Child Programme (DoH, 2009) have set a clear framework for universal and targeted children's services starting from conception. The first part of this chapter explores the implications of well-being in the pre- and post-natal periods, and reflects on the impact of the parent's relationship with the infant, both in-utero and afterwards, on later development. The second half of the chapter examines the ways in which policy and practice have evolved to support parents and early parenting during this crucial period. The implementation in England of the Healthy Child Programme (DoH, 2009) is discussed, and key concepts such as 'progressive universalism' are explored alongside innovative programmes designed to promote infant mental health.

Defining infant mental health

The study of infant mental health is relatively new and is the result of a synthesis of research and theory from a wide range of disciplines. For example, research in the field of developmental psychology has begun to demonstrate the crucial ways in which an infant's secure attachment to a primary caregiver, enables infants to begin to regulate their emotions. Indeed, this developing body of research shows that one of the key developmental tasks that takes place within the first year is emotional and behavioural regulation (Schore, 1994) (see also Chapter 5).

Emotional and behavioural regulation refers to the process by which babies learn to manage their feelings and behaviour, and one of the central findings of recent years has been that this process, known as 'co-regulation', is a central aspect of the infant's relationship with their main caregivers. So, for example, a mother may contain his 6-month-old son's cries of hunger by gentle talking and reassurance that his dinner is coming as quickly as possible! Over repeated episodes, the baby begins to be able to trust that his cries of hunger have been heard, and can begin to regulate his feelings and behaviour, and thereby wait for food to arrive. For infants experiencing erratic care, the process of co-regulation is more challenging.

The young child's capacity to experience, regulate and express emotions, and form close and secure relationships is a key developmental task, undertaken within the context of a care-giving environment that includes family, community and cultural expectations. These capacities are synonymous with healthy emotional and social development (Zeanah, 2009).

Infant development can thus be considered within the context not only of intimate relationships, but the broader set of factors that influence interactive exchanges. Bronfenbrenner's ecological systems theory (Figure 4.1) demonstrates the interplay of influences on infant mental health. This dynamic framework is useful in helping us to understand how healthy child development can best be supported. The framework can be used to help identify influential factors within any culture or setting, and the example below explores the systems in relation to women and men in the transition to parenthood.

The **MICROSYSTEM** represents the innermost layer in which parents-to-be are influenced by interactions with each other and those with whom they are in day-to-day contact. Support during this period has been shown to be important and conflict may increase stress hormones, which in turn can impact on the unborn child. Stress and conflict also impact on the woman's capacity to reflect on what her unborn child might be like – the beginning of her bonding with the infant.

The **EXOSYSTEM** surrounds the microsystem and highlights the way in which expectant parents are constantly interacting with and being influenced by relationships and events in the workplace, community and local services.

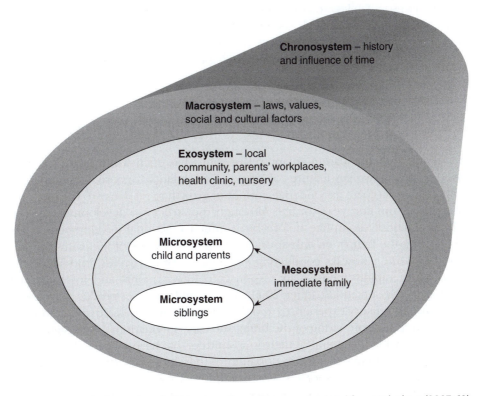

Figure 4.1   Bronfenbrenner's ecological systems theory. Diagram reproduced from Underdown (2007: 11)

The **MACROSYSTEM** represents the wider social and cultural systems within which the parents-to-be live. In some societies or cultures, there may be, for example, extensive protective birth rituals, while in others the birth may have become medicalised with short periods of maternity and paternity leave. Similarly, perceptions about teenage parenthood vary cross-culturally, with significant implications in terms of the experiences of the pregnant teenager.

The **CHRONOSYSTEM** represents the various historical factors that continue to influence a parent-to-be over time. For example, the research highlights a process during pregnancy in which women re-think their relationship with their own mother, and may experience a psychic re-organisation that influences their attitudes towards and representations of their developing infants (Huth-Bocks et al., 2004).

There is a developing body of research examining the above factors for parents-to-be (Huth-Bocks et al., 2004; Stern, 1998). For example, the evidence shows that for some men and women, the transition to parenthood and future child development may be compromised by poverty, domestic violence, mental health problems or addictions, which impact on the capacity for sensitive parenting and attachment (Zeanah, 2009). There is also a significant body of research demonstrating a direct impact of factors such as chronic maternal anxiety and depression, on the developing central nervous system of the foetus, and on later infant and child development. This shows, for example, that depression during pregnancy contributes to newborn fussiness and non-soothability, and in conjunction with anxiety is associated with negative reactivity in 2- and 4-month-olds (Bergner et al., 2008). Similarly, anxiety during pregnancy doubles the risk for hyperactivity in boys at 4 years, contributes to emotional and behavioural problems at 47 months and is predictive of impulsivity on performance tasks at 14–15 years (2008).

How does sensitive care underpin healthy development?

The reason that the parent–infant relationship has such a big impact at this period relates to two key features of infancy. First, infants are born with immature brains that undergo an exponential amount of growth in response to the environment during the first years of life. Although the structural development of the brain is practically complete before birth, much functional development takes place during the brain's growth spurt in the first two years of life, with a proliferation of nerve pathways conducting electrical messages across fluid-filled synapses, which rapidly increase in response to interpersonal and intrapersonal experiences (Nelson and Bosquet, 2000). The infant brain over-produces synapses in response to sensory experiences and then 'prunes' away those that are unused. In addition to the soft wiring of the brain, the early interactions play a significant role in influencing the chemical neurotransmitters that have a direct effect on the brain (e.g. neuropeptides such as dopamine), thereby setting the thermostat for later control of stress responses. For example, excessive stress during infancy results in the baby's brain being flooded with cortisol for prolonged periods, and an eventual lowering of the threshold for activation of fear/anxiety, resulting in the child experiencing more fear/anxiety and difficulty in dampening this response (Gerhardt, 2004).

In her book *Why Love Matters*, Sue Gerhardt (2004) shows the way in which looks and smiles between parent and baby help the baby's brain to grow, by stimulating the baby's nervous system and heart rate, leading to a biochemical response in the baby's brain and the release of pleasure neuropeptides (such as betaendorphin and dopamine). Negative looks, on the other hand, trigger a different biochemical response involving the release of cortisol, which is detrimental in terms of the growth of the brain.

The second important factor about infancy is that babies are born to relate. Indeed, they begin doing so immediately following birth. In the first 15 hours, they can distinguish their mother's voice and prefer it to a stranger; they also prefer her smell and her face. Neonates can discriminate among surprise, fear and sadness expressions in caregivers, and produce corresponding facial expressions of their own. Infants are able to detect contingencies between what they do and what the environmental response is to their actions, thereby facilitating an early sense of agency; they also develop expectancies regarding what to expect from social interactions based on earlier experiences, and babies' exposure to affect (emotion) from 10 months on influences the lateralization of their brain (summarized in Beebe and Lachmann, 2002). So, for example, evidence shows that babies of depressed mothers have reduced brain activity and, in particular, much lower levels of left-frontal brain activity (Dawson et al., 2006), thereby predisposing such babies to more depressive responses later in life. Early experiences of seriously sub-optimal parenting, such as persistent neglect and trauma, have been shown to result in overdevelopment of the neurophysiology of the brainstem and midbrain (leading to anxiety, impulsivity, poor affect regulation and hyperactivity), and deficits in cortical function (leading to difficulties with problem solving) and limbic function (leading to a reduced capacity for empathy) (Gerhardt, 2004). Research shows that early disturbances in parent–child interactions are implicated in a range of longer-term adverse child cognitive and emotional outcomes, including behavioural problems (Kobak and Madsen, 2008).

Which aspects of parenting are important for infants?

The key aspects of parenting that are now recognised to be important to infant mental health, in terms of facilitating the infant's ability for affect regulation, are illustrated in Figure 4.2.

Sensitivity and warmth in response to infants have been identified as crucial elements in healthy interactions and this is conveyed through eye contact, voice tone, pitch and rhythm, facial expression and touch. When two people are attuned (Stern, 1985), an empathetic understanding of shared emotions may be experienced. However, infant and adult are not attuned all the time and it is through frequent

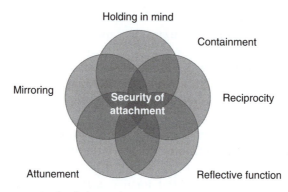

Figure 4.2   The key aspects of early interaction

healthy 'ruptures and repairs' of attunement that much learning about interaction and the regulation of emotions and behaviour takes place. Reciprocity involves turn-taking and occurs when an infant and adult are involved in initiating, sustaining and terminating interactions. Young babies are socially interactive and seek to initiate interaction from an early age. When babies fail to elicit responses, they eventually stop trying to engage, and this can be seen happening in videotape footage of babies in orphanages who receive little interaction. Mirroring (Winnicott, 1971) happens when a parent shows a contingent response to an infant, such as looking sad when the baby is crying. It is important that mirroring is 'contingent' to show the infant that their emotion is understood but also that it is 'marked' or sufficiently different to demonstrate that things can be made better (Gergely and Watson, 1996). This is closely linked with containment (Bion, 1962), which occurs when the adult takes on board the infant's powerful feelings and makes them more manageable, using touch, gesture and speech. Parents rocking a crying infant and saying sensitively 'there, there, you are going to be alright' are helping the baby manage his or her emotions both now and in the future. Reflective function (Fonagy et al., 1991), mentalisation (Allen and Fonagy, 2006) and mind-mindedness (Meins and Fernyhough, 1999) are similar and refer to parents' capacities to experience their baby as an 'intentional being' and to understand the child's behaviour in terms of internal states such as feelings. Recent research showed that a parent's capacity for 'mind-mindedness' (i.e. her ability to interpret her baby's feelings) in the first two years of life, was a better predictor of development (including the child's ability to represent her thoughts and feelings through language and play) than background, income or socio-economic status (Meins, 2004).

The security of attachment

Through everyday interactions, most parents recognise their infants' unique personalities, including their individual likes and dislikes, sensitivities and strengths.

Research from a range of disciplines has demonstrated the particular importance of the first and second years of life in terms of the infant's *emotional attachments*, and their role in establishing later mental health (Bowlby, 1969, 1988; Fonagy et al., 2004; Schore, 1994, 2001; Sroufe, 1995; Steele et al., 1996; Stern, 1998). Bowlby (1958) first identified the crucial role that the loving attachment between an infant and his mother plays in the development of mental health. Infants attach to familiar carers when they respond appropriately to their physical and emotional needs, and by about 6 or 7 months, they will begin to demonstrate appropriate attachment behaviours such as seeking out the parent when they are distressed, and being wary of strangers and clinging on to their main caregivers. Bowlby referred to these babies as 'securely attached' and suggested that this provides such infants with a 'secure base' from which to begin to explore the world. Subsequent research has confirmed the work of Bowlby, including the way in which the infant uses early interactional exchanges, to build up 'internal working models' that provide a template for later relationships. Approximately one-third of children who have experienced the type of parenting in which their bids for comfort and security from their parent were either rejected, or treated with an unpredictable mixture of acceptance and rejection, are insecurely attached (Cassidy and Shaver, 2008). Infants who have experienced attuned and responsive early parenting will have built up internal working models of themselves as lovable, and of other individuals as responsive and caring. Infants who have experienced erratic and unresponsive early care giving may feel insecure about the extent to which they are lovable, and less certain about the reliability of other people. Research suggests that insecure attachment is associated with less optimal outcomes across a range of developmental domains, including peer relations, intimacy, care giving and caretaking, sexual functioning, conflict resolution and relational aggression (Cassidy and Shaver, 2008).

More recently, research has shown that children who experience emotionally abusive and neglectful relationships during the first two years of life, are more likely to develop a 'disorganised' insecure attachment, which reflects a failure to establish a coherent attachment strategy, and is strongly associated with a range of seriously adverse developmental outcomes including social and cognitive difficulties, and a number of aspects of severe psychopathology (Cassidy and Shaver, 2008). There is evidence that the earlier the onset of insensitive care, the greater the likelihood of serious psychopathology (Zeanah, 2009). There is also increasing evidence that infants who are exposed to unmitigated distress, perhaps through exposure to violence or other traumas, may become chronically anxious (Lyons-Ruth and Block, 1996; Perry et al., 1995).

The above evidence points to the importance of a primary preventative approach to supporting infant mental health within early relationships. It is also far more effective and less costly to prevent emotional problems than to deal with the consequences later (Scott et al., 2001). In the next section, we describe the key policy and practice changes that have occurred in response to this growing body of evidence about the importance of early relationships.

Policy context

In 1998, a consultation paper *Supporting Families* (Home Office, 1998) outlined how Sure Start projects were to be established in areas of disadvantage, specifically to work with families with infants from conception to nursery age. Sure Start projects provided innovative ways of supporting early relationships and interventions, such as teaching parents to massage their infants. However, the subsequent National Evaluation of Sure Start (NESS) found wide variability in the quality of Sure Start programmes generally (DfES/DH/Sure Start, 2006) (see Chapter 2 for further discussion).

The next decade witnessed a raft of policies that included early intervention and parenting support. The public health White Paper *Choosing Health* (DoH, 2004a) and *Every Parent Matters* (DCSF, 2007) highlighted the importance of supporting parenting in terms of later outcomes for children. The government White Paper *Aiming High for Children: Supporting Families* (HM Treasury and DfES, 2007) recognised the need for 'early intervention' and introduced the concept of 'progressive universalism'. A progressive universal approach to the delivery of services involves the provision of universal services to all families, with such services being used to identify families in need of more progressive or intensive levels of support. This policy document also introduced the Family Nurse Partnership programme (based on Olds, 2006) which provides intensive support to pregnant teenagers, that continues for the first two years following birth. *The National Service Framework for Children, Young People and Maternity Services* (NSF) (DoH, 2004b) set out a 10-year plan that was aimed at stimulating long-term and sustained improvement in children's health and well-being, and *Every Child Matters* (DfES, 2003) outlined five key areas for children: being healthy; staying safe; enjoying and achieving; making a positive contribution; and achieving economic well-being. The creation of Children's Centres in deprived neighbourhoods was seen as being key to improving these five aspects. Most recently, the *Health Visitor Implementation Plan 2011–2015: A Call to Action* (DoH, 2011) provides a core 'offer' to all families that ranges from the provision of community-based services, through universal, universal-plus and universal partnership levels of provision, and is being tested in a number of early implementation sites across England.

A public health approach to early interventions

Public health aims to promote optimum health and development, and has been defined as the science and art of promoting health, the prevention of disease and the prolonging of life through organised efforts within society (Acheson, 1998). A public health approach to the mental health of infants involves the implementation of high quality, universal interventions that can support family relationships. Such provision is underpinned by a primary preventative approach, which involves the use of supportive interventions that serve all families in the population with the goal of promoting sensitive parenting practices. Primary preventative approaches begin in pregnancy, and involve primary care and early years practitioners' identifying problems early, and offering progressively more intensive services where need is identified (progressive universalism). A public health approach also involves the implementation of targeted interventions aimed at the primary prevention of insensitive, neglectful or abusive care.

The Healthy Child Programme

The revised Healthy Child Programme (HCP) (DoH, 2009) provides guidance for supporting parents from the ante-natal period onwards. The HCP states that 'an effective and high-quality preventive programme in childhood is the foundation of a healthy society' (DoH, 2009: 2), and is based on a model of progressive universalism. The HCP promotes services that begin during pregnancy, with support for men and women to negotiate the emotional and social transition to parenthood and the first year of life, and to help parents to provide sensitive and attuned parenting to underpin healthy attachments.

The HCP recognises that children who are emotionally healthy are also ready to learn and enjoy educational opportunities. If the HCP is implemented effectively, it should lead to:

- strong parent–child attachment and positive parenting, resulting in better social and emotional well-being among children
- care that helps to keep children healthy and safe
- healthy eating and increased activity, leading to a reduction in obesity
- prevention of some serious and communicable diseases
- increased rates of initiation and continuation of breastfeeding
- readiness for school and improved learning
- early recognition of growth disorders and risk factors for obesity
- early detection of – and action to address – developmental delay, abnormalities and ill health, and concerns about safety
- identification of factors that could influence health and well-being in families
- better short- and long-term outcomes for children who are at risk of social exclusion. (DoH, 2009: 6)

The HCP is led by health visitors and is increasingly being delivered through integrated services that bring together Sure Start Children's Centre staff, GPs, midwives, community nurses and others. There is also an increasing role for the voluntary sector (Coe and Barlow, 2010). Children's Centres offer a unique opportunity for integrated delivery of community-based services, and are both visible and involve partnership working across a range of agencies. This model of working increases families' exposure to a wider range of skills and expertise, and increases the delivery of effective services to families. (For a summary of research on integrated working, see Barlow with Scott [2010].) Early years practitioners have a key role, both in identifying and supporting parents during this important period in terms of children's development. The next two sections examine a range of evidence-based methods of achieving this.

A partnership approach

The Healthy Child Programme is underpinned by recognition that early years workers are most effective when they adopt a partnership approach to working with parents. Traditionally, health workers have assumed an expert role, in which they aim to identify problems, and then provide brief advice and solutions. In contrast, a partnership approach involves developing the expertise of the parent, and working alongside them to promote the best outcomes for themselves and their children. This model of working requires particular qualities and skills in the helper to enable them to be in contact with mothers and infants by observing and listening, and the kind of relationship that enables empathy to develop (Egan, 1990). Rogers (1959) suggests that the qualities of empathy, respect and genuineness are necessary if support and change are to be fostered through working in partnerships with others. Partnership relationships are built on mutual respect and open communication where the two partners share a common aim. Table 4.1 summarises the skills that have been identified as being intrinsic to the helping process (Davis et al., 2002).

Qualities may also be defined as 'personal characteristics' and skills defined as 'competencies'. Although Egan (1990) argues that helpers cannot respond effectively unless they have empathic qualities, he also argues that the skills of listening and understanding that underpin empathy can be learnt. It is therefore important to consider helper qualities and skills holistically and as interdependent.

The Family Partnership Model is underpinned by a recognition of the importance of both skills and qualities (Davis et al., 2002), and an understanding of the 'helping process' of which relationship building is an integral part. The process of helping involves a number of key stages (including exploration, understanding, goal setting, strategy planning, implementation and review) (2002), with the aim of enabling parents to develop more helpful or effective 'constructions' or understanding about their situation and the possible solutions (2002). The partnership stages are all based on building an effective partnership relationship between the helper, the parents and

Table 4.1   Helper qualities. Adapted from Davis et al. (2002) and Rogers (1959)

Quality	Description
Respect	Rogers (1959) refers to this as 'unconditional positive regard', accepting the mother and infant in a constructive, warm and positive way
Genuineness	Involving honesty, sincerity and reliability
Humility	Being realistic about what one has to offer and being able to communicate openly with parents (without the defences of the 'expert' model)
Empathy	Attempting to perceive the situation from the parents' perspective and supportively facilitating them to explore aspects they may want to change
Personal integrity	The capacity to support vulnerable parents and infants without being overwhelmed so that parents can be objectively helped to explore other possibilities
Enthusiasm	This is linked with respect and integrity and refers to the positive energy that a helper brings to their role

Table 4.2   Skills of helpers. Adapted from Davis et al. (2002)

Skill	Description
Partnerships skills	It takes time to build a trusting relationship; it requires power sharing which recognises the parents as the 'senior' partners with individual knowledge of their infants; the facilitator may help to 'scaffold' the parents to 'unfold' their knowledge and understanding about their infant's individual strengths and sensitivities
Listening and relating skills	Effective communication requires focus and concentration in listening to what the parent and the infant are saying. Infant massage programmes are unusual in having infants as active participants. Facilitators' roles involve working in partnership to 'scaffold' the interaction between parent and infant. Effective facilitators also bring energy or 'quiet enthusiasm' and encouragement
Enabling change in feelings and ideas and actions	Change may be enabled through the process of listening to parents; through observing interactions through touch, vocalisation, facial and body language modelled by peers and the facilitator; and through informal discussion with peers and facilitator
Technical expertise	Sharing knowledge and expertise in a meaningful and useful manner
Problem management	Enabling parents to share and explore problems, think through priorities, set goals, plan and implement strategies, in order to make the problem more manageable

their children. This trusting relationship acts as a foundation for working with parents to promote children's health and well-being, and this approach has been found to be more effective than traditional expert-led advice giving (Miller and Rollnick, 2002). A partnership model acknowledges the parents' knowledge about the child and helps the parents explore and reframe problems so that goals can be jointly set and strategies implemented and reviewed. The partnership model may be more time-consuming and emotionally demanding because the helper seeks an in-depth understanding of the problem. Helpers using the partnership model need to have training and skilled supervision to support them to work in this way.

Interventions

The Healthy Child Programme (HCP) supports the delivery of a range of evidence-based methods of supporting parents and parenting during the perinatal period. In pregnancy the HCP recommends the provision of group-based methods of supporting the emotional transition to parenthood, and a range of organisations are offering innovative provisions. So, for example, the Solihull Approach (Douglas and Rheeston, 2009) has developed an ante-natal education programme, and the NHS has commissioned National Childbirth Trust (NCT) classes in some areas. These comprise six hours of classes over three weeks plus a breastfeeding workshop, and numbers are capped at 10 couples. The course has been evaluated positively (NCT, 2007), with users speaking very highly about the content and delivery.

Other highly innovative methods that have not yet been formally evaluated are aimed explicitly at developing the relationship between the mother and her baby in-utero, and include practitioners encouraging pregnant women to massage their abdomens and have conversations with their unborn babies. Similarly, Bookstart (Book Trust, at www.bookstart.org.uk/about-us/) have produced a pack of books that can be shared by practitioners, particularly with deprived parents, as a way of encouraging pregnant women to read to and thereby connect with the unborn child.

The HCP (DoH, 2009) advocates that parents should be offered promotional narrative interviews, and health visitors are being trained to conduct these before and after all new births. This consists of an ante- and post-natal home visit, aimed at supporting the transition to parenthood and promoting positive interaction between parent and infant. So, for example, pre-natal interviews focus on: feelings about pregnancy and emotional preparation for birth; parents' perceptions of their unborn child; the parent–infant relationship; and new roles. As part of this interview, the health visitor explores with and encourages the woman to identify her perceptions and anticipation of her unborn child with questions such as 'how is your baby?'; 'how do you imagine your baby now?'; 'what do you think your baby is going to be like?' Positive feelings are then endorsed and negative feelings explored further and talked about.

The post-natal promotional interview is conducted at home 6–8 weeks after the birth, with the infant present, so that interaction can be observed, and focuses on: the birth experience; perceptions of the baby; parents' emotional resources for the baby; parent–infant interaction; and the development of new roles. Promotional interviews therefore comprise both a universal intervention and a supportive method of identifying families at risk of developing child mental health problems.

The HCP also recommends the use of a wide range of evidence-based, universal and targeted methods of supporting families during the post-natal period (Barlow et al., 2010). These comprise simple media-based tools such as the use of *The Social Baby* book and DVD (Murray and Andrews, 2000) to increase parental awareness about early perceptual and cognitive abilities, skin-to-skin care and the use of baby carriers to promote bonding, as well as group-based support such as infant massage that is aimed at improving parent–infant interaction and raising awareness about infant states and cues (Underdown and Barlow, 2011). More progressive and intensive methods of support include parenting and home-visiting programmes, video-interaction guidance, and parent–infant psychotherapy.

In addition to the more formal methods of supporting parents, the HCP recommends that practitioners act as role models, use every exchange with parents to encourage sensitive interaction, and identify parents who may be having problems in relating to their baby, and may be in need of additional support. The latter includes parents experiencing mental health problems, using alcohol or drugs, and families experiencing domestic violence.

Final thoughts

The mental health of infants is important because it provides the foundation for all aspects of later development and well-being. Research across a range of disciplines points to the importance of pregnancy and the first two years of life in the development of infant mental health, and emphasises, in particular, the importance of the parent–infant relationship in helping the baby to develop good affect regulation. The Healthy Child Programme involves the provision of a range of evidence-based interventions on a progressive universal basis, during pregnancy and the post-natal period, with the aim of supporting parents, and the early parent–infant relationship. Early years practitioners have a key role in promoting infant mental health, by working alongside other practitioners in the delivery of the HCP.

Summary

- In this chapter, theory and research from a range of disciplines has been used to highlight the crucial nature of how early infant development takes place within relationships.
- We describe the key aspects of early interaction and link these with infants' developing attachments to their carers.
- A public health approach to supporting infant mental health is used to explore early interventions in pregnancy and early infancy.
- The HCP has been introduced and partnership approaches to working with families have been reviewed.

Questions for discussion

1 Why do you think sensitive relationships are important for the developing infant?
2 What do you think is the difference between an expert model and a partnership model of helping parents?
3 In what ways might practitioners work to encourage parents to build a relationship with their infant ante-natally?
4 How effective do you think the Healthy Child Programme may be in meeting the aim of promoting infant mental health within families? *(Higher-level question)*

Further reading

Levels 5 and 6

Barlow, J. and Underdown, A. (2008) Attachment and infant development. In: C. Jackson, K. Hill and P. Lavis (eds) *Child and Adolescent Mental Health Today: A Handbook.* Mental Health Foundation/Pavillion.

This chapter discusses the essential role that attachment plays in infants' emotional and neurological development.

Barlow, J. and Underdown, A. (2008) Supporting parenting during infancy. In: C. Jackson, K. Hill and P. Lavis (eds) *Child and Adolescent Mental Health Today: A Handbook.* Mental Health Foundation/Pavillion.

This reading explores different preventative models of intervention that have been developed to support positive parenting.

The Healthy Child Programme (DoH, 2009) www.dh.gov.uk/prod_consum_dh/groups/dh_digital assets/@dh/@en/@ps/documents/digitalasset/dh_118525.pdf (accessed March 2011).

The Healthy Child Programme was published as Guidance by the Department of Health and the Department of Children, Schools and Families in March 2009. The programme starts in pregnancy and is led by health visitors and delivered by the early years workforce in primary health care and Children's Centres. The programme is based on principles of primary prevention and progressive universalism.

Levels 6 and 7

Slade, A., Grienenberger, J., Bernbach, E., Levy, D. and Locker, A. (2005) Maternal reflective functioning, attachment, and the transmission gap: a preliminary study. *Attachment and Human Development*, 7(3): 283–98.

This article considers how reflective functioning (the parent's capacity to hold her baby and her mental states in mind) enables a psychological experience of comfort and safety to be created for the child and the impacts on attachment.

Underdown, A. and Barlow, J. (2011) Interventions to support early relationships: mechanisms identified within massage programmes. *Community Practitioner*, 84(4): 21–6.

This article reports on a study into infant massage programmes and identifies mechanisms that support early relationships.

Websites

www.aimh.org.uk
The Association for Infant Mental Health AIMH (UK) is an autonomous body affiliated to the World Association for Infant Mental Health (WAIMH). Infant mental health is the study of mental health as it applies to infants and their families. The field investigates optimal social and emotional development of infants and their families in the first three years of life.

www.zerotothree.org
Zero to Three is a national, non-profit organisation that informs, trains and supports professionals, policy makers and parents in their efforts to improve the lives of infants and toddlers.

References

Acheson, D. (1998) *Independent Inquiry into Inequalities in Health Report.* London: The Stationery Office.

Allen, J. and Fonagy, P. (eds) (2006) *Handbook of Mentalization-based Treatment.* Chichester: Wiley.

Barlow, J. with Scott, J. (2010) *Safeguarding in the 21st Century: Where to Now?* London: Research in Pratice [Monograph].

Barlow, J., Schrader McMillan, A., Kirkpatrick, S., Ghate, D., Barnes, J. and Smith, M. (2010) Evidence for health-led interventions in the postnatal period to enhance infant and maternal mental health: a review of reviews. *Child and Adolescent Mental Health*, 15(4): 178–85.

Beebe, B. and Lachmann, F. (2002) *Infant Research and Adult Treatment: Co-constructing Interactions*. Hillsdale, NJ: The Analytic Press.

Belsky, J. (2001) Developmental risks (still) associated with childcare. *Journal of Child Psychology and Psychiatry*, 42(7): 845–59.

Bergner, S., Monk, C. and Werner, E.A. (2008) Dyadic intervention during pregnancy? Treating pregnant women and possibly reaching the future baby. *Infant Mental Health Journal*, 29(5): 399–419.

Bion, W. (1962) *Learning from Experience*. London: Heinemann.

Bowlby, J. (1958) The nature of the child's tie to his mother. *International Journal of Psychoanalysis*, 39(5): 350–73.

Bowlby, J. (1969) *Attachment and Loss, 1: Attachment*. New York: Basic Books.

Bowlby, J. (1988) *A Secure Base*. London: Routledge.

Cassidy, J. and Shaver, P. (eds) (2008) *Handbook of Attachment: Theory, Research and Clinical Application*. New York: Guilford.

Coe, C. and Barlow, J. (2010) Working in partnership with the voluntary sector: Early Explorer clinics. *Community Practitioner*, 83(11): 33–6.

Davis, H., Day, C. and Bidmead, C. (2002) *Working in Partnership with Parents: The Parent Adviser Model*. London: Harcourt Assessment.

Dawson, G., Frey, K., Panagiotides, H., Osterlind, J. and Hessl, D. (2006) Infants of depressed mothers exhibit atypical frontal brain activity: a replication and extension of previous findings. *Journal of Child Psychology and Psychiatry*, 38(2): 179–86.

Department for Children, Schools and Families (DCSF) (2007) *Every Parent Matters*. London: DfES.

Department for Education and Skills (DfES) (2003) *Every Child Matters*. London: DfES.

Department for Education and Skills (DfES) (2007) *Family and Parenting Support in Sure Start Local Programmes*. National Evaluation Sure Start Report 023, July. Nottingham: DfES.

Department for Education and Skills (DfES), Department of Health (DH) and Sure Start (2006) *Sure Start Children's Centres: Practice Guidance*. London: DfES/DH/Sure Start.

Department of Health (DoH) (2004a) *Choosing Health*. London: The Stationery Office.

Department of Health (DoH) (2004b) *National Service Framework for Children, Young People and Maternity Services: The Mental Health and Psychological Wellbeing of Children and Young People*. Available at: www.dh.gov.uk/en/Publicationsandstatistics/Publications/PublicationsPolicyAndGuidance/DH_4089114 (accessed 12 May 2011).

Department of Health (DoH) (2009) *Healthy Child Programme: Pregnancy and the First Five Years of Life*. London: DoH.

Department of Health (DoH) (2011) *Health Visitor Implementation Plan 2011–2015: A Call to Action*. Available at: www.dh.gov.uk/en/Publicationsandstatistics/Publications/PublicationsPolicyAndGuidance/DH_124202 (accessed 12 May 2011).

Douglas, H. and Rheeston, M. (2009) The Solihull Approach: an integrative model across agencies. Chapter 3 in: J. Barlow and P.O. Svanberg (eds) *Keeping the Baby in Mind: Infant Mental Health in Practice*. Hove: Routledge.

Egan, G. (1990) *The Skilled Helper: A Systematic Approach to Effective Helping*. Belmont, CA: Brookes/Cole Publishing.

Fonagy, P., Gergely, G., Jurist, E. and Target, M. (2004) *Affect Regulation, Mentalization and the Development of the Self*. London: Karnac Books.

Fonagy, P., Steele, M., Moran, G., Steele, H. and Higgitt, A. (1991) The capacity for understanding mental states: the reflective self in parent and child and its significance for security of attachment. *Infant Mental Health Journal*, 13: 200–16.

Gergely, G. and Watson, J. (1996) The social biofeedback model of parent–affect mirroring. *International Journal of Psycho-Analysis*, 77: 1181–212.

Gerhardt, S. (2004) *Why Love Matters: How Affection Shapes a Baby's Brain*. Hove: Brunner-Routledge.

HM Treasury and Department for Education and Skills (DfES) (2007) *Aiming High for Children: Supporting Families*. Available at: http://publications.education.gov.uk/eOrderingDownload/PU188.pdf (accessed January 2009).

Home Office (1998) *Supporting Families*. London: HMSO.

Huth-Bocks, A., Levendosky, A., Theran, S. and Bogat, A. (2004) The impact of domestic violence on mothers' prenatal representations of their infants. *Infant Mental Health Journal*, 25(2): 79–98.

Kobak, R. and Madsen, S. (2008) Disruptions in attachment bonds: implications for theory, research and clinical intervention. Chapter 2 in: J. Cassidy and P. Shaver (eds) *Handbook of Attachment: Theory, Research and Clinical Application*. New York: Guilford.

Lyons-Ruth, K. and Block, D. (1996) The disturbed care-giving system: relations among childhood trauma, maternal caregiving, and infant affect and attachment. *Infant Mental Health Journal*, 17: 257–75.

Meins, E. (2004) Infants' minds, mothers' minds and other minds: how individual differences in caregivers affect the co-construction of mind. *Behavioral and Brain Sciences*, 27(1): 116.

Meins, E. and Fernyhough, C. (1999) Lingusitic acquisitional style and mentalizing development: the role of maternal mind-mindedness. *Cognitive Development*, 14: 363–80.

Miller, W. and Rollnick, S. (2002) *Motivational Interviewing: Preparing People for Change,* 2nd edition. New York: Guilford Press.

Murray, L. and Andrews, L. (2000) *The Social Baby*. London: The Children's Project.

National Childbirth Trust (NCT) (2007) *Preparing for Birth: What Do Parents Think of Antenatal Education at Birmingham Women's Hospital?* London: National Childbirth Trust.

Nelson, C. and Bosquet, M. (2000) Neurobiology of fetal and infant development: implications for infant mental health. Chapter 3 in: C.H. Zeanah Jr. (ed.) *Handbook of Infant Mental Health*, 2nd edition. New York: Guilford Press.

Olds, D.L. (2006) The nurse–family partnership: an evidence-based preventive intervention. *Infant Mental Health Journal*, 27: 5–25.

Panksepp, J. (1998) *Affective Neuroscience: The Foundations of Human and Animal Emotions*. Oxford: Oxford University Press.

Perry, B., Pollard, R., Blakely, R., Baher, W. and Vigilanti, D. (1995) Childhood trauma, the neurobiology of adaptation and user-dependent development of the brain: how 'states' become 'traits'. *Infant Mental Health Journal*, 16: 271–91.

Rogers, C. (1959) A theory of therapy, personality and interpersonal relationships as developed in a client-centred framework. In: S. Koch (ed.) *Psychology: A Study of Science*, vol. 3. New York: McGraw-Hill.

Schore, A. (1994) *Affect Regulation and the Origin of the Self: The Neurobiology of Emotional Development*. Hillsdale, NJ: Lawrence Erlbaum.

Schore, A. (2001) The effects of secure attachment relationship on the right brain development, affect regulation and infant mental health. *Infant Mental Health Journal*, 22: 7–66.

Scott, S., Knapp, M., Henderson, J. and Maughan, B. (2001) Financial cost of social exclusion: follow-up study of antisocial children into adulthood. *British Medical Journal*, 323: 1–5.

Sroufe, L. (1995) *Emotional Development: The Organization of Emotional Life in the Early Years*. Cambridge: Cambridge University Press.

Steele, H., Steele, M. and Fonagy, P. (1996) Associations among attachment classifications of mothers, fathers and their infants. *Child Development*, 67: 541–55.

Stern, D. (1985) *The Interpersonal World of the Infant*. London: Karnac Books.

Stern, D. (1998) *The Motherhood Constellation*. London: Karnac Books.

Underdown, A. (2007) *Young Children's Health and Well-being*. Maidenhead: Open University Press.

Underdown, A. and Barlow, J. (2011) Interventions to support early relationships: mechanisms identified within massage programmes. *Community Practitioner*, 84(4): 21–6.

Winnicott, D. (1971) Mirror-role of mother and family in child development. In: *Playing and Reality*. London: Tavistock, 111–18.

Zeanah, C. (ed.) (2009) *Handbook of Infant Mental Health*, 3rd edition. New York: Guilford Press.

CHAPTER 5

ENHANCING THE POTENTIAL IN CHILDREN (EPIC)

Stuart Shanker and Roger Downer

Overview

We are currently in the midst of a profound revolution in educational thinking and practice. Of particular significance is our recognition that the well-established difficulty of altering a child's educational trajectory following commencement of formal schooling is not due to failings of the parents, teachers or, indeed, the educational system. Rather, the child's educational achievement is, in large part, shaped by basic neurological traits that influence her ability to cope with the challenges of formal schooling. Principal among these factors is the child's capacity for self-regulation, which is critical in enabling her to respond efficiently and effectively to the various stressors to which she is exposed. Recognition and

(Continued)

(Continued)

understanding of the nature of self-regulation has enabled the successful design and implementation of intervention strategies to enhance a child's capacity to learn. To date, the successes have been achieved in the laboratory through intensive, customised therapy sessions, and the next challenge is to take the lessons learned from the laboratory and apply them in pre-school and classroom settings.

This chapter explains the scientific basis of self-regulation and the policy response in one province of Canada (Ontario) that includes the development and adoption of curricula that embrace this new understanding in order to increase the ability of children to achieve their full educational potential.

Background to the EPIC programme

The Sherritt-sponsored Enhancing Potential In Children (EPIC) Foundation was established[1] to support implementation of findings emanating from research on childhood brain development and early childhood education at the Milton and Ethel Harris Research Initiative (MEHRI) at York University, Ontario, Canada. MEHRI is a state-of-the-art cognitive and social neuroscience centre. For the past six years, clinicians have been working with young children with autism aged 2–4, while scientists have been studying the effects of a parented mediated form of therapy based on Stanley Greenspan and Serena Wieder's Individual Differences and Relationship-Based Therapy (DIR® Greenspan and Wieder, 2007). Parents are taught how to adjust their interaction style so as to enhance their child's ability to stay calmly focused and alert. Families receive two hours of coaching each week with a team composed of a speech-language therapist, occupational therapist and a mental health expert. After 12 months, outcomes are measured to determine changes in the children's social behaviours and accompanying changes in their 'social brain' network (Casenhiser et al., 2011).

The ultimate goal of EPIC is to see the knowledge gained from research at MERHI translated into programs that will enhance the potential of each and every child to learn.

The dream of universal education

The recognition of education as a basic, constitutional human right was, without question, one of the most significant and far-reaching consequences of the American Revolution. The enlightened advocacy of universal education was prompted not only by altruistic motives but also by the realisation that true participatory democracy is possible only if the citizenry is educated to a level that enables understanding of issues and informed decision making. Thomas Jefferson's writings on universal education were suffused with the optimistic belief that every individual is *educable*, i.e. capable of rational and disciplined thought.

In opposition to Jefferson's view of the *plasticity* of human potential – i.e. that an individual's learning potential is indeterminate – Jensen espoused a *determinate* view according to which initial biological factors limit the extent that an individual can be educated. Jensen's view was inspired by studies such as those showing that an IQ test administered to a child at school entry is a strong indicator of her eventual educational attainment (McCall, 1978). It was tempting to conclude that genetic factors, for example, influence the speed at which a child processes or retains information, thereby limiting her educational potential, in much the same way that the number of horsepower limits how fast a car can go. But if that is the case, then while tinkering with higher grades of fuel may coax a few more mph out of the engine, it will not be enough, according to Jensen, to warrant the sort of massive spending that we have committed to universal education.

These two views of the concept of *human potential* – the plastic and the determinate – reflect the fundamental divide in psychology about the importance of nature versus nurture that has dominated the debate over universal education from the start. In other words, is the reason for the difficulty in changing a child's educational trajectory after she enters school due to genetically determined limitations on the processing of information (nature), or is it because early, pre-school experiences (nurture), which are inextricably bound up with the child's biology (nature), have influenced her abilities to, for example, focus on a problem, ignore distractions and cope with frustration?

This conceptual distinction is important because if it were possible to identify biological factors affecting a child's ability to pay attention before they become deeply entrenched, then perhaps a child's potential to learn could be significantly enhanced. Recent advances in developmental neuroscience are lending considerable support to this view.

Biological determinism

Many studies appear to support the biological determinist thesis, such as research showing how identical twins have much stronger IQ correlations than siblings or fraternal twins (Bouchard Jr. and McGue, 1981), or how the IQs of adopted children correlate more with their biological mother than their adoptive parents (Plomin et al., 1997).

Schools have been largely ineffective in closing the achievement gap between socially advantaged and disadvantaged children (Hanushek, 2003). Even successes like the American Head Start programme, which provides comprehensive education, health, nutrition and parent involvement services to low-income children and their families, are cited as bearing out the biological determinist thesis; for, as Jensen has claimed, 'Compensatory education has been tried and it apparently has failed' (Jensen, 1969: 2).

Jensen proposed that a phenomenon like fade-out occurs because a child, removed from the influence of an enriching environment, will regress to her 'natural' intelligence level. He insisted that even a highly successful program like the Carolina Abecedarian project, a carefully controlled scientific study of the potential benefits of early childhood education for poor children, did not challenge his hypothesis (Jensen, 1998). He accepted that the Abecedarian project showed how, if sustained, a child could preserve a gain of about 5 IQ points; but he was adamant that this shows only how sustained enrichment enables us to squeeze out the last few drops of a child's potential, but not to increase that potential (Jensen, 2002).

Biological determinists need not be opposed to universal education; on the contrary, they can still support it for the sorts of reasons that Heckman spelled out in his report *Inequality in America* (Heckman et al., 2004), and which he has since applied to pre-school programs (Heckman, 2006), i.e. that educating the masses acts as a prophylactic against anti-social behaviour. So it may well be in a society's interest to help at-risk children achieve the important social gains that have been documented from early intervention programs (Brooks-Gunn, 2003). Yet it has been more common to find determinists arguing that it is in society's interest, and indeed the child's, to match a child's educational experience to her biological potential (Wooldridge and Daily, 1997).

Recent, compelling evidence indicating examples of successful interventions to enhance intellectual attainment has been demonstrated at the level of the child (Stacey, 2004), the school (Meier, 1995), the community (Tough, 2009) and a nation (Carnoy, 2007). Studies have also revealed a much more nuanced picture of school effectiveness (see Wyatt, 1996). Furthermore, an abundance of research over the past decade has exposed the methodological as well as conceptual inadequacies of the IQ studies upon which much of the determinist theories are based (for an important review, see Richardson and Norgate, 2006).

There are several reasons why the determinate view of human potential has proved to be persistent. In spite of considerable investment of resources, our educational systems have failed to close the achievement gap between rich and poor, tempting some determinists to argue that social stratification is a reflection of genetic potential (Gould, 1991). Moreover, biological factors are clearly a critical element in a child's learning trajectory (Sheppard, 2008).

However, recent advances in the science of early development suggest that if we intervene early, it is possible to mitigate serious 'downstream' consequences of biological factors such as problems with behaviour or mood, before they become too entrenched (Fogel et al., 2008). For example, individuals with autism frequently have difficulty processing multi-sensory dynamic stimuli, and as a result, they have difficulty constructing meaningful patterns and reacting appropriately. Importantly, these difficulties decrease as the presentation of stimuli is slowed (Gepner and Féron, 2009). The implication here is that children with autism do not have a malfunctioning 'mindreading' module, i.e. a mechanism for intuitively understanding what other people are thinking, feeling or intending, but that basic biological challenges (such as a hypersensitivity to visual and auditory stimuli, or deficits in integrating different kinds of sensation) can result in the appearance of a 'mindreading' deficit (Greenspan and Shanker, 2004; Shanker, 2008). A child who finds it difficult to recognise the patterns involved in, for example, affect signalling or language, will find social interaction extremely stressful, leading, perhaps, to problems in behaviour or mood.

Similarly, the reason why a child demonstrates a learning disorder may be because the information has been presented at too fast a pace for her to process, or in a sensory modality in which she is weak, or in a setting which stresses the child's nervous system, leading to all sorts of problems in motivation and self-confidence that further exacerbate the child's learning problems. Even more important are biological factors that drain the child's capacity to pay attention, such as sensory and motor challenges that, if addressed early, can be significantly mitigated. Clearly, a much deeper understanding of underlying processes is required.

Changing educational trajectories

A number of recent advances are causing major revision to our views about *enhancing children's educational potential*. These include progress in developmental neuroscience; the advances that have been made in our understanding, not just of the importance of early stimulation, but the experiences that promote the development of social skills, problem solving, symbolic thinking, language and logical thinking (Greenspan and Shanker, 2004); the growing understanding of the effects of excessive stress on a child's physical and psychological development (Lillas and Turnbull, 2009); and, perhaps most important of all, our growing understanding of the importance of self-regulation at the levels of biological, emotional, cognitive, social and moral functioning (Shanker, 2010).

A constriction in any one of these interconnected aspects of development can result in cascading effects that can severely affect a child's performance in school. For example, children who have difficulty modulating their anger or frustration receive less attention from their teachers or are treated in a manner that exacerbates their negative emotions. This argument suggests an entirely new explanation of why it has been so difficult to change educational trajectories based on self-regulation (Hart and Risley, 1995), which involves the child's ability to smoothly modulate arousal states, the ability to monitor and modify emotions, focus or shift attention, control impulses, tolerate frustration and delay gratification (Shanker, 2010; Shonkoff and Phillips, 2001).

Current research suggests that, in place of the static determinist view of IQ, a child's intelligence should be seen as open-ended and fluid, and hence only assessable over time. If a social or biological impediment has constrained a child's development in an area of functioning, as, for example, we see in the case of children with autism, whose sensory impediments seriously impair their ability to engage in those early interactive experiences that wire the 'social brain network', this can lead to problems in learning. But if it were possible to reduce these initial impediments, the result would be a dramatic change in the child's capacity to learn.

Clearly, the more entrenched a trajectory, the more effort is required to change it; hence the emphasis on the early years (McCain et al., 2007). But as long as a learning curve is sloping upward, it is wrong to assume that it cannot be changed at all. This implies that educators should aspire to create opportunities for a child to continue to develop her core cognitive, communicative, social and emotional capacities at whatever age; for it is not just the brain that is plastic, but the child's overall potential (Greenspan and Greenspan, 2010).

The development of self-regulation

Recent studies in the development of 'effortful control' suggest that a child's *potential to learn* is a function of her physiological capacity to meet a challenge and then recover from the effort. Physiologists refer to the process of energy modulation involved as *optimal regulation*, by which is meant 'the capacity to make both gradual and rapid state changes across the arousal continuum (that are appropriate to context), recover back to baseline, and modulate the highs and lows of energy within a given state' (Lillas and Turnbull, 2009: 119). The more smoothly a child can make these arousal state transitions, the more effectively she can respond to the myriad challenges she will be confronted with in school: challenges that are likely to be social and emotional as much as cognitive.

In order to be able to pay attention to her caregiver, the infant has to be able to modulate her arousal states so as to meet the varying challenges and stressors to which she is exposed the moment she awakes. She has to learn when and how to reduce an overly arousing stimulus, or indeed, when to seek out an interesting, i.e. arousing, stimulus. The problem is that the neural systems that sub-serve these functions are under-developed at birth. Maturation plays a critical role in the development of effortful control, as the major neural systems involved in the prefrontal cortex undergo massive growth over the early years (see Diamond, 2002). But no less important is the nature of the experiences that the child undergoes, which deliver the stimuli that wire these growing systems to sub-serve this self-regulating function.

Nature's solution for the delivery of this information was what Tantam (2009) has dubbed the 'interbrain': a sort of wireless connection whereby the primary caregiver serves as an external brain, regulating and stimulating the baby. It is via these bi-directional interactions that the infant's developing regulatory systems receive the necessary inputs to support optimal regulation (see McCain et al., 2007). That is, the critical medial prefrontal systems that sub-serve self-regulation mature over the first five years of life, and the interactive experiences that the child undergoes in these early years have a significant impact on the wiring of these systems.

Hitherto, attention has been largely focused on the role that the primary caregiver plays in shaping the growth of the baby's brain, but a recent study shows that the mother's brain also grows as a result of these interactions. Kim et al. (2010) found that the more positive a mother's perception of her baby, the greater the increase in grey area volumes in her prefrontal cortex, amygdala, parietal lobe and hypothalamus. The authors speculate that, as with similar studies on the plasticity of the maternal brain in rats, the areas affected are those involved with maternal care (i.e. motivation and reward and emotion processing). But, of course, the inference here might just as well be in the opposite direction; that is, the greater the changes in grey volume noted, the more positive the mother's perception of her baby.

So the question is: what might be driving this growth in the mother's brain? The answer likely lies in the fact that self-regulation is a dyadic phenomenon. The caregiver must not only read the baby's signals and up or down regulate the baby's arousal as necessary, but she must herself deal with the quite extraordinary demands being placed upon her own energy resources. Hence, it is no surprise that we see changes in those parts of the brain that are involved in meeting these demands; that is, what is growing are those systems in the prefrontal cortex for regulating her own energy needs and in the parietal lobe for reading the baby's affect signals.

Not surprisingly, the better self-regulated the mother in terms of modulating her own arousal states, the better she can read and respond to her baby's signals and thus regulate her baby. And the better regulated the baby, the more resources for the mother to self-regulate. In this way, both members of the dyad are developing their ability to self-regulate to meet the new stressors to which each is being exposed, and the better each can self-regulate, the better they can co-regulate, and vice versa.

Severe problems at either pole of the 'interbrain', such as acute problems of reactivity in the baby, or caregiver psychopathology, affect the ability of the other to self-regulate, as the energy expended in trying to co-regulate severely reduces the resources left for self-regulation, setting off a vicious circle. That is, *co-regulation* is the natural effect of one member of the dyad's arousal level on the other. A person's arousal level is highly contagious; think, for example, of how someone's anger can trigger an angry response in others. But anger is an extremely energy-expensive emotion, and, as any trained psychotherapist can attest, a critical part of their training involves learning how to dissociate from a patient's emotion, and indeed, how to counteract that anger with calming behaviours so as to help her down-regulate.

This, of course, is precisely what a caregiver does when, for example, she talks softly and slowly to her child when she is upset. The caregiver is using non-verbal affect signals to help the child calm down. A caregiver has to work much harder to regulate a child who is chronically hypo(under)- or hyper(over)-aroused; but the better she can stay calmly focused and alert herself, the better she can help her child to sustain a similar arousal state. We talk about 'goodness of fit' when the members of the dyad are in this state for extended periods, but it is important to bear in mind that 'communicative synchrony' is as much an effect as a cause of being in this state. For, as Thayer (1989) has shown, it is when one is calmly focused and alert that one's energy needs are most finely modulated.

The pivotal importance of these early experiences cannot be over-emphasised, and typically, a child will have acquired fairly robust optimal regulation by the time she enters school. A 7-year-old child with strong optimal regulation can concentrate on a problem for a considerable length of time, ignore distractions, resist impulsive answers and methodically test out different solutions. Such a child is driven by curiosity and interest rather than artificial rewards and shows resilience if a problem is not solved and seeks assistance.

However, a large number of children do not display these skills on starting school, in many cases because initial biological factors have significantly constrained their development of self-regulation. For many of these children, the problem is based in their sensory and limbic (the part of the brain that deals with negative emotions) systems and on how they modulate their responses. They might, for example, have challenges in overall reactivity or excitability to various kinds of sensory stimuli. This means that what, for others, might seem like moderate stimuli are experienced as extremely intense and distressing. Connected to these problems in reactivity are problems in soothability, by which we mean how quickly a child can be calmed when hyper-aroused; how easily or intensely the child becomes fearful, anxious, angry, excited; how the child responds to new situations; whether the child actively seeks out new stimulation; and the child's distractibility and attention-span persistence (Rothbart and Derryberry, 1981). Finally, of utmost importance are the child's motor planning and sequencing abilities, their sense of their body in space, their balance and their awareness of bodily cues such as hunger or thirst (Greenspan and Greenspan, 2010).

Simply put, the harder a child has to work to perform actions that we tend to take for granted – actions like sitting up in a chair, or ignoring the distraction of a fresh air vent – the less energy they have left to pay attention and work on a problem. Furthermore, it is important to recognise that the development of self-regulation is an ongoing process; it is at the very least a 0–17 and not a 0–3 phenomenon. It is never too late to work on a child's self-regulation, even though the challenges are considerable and become more difficult as the child ages. The most important point of all, however, is to recognise the importance of physiological and emotional factors in a child's ability to self-regulate, and how out-dated are antiquated views of a child who has trouble paying attention as simply needing to learn how to apply or control herself.

The biomechanics of self-regulation

At its most basic level, self-regulation is a function of the child's ability to modulate her arousal states (Shanker, 2010). *Arousal regulation* can best be understood in terms of the countervailing forces of Sympathetic Nervous System (SNS) activation and Parasymplathetic Nervous System (PNS) inhibition: in effect, putting your foot on the gas or the brakes in order to attend to a particular activity and recover from the effort (Lillas and Turnbull, 2009). One of the implications of this model is that there aren't distinct levels of activation as such, but rather a continuum of arousal, ranging from sleep to being flooded by stimulation; and how much stimulation is needed or how much recovery is necessary for any particular task, is going to vary from child to child and from situation to situation.

The driving analogy is helpful for understanding the subtle adjustments in arousal involved in regulating one's attention according to the demands of a task or activity. For example, if one's goal is to maintain a speed of 100 km/hr, one is constantly depressing and easing up on the gas pedal, depending on the state of the road incline. In some conditions, you are going to consume a great deal of gas to maintain constant speed – as you go up a steep incline, fuel consumption may leap from 10 to 40 l/100 km. Learning how to drive involves learning how to smoothly adjust the amount of gas or braking required for the current conditions.

Children vary considerably in their capacity for optimal regulation. Some children are constantly pushing too hard on the gas or the brake pedal, jumping erratically from one level to another. If this problem in the child's response to stress is habitual, the result can be a chronic over-stressed condition (McEwen, 2002). Maintaining a stable physiological state for these children requires the expenditure of draining amounts of energy, which seriously diminishes their capacity to control impulses, ignore distractions and delay gratification. Such children are not incapable of self-regulating; rather, their modes of self-regulation can interfere with learning. The more chronically hypo-aroused a child, the less inclined she will be to explore new challenges; and the more chronically hyper-aroused a child, the less able she will be to remain focused.

> ### 📁 Case study: Enhancing a child's ability to self-regulate
>
> JJ was diagnosed with the classic symptoms of Oppositional Defiance Disorder. According to his parents, he had always had trouble falling asleep, and he was irritable from the moment he awoke to the moment that he finally fell asleep. He had frequent explosions of anger, to the point where his parents feared leaving him alone with his younger sister. He was constantly testing others to see how far they could be pushed and seemed oblivious to the pain of others. He had a great deal of trouble in accepting directions, and if asked to do something other than what he wanted would refuse and run away.
>
> The affects that most forcefully struck us when we first met JJ, however, were not so much his anger and frustration as his deep longing for friends and his pronounced feelings of shame. It wasn't that he had no desire to be calm and focused but rather that he found it exceptionally difficult to stay that way. JJ had been undergoing a form of training designed to help him learn how to organise his thinking and manage his time, with limited success. Our job, then, was to dig a little deeper based on a multi-disciplinary team assessment.
>
> It quickly became apparent that JJ was a highly reactive child, extremely sensitive to sound, touch, taste and odour. Just sitting on a hard seat in a classroom, surrounded by other children, and trying to pay attention to his teacher were extremely taxing on his nervous system. The first step was to reduce the sensory demands on him by softening the lighting in the room in which we met, reducing the tempo and volume of our speech, giving him a soft cushion to sit on, and following JJ's lead in our conversations, not just in terms of what we talked about, but, even more important, in how we talked.
>
> We also worried about JJ's awareness of his 'visceral self'. For example, he seemed to be unaware of when he was hungry, tired or cold, but when we
>
> *(Continued)*

(Continued)

reduced the sensory load on him, he would eat voraciously, and even more significant, would devour the fruit, vegetables and yoghurt that he vociferously refused to eat at home. Through activities designed to help him relax, he would even begin to nod off in his favourite 'beanbag' chair and would often ask us for one of our soft, cuddly blankets because he was cold.

The changes in his behaviour were equally striking. Suddenly, the negative affects diminished and were replaced by a smiling, happy 8-year-old, eager to begin his 'play sessions' with us. Many of the games that we introduced were designed to give an insight into whether, by reducing the demands on his nervous system, we would see a marked improvement in his ability to delay gratification and inhibit his impulses. Not only was this manifestly the case, but even more striking was the deep concern he demonstrated whenever one of us was accidentally 'hurt'.

We discovered that the problem he was trying to cope with was a sensory and social world that he found overwhelming. The more his energy reserves were depleted, the fewer resources remained for him to control his impulses. Far from being irremediably aggressive, he was an extroverted child who had trouble regulating his anger and frustration when he became hyper-aroused; and because of his biology he was chronically hyper-aroused. Because of these challenges, JJ had never really experienced the subtle gradations involved in, for example, being mildly annoyed, irritated, angry and furious. For him, frustration characteristically resulted in a sudden and overwhelming rage. Unfortunately, his oppositional defiance was a coping mechanism that made matters considerably worse; for now, on top of all his biological and social sensitivities, he had to cope with the further debilitating effects of negative affects that were dramatically intensified by the negative affects that his behaviours aroused in others.

Enhancing the potential in all children (EPIC)

It is a disturbing reflection on modern western society that the capacity for optimal regulation appears to be in decline. For example, in a large, representative survey of kindergarten teachers in the USA conducted in 2000, 46 per cent of the 3595 teachers questioned reported that at least half the children in their classes lacked the self-regulatory abilities needed to function productively in school (Rimm-Kaufman et al., 2000). The seriousness of this problem is reflected in the heightened awareness of the importance of self-regulation in current educational theory (Blair and Diamond, 2008). Furthermore, the data suggest that early problems with self-regulation can be exacerbated during the school years, often as a direct result of the school experience (Kuklinski and Weinstein, 2001).

The long-term implications of the data are profound and demand a serious research effort to determine the underlying environmental, social and demographic factors that may be behind these trends. It is now clear that, if we are going to reduce the number of children entering school with serious problems in self-regulation, we need to invest in early child development and parenting programs (Government of Ontario, 2010; Pascal, 2009). However, that still leaves the immediate problem of how teachers are to deal with the very challenging classroom environments that this data portends.

In order for early years practitioners and teachers to be able to perform the role required of them, two critical macro-changes need to occur. First, we need to develop a new societal recognition of the formative role that practitioners in early childhood settings and teachers can play in children's lives. Apart from parents, only they are in a position to truly get to know a child and understand her inherent strengths and weaknesses, aptitudes and needs.

Second, we need to examine what we should be doing to support professionals in this extraordinarily demanding task. This might involve new approaches to training and mentoring, new curricula and in-class practices, and early years settings and classroom design, and most important of all, new measures designed to enhance self-regulation amongst practitioners and teachers themselves.

Final thoughts

The rhetoric of the Founding Fathers' writings on universal education has inspired countless generations around the world; but rather more sobering has been the reality of trying to implement universal education. Despite our best efforts, it has proved to be extremely difficult to close the achievement gap, leading some to speculate that the problem must lie in the child's genes. But our understanding of development has changed so much over the past decade that biological determinism is now fading as a serious explanation of something so complex as how a child performs in school (Fogel et al., 2008).

Merely telling policy makers the problem is complex is hardly going to reassure them when under pressure to realise immediate gains in educational outcomes. Moreover, policy makers are constantly bombarded with novel programs, all promising dramatic results, not to mention competing urgent demands on finances. In order to launch a massive prevention/enrichment initiative like the Early Learning Program (see below) in such a challenging environment, Ontario's policy makers needed to be provided with a convincing developmental explanation of *why* it has proved so difficult to change educational trajectories, and with research evidence demonstrating that it is, in fact, possible to enhance those core capacities that promote a child's long-term well-being.

Mustard and McCain's (1999) *Early Years Study: Reversing the Real Brain Drain* placed early brain development at the forefront of the Ontario debate over public education. This in turn paved the way for Dr Charles Pascal (2009), the Premier of Ontario's Special Advisor on Early Learning, to outline a far-reaching vision, in *With our Best Future in Mind*, of the many different elements the government must work on in order to enhance the early development of each and every child.

The first step in achieving Pascal's vision has been the phased introduction, beginning in September 2010, of the province's Early Learning Program (ELP): full-day kindergarten for 4- and 5-year-olds. The philosophy underlying the curriculum for this program is laid out in *Every Child, Every Opportunity* (ECEO) (Government of Ontario, 2010). ECEO makes clear that the goal of the ELP is to help strengthen children's social, emotional, language, cognitive and physical competencies. In particular, great emphasis is placed on enhancing children's self-regulation.

In translating the scientific evidence into policy and practice, it was crucial to have a premier in power who grasped the significance of the arguments; also, to have a number of professionals in the private and public sectors who had already been working for more than a decade on developing programs that would enhance early childhood development (Best Start Early Learning Expert Panel, 2007).

At the end of the day, however, it was science that drove this agenda. It was for precisely this reason that we remarked at the start of this chapter that we are currently in the midst of a profound revolution in educational thinking and practice. The science of early childhood development, both pure and applied, has made such important strides over the past decade that we are now in a position to understand, both why it has been so difficult to change educational trajectories, and what we should be doing differently.

☐ Summary

- Enhancing Potential In Children (EPIC) is a research-based program investigating the neurobiological and social basis of children's ability to self-regulate and the implications for learning, along with the most effective techniques to implement these ideas in universal education.
- Children vary in their sensitivity to stimuli and in their ability to self-regulate their levels of arousal. Those with chronic hyper- or hypo-arousal can find this very distressing and expend such large amounts of energy and effort in regulating their arousal level that they have little left to expend on learning.
- Parents and caregivers who are closely attuned to their infant's needs have a critical role to play in helping children modulate their arousal levels through soothing/reducing or seeking out additional stimuli – acting as an external regulator while their child's self-regulation mechanism is maturing.
- Understanding of the nature of self-regulation has enabled the design and implementation of intervention strategies, based on intensive, customised therapy sessions, to enhance a child's capacity to learn.
- The next challenge is to take the lessons learned from the laboratory and apply them in pre-school and classroom settings, through the design of soothing

(Continued)

(Continued)

environments, the availability of self-regulating aids, new teacher-training programs and the development and adoption of curricula that embrace EPIC principles.
- Policy makers in Ontario are persuaded of the scientific evidence and have assigned a high priority to helping every child achieve their full potential.

Questions for discussion

1 Thinking about your own experience of dealing with children who appear hyper-active, disruptive or difficult to engage, how might you want to change the environment of your setting or your own practice to help children cope with a chronic state of over-arousal? Are there simple techniques you can employ to help them return to a state of being calmly focused and alert?
2 Given that finely tuned interactive experiences are crucial for the development of self-regulation in infants, what do you think are the implications for the organisation of early years settings and staff training?
3 What can you learn from this example in Ontario about using evidence to shape policy in your area of work? *(Higher-level question)*

Further reading

Levels 5 and 6

McCain, M., Mustard, J.F. and Shanker, S.G. (2007). *Early Years Study II*. Toronto: The Council on Early Child Development. Toronto: The Council on Early Child Development.
This text provides an overview of the evidence relating to children's development and the implications for early years policy and practice.

Shonkoff, J. and Phillips, D. (2001). *From Neurons to Neighbourhoods: The Science of Early Childhood Development*. Washington, DC: National Academy Press.
This book provides a readable introduction to developmental neuroscience and the implications of recent findings for understanding children's development and for society in general.

Levels 6 and 7

Greenspan, S. and Shanker, S. (2004). *The First Idea*. Boston, MA: Da Capo Press.
This book outlines the developmental stages that lead to strong learning and the experiences that help a child master these stages.

Shanker, S.G. (2010). Self-regulation: calm, alert and learning. *Education Canada*, 50: 3.
This article outlines the five core domains of self-regulation and their importance for twenty-first century learning.

Websites

www.IMBES.com
This site is helpful if you are looking for technical reports and research on developmental neuroscience.

www.kidshavestresstoo.org
This site provides information on the effects of excessive stress on a child's physical and psychological development, and practical advice and techniques for supporting children and combating stress.

www.mehri.ca
This is the home site for the Milton and Ethel Harris Research Initiative (MEHRI) which funds scientific research into children's development and learning. Here you can find a wide variety of reports and information on relevant projects.

Note

1   Sherritt International is a Canadian energy company, based in Toronto, Canada. It is involved in nickel and cobalt mining, thermal coal production, oil and gas exploration and production, and electricity generation. Sherritt is one of the largest foreign investors in Cuba, and is one of the lead partners in the Ambatovy project, a long-life mining venture in Madagascar.

References

Best Start Early Learning Expert Panel (2007). *Early Learning for Every Child Today*. Toronto, ON: Ontario Ministry of Children and Youth Services.

Blair, C. and Diamond, A. (2008). Biological processes in prevention and intervention: the promotion of self-regulation as a means of preventing school failure. *Development and Psychopathology*, *20*(03), 899–911.

Bouchard Jr, T.J. and McGue, M. (1981). Familial studies of intelligence: a review. *Science*, *212*(4498), 1055–9.

Brooks-Gunn, J. (2003). Do you believe in magic? What we can expect from early childhood intervention programs. *Social Policy Report*, *17*(1), 3–14.

Carnoy, M. (2007). *Cuba's Academic Advantage*. Stanford, CA: Stanford University Press.

Casenhiser, D., Shanker, S. and Stieben, J. (2011). Learning through interaction in children with autism: preliminary data from a social communication based intervention. *Autism: The International Journal of Research and Practice*. Published online 26 September.

Diamond, A. (2002). Normal development of prefrontal cortex from birth to young adulthood: cognitive functions, anatomy, and biochemistry. In: D. Stuss and R. Knight (eds), *Principles of Frontal Lobe Function* (pp. 466–503). New York: Oxford University Press.

Fogel, A., King, B.J. and Shanker, S. (2008). *Human Development in the 21st Century: Visionary Policy Ideas from Systems Scientists*. Toronto: The Council on Human Development.

Gepner, B. and Féron, F. (2009). Autism: a world changing too fast for a mis-wired brain? *Neuroscience and Biobehavioral Reviews*, *33*(8), 1227–42.

Gould, S.J. (1991). *The Mismeasure of Man*. New York: Norton.

Government of Ontario (2010). *Every Child, Every Opportunity*. Available at: www.ontario.ca/en/ initiatives/early_learning/ONT06_023399.html

Greenspan, S. and Greenspan, N.T. (2010). *The Learning Tree: Overcoming Learning Disabilities from the Ground Up*. Boston, MA: Da Capo Lifelong Books.

Greenspan, S. and Shanker, S. (2004). *The First Idea*. Boston, MA: Da Capo Press.

Greenspan, S. and Wieder, S. (2007). *Engaging Autism*. Boston, MA: Da Capo Press/Perseus Books.

Hanushek, E.A. (2003). *The Economics of Schooling and School Quality*. Cheltenham: Edward Elgar.

Hart, B. and Risley, T.R. (1995). *Meaningful Differences in the Everyday Experiences of Young American Children*. Baltimore, MD: Brookes Publishing.

Heckman, J.J. (2006). Skill formation and the economics of investing in disadvantaged children. *Science*, *312*(5782), 1900–2.

Heckman, J.J., Krueger, A.B. and Friedman, B.M. (2004). *Inequality in America*. Boston, MA: MIT Press.

Jensen, A.R. (1969). How much can we boost IQ and scholastic achievement? *Harvard Educational Review*, *39*(1), 1–123.

Jensen, A.R. (1998). *The G Factor: The Science of Mental Ability*. London: Westport.

Jensen, A.R. (2002). Galton's legacy to research on intelligence. *Journal of Biosocial Science*, *34*(2), 145–72.

Kim, P., Mayes, L.C., Wang, X., Leckman, F., Feldman, R. and Swain, J.E. (2010). The plasticity of human maternal brain: longitudinal changes in brain anatomy during the early postpartum period. *Behavioral Neuroscience*, *124*(5), 695–700.

Kuklinski, M.R. and Weinstein, R.S. (2001). Classroom and developmental differences in a path model of teacher expectancy effects. *Child Development*, *72*(5), 1554–78.

Lillas, C. and Turnbull, J. (2009). *Infant Child Mental Health, Early Intervention, and Relationship-based Therapies*. New York: Norton.

McCain, M., Mustard, J.F. and Shanker, S.G. (2007). *Early Years Study II*. Toronto: The Council on Early Child Development.

McCall, R.B. (1978). Childhood IQs as predictors of adult educational and occupational status. *Obstetrical & Gynecological Survey*, *33*(3), 150.

McEwen, B. (2002). *The End of Stress as We Know It*. Washington, DC: National Academy Press.

Meier, D. (1995). *The Power of their Ideas*. Boston, MA: Beacon Press.

Mustard, J.F. and McCain, M. (1999) *Early Years Study: Reversing the Real Brain Drain*. Toronto: The Council of Early Child Development.

Pascal, C. (2009). *With our Best Future in Mind: Implementing Early Learning in Ontario*. Report to the Premier, Government of Ontario. Available at: www.ontario.ca/en/initiatives/early_learning/ONT06_023399.html (accessed 12 November 2009).

Plomin, R., Fulker, D.W., Corley, R. and DeFries, J.C. (1997). Nature, nurture, and cognitive development from 1 to 16 years: a parent–offspring adoption study. *Psychological Science*, 442–7.

Richardson, K. and Norgate, S.H. (2006). A critical analysis of IQ studies of adopted children. *Human Development*, *49*(6), 319–35.

Rimm-Kaufman, S.E., Pianta, R.C. and Cox, M.J. (2000). Teachers' judgments of problems in the transition to kindergarten. *Early Childhood Research Quarterly*, *15*(2), 147–66.

Rothbart, M.K. and Derryberry, D. (1981). Development of individual differences in temperament. *Advances in Developmental Psychology*, *1*, 37.

Shanker, S. (2008). In search of the pathways that lead to mentally healthy children. *Journal of Developmental Processes*, *3*(1), 22–3.

Shanker, S.G. (2010). Self-regulation: calm, alert and learning. *Education Canada*, *50*, 3.

Sheppard, L.D. (2008). Intelligence and speed of information-processing: a review of 50 years of research. *Personality and Individual Differences*, *44*(3), 533–49.

Shonkoff, J. and Phillips, D. (2001). *From Neurons to Neighbourhoods: The Science of Early Childhood Development*. Washington, DC: National Academy Press.

Stacey, P. (2004). *The Boy who Loved Windows: Opening the Heart and Mind of a Child Threatened with Autism*. Boston, MA: Da Capo Press.

Tantam, D. (2009). *Can the World Afford Autistic Spectrum Disorder?* London: Jessica Kingsley.

Thayer, R.E. (1989). *The Biopsychology of Mood and Arousal.* New York: Oxford University Press.

Tough, P. (2009). *Whatever it Takes: Geoffrey Canada's Quest to Change Harlem and America.* New York: Mariner Books.

Wooldridge, A. and Daily, A. (1997). Measuring the mind: education and psychology in England, c. 1860–c. 1990. *History of Science*, 35: 485–7.

Wyatt, T. (1996). School effectiveness research: dead end, damp squib or smouldering fuse? *Issues in Educational Research*, 6(1): 79–112.

CHAPTER 6

PARENTING POLICY AND SKILLS STRATEGIES

Mary Crowley

Overview

In this chapter, I consider the gradual expansion of services and support for parents in England from the early 1990s until 2010. I describe some of the research which made clear the impact of parenting on outcomes for children and hence was influential in this expansion and also the different policy areas involved in this work. I discuss the issue of quality standards for parenting programmes, together with the kinds of training and support that have been shown to provide the most effective services.

Development of parenting policy

During the 1980s and the first years of the 1990s, policy makers concerned with the welfare of children talked about services delivered by schools to children in order to improve their life chances. *Better Schools*, a Department for Education and Skills (DfES) policy paper published in 1985, envisaged that the best role for parents was in learning how to support the school's daily work. It pointed out that some parents wanted to be involved but lacked the confidence to come forward and that it was in schools' interests to encourage their participation. Otherwise, parents tended to be mentioned in government policy documents only when referring to improvements in maternity leave, health and childcare provision.

The pressure on government to provide services for parents around the parent–child relationship came in the first instance from small but persistent voluntary organisations working in the United Kingdom (UK) during the 1980s and 1990s. They included Parent Network (now ParentLine Plus), The Family Policy Studies Centre, The Parenting Education and Support Forum (now Parenting UK), The Trust for the Study of Adolescence, Family Links, and Fathers Direct. They pointed out that explicitly providing services directly to parents had the potential to improve the life chances of children. They talked about the impact of poor parenting on mental health, crime, domestic violence and educational achievement and about the need to break the intergenerational cycle of 'bad parenting'. This resonated with policy makers who were familiar with the view expressed by Sir Keith Joseph in 1972 (then Secretary of State for Social Services) that 'Problems reproduce themselves from generation to generation ... I refer to this as a "cycle of deprivation"' (cited in Rutter and Madge, 1976: 413). The seminal work in which this quote is cited is *Cycles of Disadvantage* which is government-sponsored research into transmitted disadvantage.

In 1998, the Home Office published a Green Paper *Supporting Families* which described existing services for parents and families and pledged to expand and improve what was available (Home Office, 1998). The Home Office interest in parenting stemmed in part from the interim findings of the longitudinal Cambridge Study of Delinquent Development (a Home Office funded research project which linked poor parenting to crime; reported in Farrington and Walsh, 2007). According to this study, 55 per cent of boys observed as being poorly supervised at the age of 8 had been convicted of offences by the age of 32, compared with a third of the overall sample. To deliver on the promise to expand services, the then Home Secretary announced on 23 July 2000 that he was setting up a National Family and Parenting Institute in order to assist parents and families.

Parenting Orders

The media profile of work with parents to improve the parent–child relationship was considerably raised when the Crime and Disorder Act 1998 introduced Parenting

Orders – compulsory court-mandated programmes for parents of young offenders. They received widespread press coverage from journalists intrigued by the concept of 'sentencing' parents to attend classes. Many parents who were served with Parenting Orders reported that they had regularly requested help in the past but that this was only forthcoming when their child was convicted of a crime. For the first time, parents whose children were not subject to interest from the criminal justice system became aware of the possibility of obtaining help with the parent–child relationship.

These programmes varied depending on the provider, but a typical group-based course would be likely to include topics such as: how to listen to children and young people; how to talk so that children and young people listen; encouragement versus praise; 'labels'; building parents' self-esteem and helping parents to look after themselves; how to build children and young people's self-esteem; setting limits and goals.

According to Ghate and Ramella (2002), whose work was based on a substantial sample of 4097 parents, they showed high attendance rates at the programmes and attended three-quarters of all sessions provided for them. By the time the parents left their programmes, the researchers reported statistically significant positive changes in parenting skills and competencies, including:

- improved communication with their child
- improved supervision and monitoring of young people's activities
- reduction in the frequency of conflict with young people and better approaches to handling conflict when it arose
- better relationships, including more praise and approval of their child and less criticism and loss of temper
- feeling better able to influence young people's behaviour
- feeling better able to cope with parenting in general.

Many parents and staff commented that the parenting of younger siblings might also change as a result of things parents had learned (Ghate and Ramella, 2002: 3).

This overwhelmingly positive evaluation of the impact of Parenting Order interventions helped raise awareness of the value of providing help and support to all parents.

Every parent matters

At the beginning of the new millennium, the policy lead for parenting moved from the Home Office to the then Department for Education and Skills (DfES) which held the overarching policy lead for integrated children's services. Working with and through local authorities and major voluntary bodies, the DfES rolled out a comprehensive set of services for parents across the country. It required all local authorities to have a named Parenting Services Commissioner with responsibility for ensuring access to a range of services for all parents. A Parenting Plan had to be produced and local parents consulted. Family Information Services were required to signpost parents to sources of support around the parent–child relationship. Parents of pre-school children could access services through their local Sure Start centre. Parents of older children would receive information through their children's school in a move to make schools the hub of all services for school-aged children under the Extended Schools Initiative (DfES, 2002).

In 2007, the then Secretary of State for Education published *Every Parent Matters* (DfES, 2007) which brought together in one place the list of interventions available to help parents. The report was a public information document produced to highlight the extent of services for parents now being routinely provided. These included:

- health-led parenting projects in 10 areas across England, jointly run by the Primary Care Trust (PCT) and Local Authority (LA) and linking with Sure Start Children's Centres
- support for teenage parents to help them build a secure future for themselves and their children. This support was to include developing strong and confident parenting skills, and continuing or re-engaging with education and training
- a universal Parent Know-How service providing integrated access to quality web-based materials with targeted information via helplines and printed material for parents at higher risk or unable to access other channels of information
- the National Academy for Parenting Practitioners with a brief to deliver the following main areas of work:
  - training and support for the parenting workforce
  - acting as a national centre and source of advice on research evidence on parenting and parenting support, combined with practical knowledge of what works in different situations
  - supporting the government's parenting agenda as it developed
  - developing parental engagement

- Parent Support Advisers (PSAs) who were introduced into a number of pilot schools and later into all schools. These advisers were specially trained members of staff who could visit a child's home where there was concern that problems at home could be preventing the child from learning. The models of operation varied but many PSAs also offered school-based parenting programmes and in general it was found that when parents were engaged with the school, they were also more likely to share information, allowing problems and misunderstandings to be reconciled before they escalated
- the Family Nurse Partnerships, an intensive programme adapted from the USA, in which specially trained health visitors or community midwives deliver one-to-one support designed to:
  - improve interaction between babies and parents, with parents perceived to be at risk of poor outcomes
  - improve mother and child health
  - build family and neighbourhood support structures
  - help parents develop in their own lives, for example through participation in the workforce or re-engagement with education.

A longitudinal study carried out in three areas of the USA showed this programme to be effective in improving outcomes for the children of poor, young uneducated parents from white, Hispanic and black backgrounds (summarised in Barnes et al., 2011).

This raft of new initiatives represented a sea change in policy relating to parents. The reasons why this change had come about at this point in time are discussed below.

Why the policy emphasis on parents?

An important factor in awakening the interest of policy makers in parents was the range of research which made clear the potential of parents to affect the life chances of their children and hence the importance of ensuring that parental impact was a positive one.

There were also indications that the existing help was not always meeting the needs of parents. Ghate and Hazel (2002), in a study entitled *Parenting in Poor Environments*, made clear that parents did not feel supported by the available services at that time and in fact felt undermined rather than supported by what was provided. Parents felt that some professionals treated them as though they were stupid and didn't know anything, whereas they saw the essence of parent support programmes as being that they as parents were still in charge, but that they were being helped and supported in their role.

Leon Feinstein's analysis of children's learning attainment as being related to the social class of their parents (Feinsten, 2003) powerfully underscored the impact of parents on outcomes for their children. He analysed test scores of children from different social backgrounds at age 22, 42, 60 and 120 months. His findings highlighted the seemingly inexorable tendency towards low achievement of many children born into poor or deprived backgrounds, initially detectable at 22 months and getting progressively worse; while, at the same time, the outcomes for children from richer or more privileged families remained stable or improved.

In the same year, Charles Desforges and Alberto Abouchaar were commissioned by the DfES to produce a review of research on the impact of parenting on children's education (Desforges and Abouchaar, 2003: 4). Their report concluded categorically that:

> Parental involvement in the form of 'at-home good parenting' has a significant positive effect on children's achievement and adjustment even after all other factors shaping attainment have been taken out of the equation. In the primary age range the impact caused by different levels of parental involvement is much bigger than differences associated with variations in the quality of schools. The scale of the impact is evident across all social classes and all ethnic groups.

The need for parents and other caregivers to interact with newborn babies because of the positive effect on their brain development (see also Chapter 5) was a key theme of Sue Gerhardt's book *Why Love Matters* (Gerhardt, 2004). The author sent a copy to every Member of Parliament in England which led to apocryphal tales of civil servants being confronted by ministers demanding to know what was being done to raise the awareness of these facts amongst parents.

Services for parents and young children

Recognition of the importance of raising parents' awareness of the needs of their young children was one of the factors which led to the decision to create local Sure Start centres which offered a range of services to parents with children from birth to 5 years old, the first of which opened in 1999.

The first report of the national evaluation of Sure Start (NESS, 2005) found, however, that the parents about whom there was greatest cause for concern were often not the ones attending the centres (see Chapter 2). Staff in Sure Start centres were mostly trained to work directly with children in the early years or in health-based settings; few had specific training for work with parents and parent–child relationships. Even smaller numbers of staff were trained for the demanding work of helping parents with additional problems such as marital violence, mental health issues or difficulties arising from their own or their children's disability or chronic ill health. It is therefore not surprising that their efforts to engage the 'hardest to reach' parents were not proving successful as services were rapidly colonised by the more advantaged and better informed.

Health services and parenting support

Health visitors (nurse-trained practitioners employed by local health authorities) already provided a universal post-natal service. They visited all new mothers in their area at least once and provided expert health advice and reassurance. Some health visitors were specifically trained in infant mental health and in parent–child relationships. However, training in these areas was often undertaken post-basic health visitor education and was often dependent on specific practitioner interest in this topic.

The National Service Framework for Children, Young People and Maternity Services (DoH, 2004) set out a vision of services to be available to parents in the future:

> Parents or carers are enabled to receive the information services and support which will help them to care for their children and equip them with the skills they need to ensure their children have optimum life chances and are healthy and safe. (Executive summary, p. 6)

Endorsement by The National Institute for Clinical Excellence (NICE) in July 2006, of what it called 'Parent Training Programmes', found them 'effective and cost-effective in the treatment of conduct disorder' (NICE Guidance, 2006: 4) and went some way to persuade health service providers of the evidence base for the work.

The most intensive intervention for parents in need of help offered by health providers was the Family Nurse Partnership model, referred to earlier, offered to young mothers and fathers with high levels of need and living in 10 selected areas of the country. Specially trained nurses on the programme visit vulnerable first-time parents in their homes, from early pregnancy until the child is 2 years old. Ten sites across England have been piloting the government-backed project since 2007 and the programme is still being evaluated (Barnes et al., 2011).

Work with fathers

A striking feature of the recent development of services for parents has been the increasing recognition that it is vital to provide services for fathers as well as mothers. It has sometimes seemed that early years service providers were in danger of forgetting that children have two parents and indeed that half the world's parents are men.

The study by Buchanan and Flouri (2002) based on data from the National Child Development Study – an ongoing longitudinal cohort study – found that father involvement played a protective role, particularly in relation to girls, against emotional and behavioural problems in adolescence. The effect was noticeable even when parents were separated. Positive relationships with fathers at age 7 was linked to greater commitment to schooling and higher educational attainment at age 20. In addition, children, especially boys, were less likely to get into trouble with the police in adolescent years.

Credit is due to the voluntary organisations that have worked to raise awareness of the importance of including fathers – in particular, The Fatherhood Institute, Working with Men, and Families Need Fathers – for their persistence and eventual success in convincing a female-dominated sector of the importance of fathers. It would appear that the best time to engage fathers is during the peri-natal period when they are anxious to do their best. A study of fathers' views on fatherhood with special reference to infancy, by Cordell, Parke and Sawin, published as early as 1980, found that fathers' willingness to assume infant care responsibilities was related to their sex-role concepts and the amount of time they were available. Fathers who felt that they should undertake a greater number of functions with their children were more likely to have been present in the delivery room at the infant's birth; 88 per cent thought there was some difference between men and women in relation to infant care, however over half of the sample mentioned that recognising their children's emotional needs was a critical function of fatherhood.

Findings from the study suggested that to capitalise on their heightened interest, preparation for parenthood classes should be routinely offered to expectant fathers as well as mothers during the months before the baby arrives, focusing particularly on the period directly after birth, the emotional and relationship impact of the new arrival, and hopes and expectations for their baby. Over a decade later, Dr Kevin Nugent, Director of the Brazelton Foundation in Boston, USA, in an address to their London conference (Nugent, 2004) urged prospective and new parents to speak to their babies. Based on observational research, he suggested that newborn babies are more likely to recognise their father's voice, possibly because its deeper timbre reverberates better through the abdominal wall during pregnancy and is hence more likely to be familiar to babies after birth.

Greater involvement of some fathers in their children's lives can make it more difficult when parents separate and fathers risk losing contact with their children. The organisation Families Need Fathers has campaigned for the rights of fathers in continuing involvement, and supports fathers who are separated from their children, assisting them in maintaining regular contact (www.fnf.org.uk).

Training the parenting workforce

In the 1980s and 1990s, companies offering 'branded' parenting programmes such as 'Triple P', 'The Incredible Years' and 'Strengthening Families, Strengthening Communities' provided preparatory training programmes for those engaged in work with parents. However, for those who had little existing relevant knowledge and experience, the brief training offered was found to be insufficient to meet their needs, resulting in a lack of confidence in delivering programmes to parents. Some practitioners working, for example, in health, early years and youth justice, realised that the task of supporting parents around the parent–child relationship was one which required a specific underpinning body of knowledge and skills that had not been identified or included in their previous professional training. Practitioners who were members of Parenting UK often commented that they felt the need for generic training in working effectively with parents as well as programme-specific training.

From 1990 onwards, The Parenting Education and Support Forum (now Parenting UK) worked to raise awareness of the need for quality standards and generic training for work with parents. Their efforts led to the development of National Occupational Standards for Work with Parents – nationally agreed statements of competence describing what practitioners need to know and be able to do to deliver quality parenting education and support services, and used as the basis for accredited vocational awards.

Finalised in 2005 and recently revised, these standards are underpinned by 15 core principles:

1 All work with parents should reflect the rights of the child set out in the United Nations (UN) Convention on the Rights of the Child (1989) ratified by the UK in December 1991.
2 Practitioners need to work in partnership with parents at all times, encouraging independence and self-reliance.
3 Mothers, fathers and those in a parenting role are acknowledged as having unique knowledge and information about their children and are the primary educators of their children.
4 Children are the responsibility of, and make a positive contribution to, the wider society as well as their families.

5 Work with parents should value and build on parents' existing strengths, knowledge and experience.

6 Parenting information, education, support and interventions should be available to, and practitioners should engage with, all those in a parenting role.

7 Services should aim to offer a range of appropriate support according to both child and parent level of need, and what is available in the family already, and in communities.

8 Respect for diversity and different needs, promotion of equality and taking action to overcome threatening, offensive or discriminatory behaviour and attitudes are of fundamental importance to work with parents.

9 Anyone who works with parents should have specific training, qualifications and expertise that are appropriate to the work they are undertaking.

10 Good practice requires reflection, regular and appropriate supervision and support as well as a continuing search for improvement.

11 Parenting practitioners should utilise effective working partnerships with agencies and individuals in providing support to parents and families. Integrated working and the sharing of approaches across services is a key element of this role.

12 Parenting information, education, support and interventions should utilise the best known evidence for good outcomes for children and parents.

13 Parenting practitioners should be committed to engaging with children, young people and families fully through identifying goals, assessing options, making decisions and reviewing outcomes. They should support children's and families' involvement in the development, delivery and evaluation of children's services.

14 Work with parents should place the interests of children and young people at the heart of the work. Practitioners are committed to working with parents and families so that children and young people have the chance to achieve positive outcomes.

15 Work with parents recognises the need for innovation and creativity to address both emerging and local needs and to build self-regulating and supportive community networks. (Parenting UK, 2010)

Involving parents

A crucial element in the provision of successful services for parents is effective recruitment to programmes. Earlier in this chapter, I discussed the use of Parenting Orders requiring parents of young offenders to attend parenting classes. This initiative was initially considered to be shocking but turned out to be surprisingly popular with parents and effective in helping deliver improvements in the parenting of young offenders. Some parents whose children were not offenders, but who were experiencing difficulties with the parenting role, demanded access to the support given by these programmes. Others were extremely reluctant to access any form of external support, being wary of exposing their family life and deepest feelings to the scrutiny and possibly condemnation of strangers.

Anecdotal reports from experienced practitioners who were members of Parenting UK suggest a number of strategies that could be helpful in marketing parent support and recruiting initially reluctant parents to programmes:

- ensuring parents know what services are available through advertising in places where parents go, for example supermarkets, schools, pre-schools and doctors' surgeries
- radio advertising using local radio stations
- sharing examples of what happens at a parenting programme in order to reassure concerned parents they will not be found wanting or humiliated in public
- holding an introductory session and offering refreshments at a convenient time and place, for example in the school or pre-school, just after parents have dropped off their children
- offering one-to-one support in community venues for those who may have had unhappy experiences at school and are reluctant to attend any events held in school premises
- recruiting fathers, for example by including in a letter of invitation a summary of research evidence about the importance of fathers' involvement to outcomes for children; ensuring that the invitation looks business-like and, if possible, offering a choice of times to attend an introductory session
- fathers being met by a least one man on arrival at a session, as this can be reassuring for men not used to an all-female environment
- ensuring the venue is comfortable, with the provision of adult furniture and refreshment facilities
- possibly offering some reward such as a small gift to children whose parents attend an introductory session (though this is an extreme and somewhat controversial strategy). Some practitioners are reluctant to take this route although others consider that, since the children are the ultimate beneficiaries of improved parenting, it can be justified.

Final thoughts

Despite the enormous growth in awareness of the needs of parents amongst policy makers and the variety and scope of new services for parents which have been developed over the last 10 years, it is still common to meet parents who are unaware that support and help is available. Investment in raising awareness and in training people to deliver effective parent support services and programmes has the potential to contribute to reduced calls on specialist services such as social work, child protection, criminal justice and mental health, and hence to financial savings.

It is encouraging that the first ever UNESCO World Conference on Early Childhood Care and Education held in Moscow in September 2010 included the following statements in its Moscow Framework for Action and Co-operation:

> Empower and strengthen the capacity of parents, families and service providers, so that they can provide protective relationships, quality care and education to the young child … Place a key emphasis on achieving good birth outcomes to mitigate poor outcomes for neonates through developing and expanding parenting programmes to orient families in good ECCE pratice, with particular emphasis on the 0–3 age group. (UNESCO, 2010: 3)

Summary

- Interest in parents in the 1980s predominantly focused on their role in support of schooling. Since that time, the focus has switched to the quality of parenting as a determinant of social and educational outcomes for children.
- Parent education and training programmes have developed to meet identifiable needs for more support.
- The introduction of Parenting Orders had a positive side effect in raising awareness of education and support opportunities amongst wider groups of parents whose children were not (yet) involved in the Criminal Justice system.
- The publication of *Every Parent Matters* in 2007 marked a policy watershed in terms of the services and support available to parents, including the piloting of Nurse Family Partnerships.
- The continuing involvement of fathers, including after marital separation, has been shown to impact positively on children's development and well-being in the long term.
- The importance of specific training for work with parents has been recognised and appropriate standards and qualifications are now in place.

 Questions for discussion

1 Do you think parenting education and support should be offered to all parents? If so, can you say why?
2 How best do you think fathers can be involved as well as mothers?
3 In your view, what practical considerations should inform planning services for parents around the parent–child relationship?
4 At a time of financial stringency, should policy makers prioritise and extend support and education for parents or provide services directly to children? *(Higher-level question)*

Further reading

Levels 5 and 6

Ghate, D. and Hazel, N. (2002) *Parenting in Poor Environments: Stress, Support and Coping*. London: Jessica Kingsley.
With a unique focus on the effects of poverty on parenting in Britain, this book explores what professionals and policy makers can do to support families living in poverty.

Miller, S. (2010) *Supporting Parents: Improving Outcomes for Children, Families and Communities*. Maidenhead: Open University Press.
This is an excellent introduction to work with parents, with helpful and clear information on different styles of parenting and parenting programmes.

Levels 6 and 7

Hilton Davis, H., Day, C. and Bidmead, C. (2002) *Working in Partnership with Parents: The Parent Adviser Model*. London: Harcourt Assessment.
This book describes a model of working with parents in which practitioners view parents as a partner in identifying solutions to the issues and problems they identify.

Quinton, D. (2004) *Supporting Parents: Messages from Research*. London: Department of Health.
This overview covers 14 studies describing different models and contexts for supporting parents.

Stewart-Brown, S.L., Fletcher, L. and Wadsworth, M.E.J. (2005) Parent–child relationships and health problems in adulthood in three national birth cohort studies. *European Journal of Public Health*, 15: 640–6.
Studies such as these three UK national birth cohort studies examined by Stewart Brown et al. show the long-term health impact on children of family conflict, harsh discipline or lack of affection and indicate that poor quality parent–child relationships can be a remediable risk factor for poor health in adulthood.

Websites

www.fiep-ifpe.fr/
This is the home site of the International Federation for Parent Education which is hosted in France and published in French and English. It brings together information and links to resources about parent education provision from across 40 countries worldwide.

www.parentchannel.tv
This site has a range of videos for parents about parenting issues across the children and young people age range, from supporting early literacy to going to university and choosing careers.

www.parentinguk.org
This is the home site for Parenting UK – a national membership organisation linking parent education programmes across the UK. Resources include information for

parents and papers relating to practice, as well as access to national standards for parent educators.

www.parentsadvicecentre.org
The Parents Advice Centre in Northern Ireland has developed a model process to measure organisations against the National Occupational Standards for work with parents. Organisations which have successfully completed this process report that they have found it helpful in assuring potential funders, as well as parents and fellow professionals, that their work meets the Standards.

References

Barnes, J., Ball, M., Meadows, P., Howden, B., Jackson, A., Henderson, J. and Niven, L. (2011) *The Family–Nurse Partnership Programme in England: Wave 1 Implementation in Toddlerhood and a Comparison between Waves 1 and 2a of Implementation in Pregnancy and Infancy.* Report to the Department of Health. Available at: www.dh.gov.uk/publications (accessed 26 March 2011).

Buchanan, A. and Flouri, E. (2002) *Fathers' Involvement and Outcomes in Adolescence* (end of award report). London: ESRC.

Cordell, A.S., Parke, R.D. and Sawin, D.B. (1980) Fathers' views on fatherhood with special reference to infancy. *Family Relations*, 29(3): 331–8.

Department for Education and Skills (DfES) (1985) *Better Schools.* London: HMSO.

Department for Education and Skills (DfES) (2002) *Extended Schools: Providing Opportunities and Services for All.* Nottingham: DfES.

Department for Education and Skills (DfES) (2007) *Every Parent Matters.* Nottingham: DfES.

Department of Health (DoH) (2004) *National Services Framework for Children, Young People and Maternity Services: Executive Summary.* London: DoH.

Desforges, C. and Abouchaar, A. (2003) *The Impact of Parental Involvement, Parental Support and Family Education on Pupil Achievement and Adjustment: A Literature Review.* Report No. 433. London: DfES.

Farrington, D. and Walsh, B. (2007) *Saving Children from a Life of Crime.* Oxford: Oxford University Press.

Feinstein, L. (2003) Inequality in the early cognitive development of British children in the 1970 cohort. *Economica*, February.

Gerhardt, S. (2004) *Why Love Matters: How Affection Shapes a Baby's Brain.* London: Routledge.

Ghate, D. and Hazel, N. (2002) *Parenting in Poor Environments.* London: Jessica Kingsley.

Ghate, D. and Ramella, M. (2002) *Positive Parenting: The National Evaluation of the Youth Justice Board's Parenting Programme.* London: Policy Research Bureau. Available at: www.yjb.gov.uk/publications/resources/downloads/posparentsum.pdf (accessed 26 March 2011).

Home Office (1998) *Supporting Families.* London: HMSO.

National Evaluation of Sure Start (NESS) Team (2005) *Early Impacts of Sure Start Local Programmes on Children and Families.* Research Report No. NESS/2005/FR/013. London: HMSO.

National Institute for Health and Clinical Excellence (NICE)/Social Care Institute for Excellence (2006) *Parent Training/Education Programmes in the Management of Children with Conduct Disorders: Technical Appraisal Guidance 102.* London: NICE.

Nugent, K. (2004) Enriching early parent–infant relationships. Paper presented at the Brazelton Institute Conference, London, March.

Parenting UK (2010) *National Occupational Standards for Work with Parents.* Available at: www.parentinguk.org/2/standards (accessed 26 March 2011).

Rutter, M. and Madge, N. (1976) *Cycles of Disadvantage.* London: Heinemann.

UNESCO (2010) *Framework for Action and Co-operation on ECCE: Harnessing the Wealth of Nations.* Moscow: UNESCO.

PART 3

MARKETISATION AND DEMOCRACY

CHAPTER 7

MAKING DEMOCRACY A FUNDAMENTAL VALUE: MEANING WHAT EXACTLY?

Peter Moss

Overview

In this chapter, I outline a possibility for early childhood education and care: democracy as a fundamental value in early childhood centres, based on an image of these centres as public spaces capable of many projects, including democratic practice. Democracy is discussed as a multi-dimensional concept that can be applied at many levels, from national government to nursery; it is both a form of governing and a way of living and relating. I consider what democracy might mean in the early childhood centre, including examples of how it might be practised by adults and children alike. I conclude by reviewing some of the conditions that may stifle democracy or enable democratic practice to establish itself and flourish in early childhood education, including active promotion by government, time, trust and a workforce for democracy.

The image of the early childhood centre

What is your image of the early childhood centre – be it the nursery, kindergarten, crèche, pre-school, school or Children's Centre? This is one of the critical questions that should be the starting point for policy, provision and practice in early childhood education and care (ECEC), or indeed in any education. It is critical questions like this one that remind us that ECEC is, first and foremost, a political and ethical practice, not simply a technical practice of applying experts' answers to the technical question: 'what works?'

The most common image of the early childhood centre in the UK today, but also, I would argue, in many other parts of the world today, is sadly impoverished. Under the sway of neo-liberalism, with its belief in competition, and advanced liberalism, with its faith in new management methods, the centre is seen as a business providing specified commodities ('childcare', 'early learning') to parent-consumers through the mechanism of the market (see Chapter 8); and as a site for the application of human technologies to children to ensure the efficient and certain production of a range of predefined and uniform outcomes. The result is a strange mixture: a rhetoric of diversity and choice with a reality of normalisation and standardisation expressed in the recurrent invocations of 'quality', 'best practice' and 'goals'.

Perhaps because I was fortunate to enter the early childhood field as part of the Children's Centre movement of the early 1970s, and came to it as a callow researcher unhampered by too much disciplinary baggage, my image of the early childhood centre has always been richer – not that I originally thought in terms of 'image', with its underpinning social constructionist perspective. The early pioneers of Children's Centres, like Jack Tizard, social researcher and founder of the Thomas Coram Research Unit in London, saw these centres as universal services for all children and families in their catchment areas, responsive to local needs and capable of many purposes – education and care certainly, but much else besides. Put another way, they were envisioned as community resources and, therefore, as a public service and a public responsibility, vital players in improving the often difficult lives of young parents and their children. The rediscovery of Children's Centres by the UK's last Labour government (1997–2010) (see Chapter 2) was a belated vindication of this pioneering work. Yet the vision, 30 years on, was greatly diluted. Instead of being the basis of a universal public system of ECEC for all our children, Children's Centres became an add-on to a fragmented and divisive system dominated by for-profit nurseries and the mantra of markets.

Sometime later, I began to clarify, broaden and articulate in more political terms my image of the early childhood institution. In the book *Beyond Quality in Early Childhood Education and Care*, Gunilla Dahlberg, Alan Pence and I wrote that 'early childhood institutions can be understood as *public forums situated in civil society, in which children and adults participate together in projects of social, cultural, political and economic significance*' (2007: 73, original emphasis). I have retained this image of the early childhood centre as a forum and place of projects, but elaborated it, so my image today of what the early childhood institution might be goes along these lines: the early childhood institution as a public responsibility, a public institution and a public space; as a forum or place of encounter between citizens young and old; and as a collaborative workshop capable of many, many purposes and projects of common interest and benefit, including:

- learning
- practising relational ethics
- providing family support
- strengthening social cohesion and community solidarity
- sustaining cultures and languages
- developing economy (including 'childcare')
- promoting gender and other equalities
- practising democracy and active citizenship.

What is important here, I think, is the image of the early childhood institution as a *public* space where *citizens encounter* each other and as a place of limitless *potential*, of constant *becoming*.

The early childhood centre as a place for democratic practice

One of the possible purposes of the early childhood institution that has become apparent to me in recent years has been as a place of democratic practice and, consequently, as a place that may contribute to re-invigorating democracy in our societies. This idea has gradually taken shape in the last 15 years, mainly as the result of encounters outside the current early childhood scene in the UK. Here, dominated by talk of businesses, markets and outcomes, democracy rarely figures. But it does elsewhere.

For example, as I became acquainted with the Swedish early childhood system, I found that the national pre-school curriculum makes a clear commitment to democracy as a fundamental value: 'Democracy forms the foundation of the pre-school.[1] For this reason, all pre-school activity should be carried out in accordance with fundamental democratic values' (Swedish Ministry of Education and Science, 1998: 6). Here is another critical question – what are the fundamental values of ECEC? And a clear answer. Other Nordic countries, too, pay explicit attention to the importance of democracy in their early childhood curricula. Wagner (2006: 292) argues that democracy is central to the Nordic concept of the good childhood: 'official policy documents and curriculum guidelines in the Nordic countries acknowledge a central expectation that pre-schools and schools will exemplify democratic principles and that children will be active participants in these democratic environments'.

The last 15 years have also involved deeper acquaintance with the early childhood centres in the Italian city of Reggio Emilia, and that has again revealed an early childhood service in which democracy is an important value (for more on this important local project, see Rinaldi, 2006 and Vecchi, 2010). Here, for example, are the words of three Reggio educators:

> The educational project [of Reggio Emilia] is by definition a participation-based project: its true educational meaning is to be found in the participation of all concerned. This means that everyone – children, teachers and parents – is involved in sharing ideas, in discussion, in a sense of common purpose and with communication as a value ... So in the Reggio Emilia experience, participation does not mean simply the involvement of families in the life of the school. Rather it is a value, an identifying feature of the entire experience, a way of viewing those involved in the educational process and the role of the school. The subjects of participation then, even before the parents, are the children who are considered to be active constructors of their own learning and producers of original points of view concerning the world ... This idea of participation, therefore, defines the early childhood centre as a social and political place and thus as an educational place in the fullest sense. However, this is not a given, so to speak, it is not a natural, intrinsic part of being a school. It is a philosophical choice, a choice based on values. (Cagliari et al., 2004: 28–9)

If we border cross from the field of early childhood into the field of compulsory education, which I think it vital to do, then we meet again with democracy and a well-established idea that democracy is an important part of education. There is, for instance, the tradition of educational progressivism, largely a product of the late nineteenth century that came to hold sway, according to which country we are considering, during the 40 years between 1930 and 1970, though its roots go back much further to writers like Comenius and Rousseau. Its legacy remains a significant presence today. Darling and Norbenbo (2003) suggest five recurring themes in progressive approaches to schooling: criticism of traditional education, the nature of knowledge, human nature, the development of the whole person – and democracy. Within this progressive tradition, there are many examples of democratic education, whether in schools or in work with marginalised or troubled young people, with protagonists such as Alex Bloom, the pioneer head teacher of St George's-in-the-East School in one of the toughest areas of London's East End, who deliberately set out to create a 'consciously democratic community ... without regimentation, without corporal punishment, without competition' (Bloom, 1948: 121; for a fuller discussion of Bloom's work and other examples, see Fielding and Moss, 2010).

Then there is John Dewey, described by Carr and Hartnett (1996: 54) as 'the most influential educational philosopher of the 20th century'. Dewey, author of the classic text *Democracy and Education: An Introduction to the Philosophy of Education* (1916), considered democracy to be a central value, practice and purpose of school education. But he also saw the school as having a vital role to play in democracy, famously asserting that 'democracy needs to be reborn in each generation, and education is its midwife'.

So instead of finding the idea of democracy in the nursery rather strange and fanciful, which I might well have done 15 years ago, today I find it familiar and quite credible. Indeed, what seems strange is the almost total silence about it in my own country. It's true we now talk sometimes about 'participation' and 'listening to young children'. But unlike Reggio Emilia, these are not folded into the larger political concept of democracy; they risk instead becoming parts in management's toolkit, a box to tick as evidence of having done some market research and having checked out 'customer satisfaction'.

Formal democracy: government and policy making

So what do I mean by democracy and how is it relevant to the early childhood centre? One starting place is what people often think of when 'democracy' is mentioned, the formal institutions and procedures of representative democratic government at national/federal, regional/state and local levels. This formal democracy has a key role to play in ECEC, being an important forum for dialogue, deliberation and decision making. As such, its health is vital.

In reality, though, formal democracy is sickly, struggling to respond to the contemporary challenges of a complex and threatened world and to retain the engagement of citizens (Morin, 1999; Bentley, 2005; Power Inquiry, 2006; Skidmore and Bound, 2008). Fewer people vote, elected representatives are distrusted and held in low esteem, whole sections of the community feel estranged from or disinterested in mainstream politics, and undemocratic political forces (from lobbyists to extremist groups) are on the rise. We are, says Morin, 'in the midst of a debased politics that lets itself be swallowed by experts, managers, technocrats, econocrats, and so on' (Morin, 1999: 112).

As Morin suggests, the weakening of effective democratic government is apparent in the degree to which it has abdicated responsibility for decision making and evaluation to markets and technocrats, transforming what is first and foremost an ethical and political endeavour, governing, into a technical and managerial exercise. Central to this process has been the growing importance attached to 'technical research' and 'evidence based' policy and practice, which seek to provide answers about means and strategies ('what works') whilst avoiding critical political and ethical questions about purposes, values and meanings. In his critique of the evidence-based approach in education, Gert Biesta argues that this technical practice suffers from a democratic deficit:

> [A democratic society is] characterized by the existence of an open and informed discussion about problem definitions and the aims and ends of our educational endeavours ... [So it] is disappointing, to say the least, that the whole discussion about evidence-based practice is focused on technical questions – questions about 'what works' – while forgetting the need for critical inquiry into normative and political questions about what is educationally desirable ... From the point of view of democracy, an exclusive emphasis on 'what works' will simply not work. (2007: 20–2)

This formal, procedural level of democracy requires not only collective choices about decisions that are of public significance, but a recognition that there is not one right answer, not one right way, and that 'all knowledge, as well as all perception is an act of translation and perception, that is interpretation' (Morin, 1999: 101). This is an agonistic idea of democracy (Mouffe, 2000), which assumes there are always differences of perspective, interest and power and where dissensus and conflict are positively valued. Democracy implies and enhances 'diversity among interests and social groups as well as diversity between ideas, which means it should not impose majority dictatorship, but rather acknowledge the right to existence and expression of dissenting minorities and allow the expression of heretical and deviant ideas' (Morin, 1999: 90). So, instead of reducing educational debate through an exclusive attention to one perspective, which purports to tell the truth, agonistic democracy would make visible (or transparent) conflicting perspectives, for example different paradigmatic and theoretical positions.

Decision making on ECEC policy in England falls far short of such democratic ideals. For example, we have adopted a policy on 'childcare' (itself a deeply problematic concept unquestioned in policy) premised on markets and for-profit providers. Yet I cannot recall this political option being seriously deliberated on, including contesting its advantages and disadvantages in comparison with alternative policies. Or to take another example, policy document after policy document on ECEC is written as if there was one truth about the subject, represented by a combination of positivistic research, the discipline of developmental psychology and economistic thinking. Critiques of this approach never appear; nor is mention made of the increasing literature documenting early childhood practice informed by other truths and knowledges and situated in different paradigms and theoretical perspectives. Many truths are rendered invisible by a mask of pseudo-consensus.

Informal democracy: democracy as a way of being and everyday democracy

Democracy is more than formal procedures and institutions. It is a multi-dimensional concept, operating in different ways, at different levels and in different settings. Democracy can be understood as a mode of being in the world, 'primarily a mode of associated living embedded in the culture and social relationships of everyday life'; it is 'a personal way of individual life … it signifies the possession and continual use of certain attitudes, forming personal character and determining desire and purpose in all the relations of life' (Dewey, 1939: 2). This is democracy understood as an approach to living and relating, an ethos and a way of acting, that should pervade all aspects of everyday life, not least in the centre or school: as such, it is 'a fundamental educational value and form of educational activity' (Rinaldi, 2006: 156).

Democracy as a way of being and acting is closely related to the idea of what Bentley (2005) terms 'everyday democracy', the enactment of democratic values in the relationships and places in which children and adults spend most of their time. Such everyday democracy has its place in formal democratic institutions, shaping the way politicians, administrators and others conduct themselves and their business. But it is particularly important at more local, institutional levels. When Skidmore and Bound talk about everyday democracy in 'the informal spheres of everyday life' (2008: 7), they include families, communities, workplaces – and public services; and when I speak about democracy in early childhood centres, or in schools, I am thinking more of 'everyday democracy' than the procedures and institutions of formal democracy. Both types of democracy – the formal and the everyday – are about democracy, but everyday democracy is about the conduct of democracy in everyday life in everyday institutions.

Bentley has argued for 'everyday democracy' as an urgent response to the crisis in traditional democratic politics, in which 'our preoccupation with making *individual* choices is undermining our ability to make *collective* choices' (2005: 19, emphasis added). Similarly, Skidmore and Bound emphasise how 'any workable approach to democracy today needs to reckon with, and be able to reconcile, our need for both a personal and a collective sense of agency' (2008: 24). The same point is taken up by the three educators from Reggio Emilia cited earlier, when they speak of participation having a communal as well as individual level, so equating, in my view, participation to everyday democracy:

> 'To participate' is a verb that can be conjugated in both the singular and the plural. Each person can participate as an individual subject who singly makes his or her contribution and singly takes in the information and contributions provided by the others ... Individual participation is, and will always be, an aspect of everyone's participation. But participation takes on further meaning if the school presents itself as a community – in relation to the wider community represented by the town – and with a broader strategy ... [the value and practice of participation means] actively engaging all the children, teachers and parents in a community dimension that involves reading and interpreting change together. (Cagliari et al., 2004: 29)

Everyday democracy in everyday institutions, such as early childhood centres and schools, is partly a case of how we live with and relate to each other. But it is also about the conduct of certain activities that involve choices, power and responsibility, which Bentley describes as:

> the practice of self-government through the choices, commitments and connections of daily life. Everyday democracy means extending democratic power and responsibility simultaneously to the settings of everyday life ... *It means that people can actively create the world in which they live.* (2005: 20–1, emphasis added)

Some examples can help to illustrate this active creation of the world through everyday democracy. It can involve the *formal governance* of institutions, for example decisions about goals and practices, personnel and resources, environments and relationships with the wider community. This may involve formal structures and procedures, such as elected governing bodies or school councils or open school meetings or other forums, deliberating on a regular basis and with set terms of reference. This is closest to the idea of democracy as a principle of government, in which either representatives or all members of certain groups are involved in decisions in specified areas. It is an expression, too, of John Dewey's principle that 'all those who are affected by social institutions must have a share in producing and managing them' (Dewey, 1937).

But this principle, applied as everyday democracy, can also involve more ad hoc and varied means to enable participation in *decision making*, ranging from small issues in daily life to larger matters such as designing the environment (see, for example, Clark, 2010) and deciding about project work (see, for example, Vecchi, 2010). Participation in formal governance bodies is more likely to be confined to adults in early childhood centres and the first years of school, gradually extending to include older children in schools. But all children can be active participants in other forms of decision making.

Case study: *Demokratie Leben* project

An example of involving very young children in decisions about their daily life comes from the *Demokratie Leben* project, conducted in day nurseries in an east German town, working with very young children. At the heart of this project was respecting the autonomy of 1- and 2-year-old children in everyday relationships and activities, for example feeding, changing nappies and planning activities for the day. What does respecting autonomy look like in practice?

> Before changing a child's diaper, one has to establish contact with the child and ask – if it is age appropriate – whether one should change his diaper now. This is not solely a yes/no question, it is rather used to talk the child through it and explain why changing the diaper is necessary from a certain point in time for hygiene. Children often don't want to relinquish the content of their diapers immediately ... (and then) there should be an agreement with the child, when the diaper will be changed. This point in time is accepted by the child and a postponement – even if it's only a matter of minutes – is often enough to grant a child his autonomy and possibly gives him the opportunity to finish a game or an activity. This also lets the child feel included in the diaper-changing situation. (Priebe, quoted in George, 2009: 13)

Democratic relations involve developing negotiating skills:

> The teacher negotiates with the children what they should do in the afternoon. This shows that negotiating means more than just voting. When the vote decides, the majority is always content but in a worst case scenario almost half the group is unhappy or – like in this example – only two children. But two discontented children are already two too many. The goals of negotiation processes are that nobody is left behind or sidelined ... Negotiation until a consensus is reached is, naturally, a perfected art. But it is always worth trying (2009: 14).

The conclusion of the project's evaluator is 'that the basis for a democratic everyday culture can indeed already be formed in the day nursery' (2009: 14).

Evaluation can be democratic when participatory forms are used, such as pedagogical documentation, which for Loris Malaguzzi, the first head of Reggio Emilia's early childhood centres, 'meant the possibility to discuss and dialogue "everything with everyone"', sharing opinions about pedagogical work on the basis of 'real, concrete things – not just theories or words, about which it is possible to reach easy and naïve agreement' (Hoyuelos, 2004: 7) (for further discussion of pedagogical documentation, see Rinaldi, 2006; Dahlberg et al., 2007; and Vecchi, 2010). We can speak, too, about democratic *learning*, based on a pedagogy that values listening, dialogue and diversity and which is understood as co-construction of meaning whose outcome is not known in advance. Carlina Rinaldi, from Reggio Emilia, epitomises democratic learning when she describes project work as evoking:

> a journey that involves uncertainty and chance that always arises in relationships with others. Project work grows in many directions, with no predefined progression, no outcomes decided before the journey begins. It means being sensitive to the unpredictable results of children's investigation and research. (Rinaldi, 2005: 19)

Everyday democracy can also entail creating opportunities for *contesting dominant discourses*, which seek to shape our subjectivities and practices through their universal truth claims and their relationship with power. This political activity seeks to make core assumptions and values visible and contestable. Yeatman (1994) refers to it as 'postmodern politics' and offers examples such as a politics of difference, which challenges those groups claiming a privileged position of objectivity on a contested subject. But we could extend the areas opened up to politics, that are repoliticised as legitimate subjects for inclusive political dialogue and contestation: the politics of childhood, about the image of the child, the good life and what we want for our children; the politics of education, about what education can and should be; and the politics of gender, in the nursery and the home. It is through contesting dominant discourses that a fifth democratic activity can emerge: *opening up for change*, through developing a critical approach to what exists, envisioning utopias and using them to provoke utopian action.

All forms of democracy – from formal democratic politics to democratic relationships among a nursery group – are important and welcome; it is not a case of 'either/ or' but of 'and … and … and'. For ultimately, the different levels and forms of democracy are interrelated and interdependent. A healthy democracy needs to be healthy in all its parts, with formal democratic government supporting everyday democracy, democracy in the nursery or school, and everyday democracy sustaining a healthy formal democracy.

Conditions for democracy

Like any other complex human endeavour, democracy can wither, through either being stifled or neglected; it needs deliberate, sustained and energetic work to create conditions in which it can flourish in its many forms and settings. Some of the conditions are broad and general, rather than specific to early childhood; they represent features of the wider context that can stifle democracy. Arguably, economic neoliberalism and political advanced liberalism come under this heading, with their suspicion and disdain for democratic politics and anything public, and their privileging of the autonomous citizen and individual choice (Moss, 2009). This incompatibility between markets and democracy is summed up by Carr and Hartnett (1996: 192): 'Any vision of education that takes democracy seriously cannot but be at odds with educational reforms which espouse the language and values of market forces and treat education as a commodity to be purchased and consumed.' It raises an important question for those who want to see democracy as a fundamental value: how might it be possible to de-marketise and de-privatise the early childhood system?

Edgar Morin identifies another example of conditions that stifle democracy, the spread of what he calls 'technobureaucratism', marked by the rule of a certain kind of thinking:

> Such thinking perceives only mechanical causality while everything increasingly obeys a complex causality. It reduces reality to that which is quantifiable. Hyperspecialization and reduction to the quantifiable produce blindness not only to existence, the concrete, and the individual, but also to context, the global, and the fundamental. They involve, in all technobureaucratic systems, a fragmenting, a dilution, and finally a loss of responsibility ...
>
> *They contribute strongly to the regression of democracy in Western countries, where all problems, having become technical, elude the grasp of citizens to the profit of experts* ... [bringing] about the domination of experts in all fields that, until then, had been answerable to political discussions and decisions. (1999: 70, 91, emphasis added)

A third negative condition, related to the previous two, is what Roberto Unger (2005: 1) refers to as 'the dictatorship of no alternatives', a way of thinking and acting personified by the powerful and totalising truth claims made by the dominant discourse of neoliberalism and its technobureaucratic backers. This dictatorship proclaims there is only one way to go, only one way of viewing the world, and only one answer to any question. As such, it is at odds with a democracy which assumes an irreducible plurality – of values, identities and ways of life – and the possibility that human beings can flourish in many ways of life.

Of course, this does not mean we can abandon the common altogether. To live in plural societies, we need certain common institutions, procedures, rules and norms, arrived at through democratic deliberation, argument and negotiation. In ECEC, for example, there needs to be a national framework of entitlements, structures, resourcing, values, goals and practices. The issue is not only how this framework is arrived at, but also the balance it strikes between coherence and diversity, what it prescribes, and how much space it leaves for interpretation, experimentation and developing additional local values, goals and practices.

Let me turn away from conditions that stifle democracy, to consider positive conditions that might enable democracy to take root and flourish specifically in early childhood centres. Given limited space, all I can do is flag some up and encourage the reader to flesh them out and add to the list:

1   government, both national and local, actively promoting democracy, for example, by recognising democracy as a fundamental value in the curriculum and by placing a duty on local authorities to promote democracy in early childhood centres in their area (replacing the current duty on English local authorities to promote the 'childcare' market)

2   an infrastructure for democracy, including *pedagogistas*, experienced educators each working intensively with a small number of early childhood centres to develop pedagogical work and democratic practice; team working in centres to create an environment for discussion; a central role for pedagogical documentation; and attention to the design of early childhood environments to create spaces that reflect and support educational values, including democracy

3   time for democracy, both for educators and for parents/other citizens. This leads on to a much larger question – vitally important for individual and collective well-being, but beyond the scope of this chapter – of the use and redistribution of time, for men and women, between paid work, caring and what Ulrich Beck (1998) calls 'public work', a term that should encompass democratic participation in a range of local services

4   trust in human capacity for democracy. Democracy, in the words of John Dewey, is a 'way of personal life controlled not merely by faith in human nature in general but by faith in the capacity of human beings for intelligent judgement and action if proper conditions are furnished' (Dewey, 1939: 2). Policies and practices need to embody and reflect that trust and faith in human capabilities

5   a workforce for democracy. This calls for a workforce of well-educated early childhood professionals who are committed to and understand the meaning of democracy; who are critical thinkers, willing to question dominant discourses; who are curious to border cross and welcome new perspectives; who are comfortable working with plurality; who can dialogue without presuming to know or control the final outcome; and who recognise that they do not have *the* truth nor privileged access to knowledge. As Paulo Freire puts it, the educator may offer her 'reading of the world', but her role is to 'bring out the fact that there are other "readings of the world"' (Freire, 2004: 96), at times in opposition to her own.

Final thoughts

What has become apparent to me is that democracy has a clear meaning and concrete practical applications in all forms of education and educational institutions. Moreover, those who choose to espouse democracy as a fundamental value in education are not alone: they can draw on rich traditions and experiences, which show a recurring desire for this value and its feasibility in practice – given the right conditions. Democracy is neither necessary nor inevitable, no more than the image of the early childhood centre as a public space and workshop, with democratic practice as one of its many realised projects. But both the value and the image are viable alternatives that a community – be it a national, local or nursery community – can collectively choose in defiance of the dictatorship of no alternatives.

Summary

- In this chapter, I have made a case for democracy as a fundamental value in early childhood education and care, involving children and adults alike and connected to a particular image of the early childhood centre.
- I have introduced the idea of critical questions, requiring democratic discussion and deliberation, which should precede policy and practice.
- I have shown that a belief in democracy as a fundamental value is not new and that there are many examples to draw on to better understand what it might mean in practice.

 Questions for discussion

1 When you hear the word 'democracy' mentioned, what do you first think of?
2 Have you seen democracy mentioned and discussed in any aspect of your professional life? In your education and professional development? In the documents that govern policy and practice? In the magazines or journals you read? If not, why do you think that is?
3 What should be the fundamental values of early childhood education? Would you include democracy here or not?
4 Identify a condition that you think would be good for democracy, such as time. How could that condition be introduced or strengthened? *(Higher-level question)*

Further reading

Levels 5 and 6

Children in Europe, Issue 6, March 2004.
This special issue of the magazine provides a good introduction to the world-famous early childhood education in Reggio Emilia, including some of the concepts and practices raised in this chapter, such as participation and pedagogical documentation.

Moss, P. (2009) *There are Alternatives! Markets and Democratic Experimentalism in Early Childhood Education and Care*. The Hague: Bernard van Leer Foundation. Available at:

www.bernardvanleer.org/There_are_alternatives_Markets_and_democratic_experimentalism_in_early_childhood_education_and_care
This discussion paper offers a critique of the marketisation that dominates ECEC in the UK, and develops an argument about democracy as a fundamental value, in particular linked to experimentation.

Levels 6 and 7

Biesta, G. (2007) 'Why "what works" won't work: evidence-based practice and the democratic deficit in educational research', *Educational Theory*, 57(1): 1–22.
This provocative essay provides a critical analysis of the idea of evidence-based practice and the ways it has been promoted in the field of education, focusing on the tension between scientific and democratic control over educational practice and research.

Fielding, M. and Moss, P. (2010) *Radical Education and the Common School: A Democratic Alternative*. London: Routledge.
This book makes the case for democracy as a fundamental value and practice in pre-school and school, drawing on rich historical and overseas examples to examine what a democratic education and school might look like. It also considers how transformation to this democratic alternative might take place.

Note

1 The 'pre-school' is the name the Swedes give to the early childhood centre that forms the basis of their universal, integrated system of early childhood education and care. The pre-school is a centre available for children from 12 months (before which age children are at home with parents taking well-paid parental leave) to around their 6th birthday, when most children start school. For more information on the Swedish ECEC system, see Cohen et al. (2004) and Kaga et al. (2010).

References

Beck, U. (1998) *Democracy without Enemies*. Cambridge: Polity Press.
Bentley, T. (2005) *Everyday Democracy: Why We Get the Politicians We Deserve*. London: Demos.
Biesta, G. (2007) 'Why "what works" won't work: evidence-based practice and the democratic deficit in educational research', *Educational Theory*, 57(1): 1–22.
Bloom, A. (1948) 'Notes on a school community', *New Era*, 30(8): 120–1.
Cagliari, P., Barozzi, A. and Giudici, C. (2004) 'Thoughts, theories and experiences: for an educational project with participation', *Children in Europe*, 6: 28–30.
Carr, W. and Hartnett, A. (1996) *Education and the Struggle for Democracy*. Buckingham: Open University Press.
Clark, A. (2010) *Transforming Children's Spaces: Children's and Adults' Perspectives in Changing Learning Environments*. London: Routledge.
Cohen, B., Moss, P., Petrie, P. and Wallace, J. (2004) *A New Deal for Children? Re-forming Education and Care in England, Scotland and Sweden*. Bristol: The Policy Press.
Dahlberg, G., Moss, P. and Pence, A. (2007) *Beyond Quality in Early Childhood Education and Care: Languages of Evaluation*, 2nd edition. London: Routledge.

Darling, J. and Norbenbo, S.E. (2003) 'Progressivism', in N. Blake, P. Smeyers, R. Smith and P. Standish (eds) *The Blackwell Guide to Philosophy of Education*. Oxford: Blackwell.

Dewey, J. (1916) *Democracy and Education: An Introduction to the Philosophy of Education*. New York: Macmillan.

Dewey, J. (1937) 'Democracy and educational administration', *School and Society*, 45: 457–68.

Dewey, J. (1939) 'Creative democracy – the task before us'. Address given at a dinner in honour of John Dewey, New York, 20 October. Available at: www.beloit.edu/~pbk/dewey.html

Fielding, M. and Moss, P. (2010) *Radical Education and the Common School: A Democratic Alternative*. London: Routledge.

Freire, P. (2004) *Pedagogy of Hope: Reliving Pedagogy of the Oppressed*. London: Continuum.

George, S. (2009) *Too Young for Respect? Realising Respect for Young Children in their Everyday Environments*. The Hague: Bernard van Leer Foundation.

Hoyuelos, A. (2004) 'A pedagogy of transgression', *Children in Europe*, 6: 6–7.

Kaga, Y., Bennett, J. and Moss, P. (2010) *Caring and Learning Together: A Cross-national Study of Integration of Early Childhood Care and Education within the Education System*. Paris: UNESCO. Available at: http://unesdoc.unesco.org/images/0018/001878/187818e.pdf (accessed 16 October 2010).

Morin, E. (1999) *Homeland Earth: A Manifesto for the New Millennium*. Cresskill, NJ: Hampton Press.

Moss, P. (2009) *There are Alternatives! Markets and Democratic Experimentalism in Early Childhood Education and Care*. The Hague: Bernard van Leer Foundation. Available at: www.bernardvanleer.org/There_are_alternatives_Markets_and_democratic_experimentalism_in_early_childhood_education_and_care (accessed 16 October 2010).

Mouffe, C. (2000) *The Democratic Paradox*. London: Verso.

Power Inquiry (2006) *The Report of Power: An Independent Inquiry into Britain's Democracy*. London: The Power Inquiry.

Rinaldi, C. (2005) 'Is a curriculum necessary?', *Children in Europe*, 9: 19.

Rinaldi, C. (2006) *In Dialogue with Reggio Emilia: Listening, Researching and Learning*. London: Routledge.

Skidmore, P. and Bound, K. (2008) *The Everyday Democracy Index*. London: Demos.

Swedish Ministry of Education and Science (1998) *Curriculum for Pre-school*. Stockholm: Ministry of Education and Science. [English translation]

Unger, R.M. (2005) *What Should the Left Propose?* London: Verso.

Vecchi, V. (2010) *Art and Creativity in Reggio Emilia: Exploring the Role and Potential of Ateliers in Early Childhood Education*. London: Routledge.

Wagner, J.T. (2006) An outsider's perspective: childhoods and early education in the Nordic countries. In J. Einarsdottir and J.T. Wagner (eds) *Nordic Childhoods and Early Education: Philosophy, Research, Policy and Practice in Denmark, Finland, Iceland, Norway, and Sweden*. Greenwich, CT: Information Age Publishing.

Yeatman, A. (1994) *Postmodern Revisionings of the Political*. London: Routledge.

CHAPTER 8

THE MARKETISATION OF EARLY YEARS EDUCATION AND CHILD-CARE IN ENGLAND

Eva Lloyd

Overview

Different models of state support for early years education and childcare provision are employed across Europe and globally. Most early years systems include both private (for-profit and not-for-profit) and publicly funded provision, often referred to as a mixed economy of childcare or the childcare market. Direct and significant public funding of universal early childhood education and care services in several European countries, including France and the Nordic countries (Scheiwe and Willekens, 2009), contrasts with the position in major English speaking countries including the United Kingdom (UK), Australia, Canada, and the USA, and many other countries. However, information is hard to come by.

(Continued)

(Continued)

Few countries collect comprehensive information on private for-profit, or even not-for-profit, provision. In the UK, the market research firm Laing and Buisson is the major source of information about the private for-profit childcare sector; this data is very costly (Laing and Buisson, 2010).

The official rationale given for adopting a market approach tends to be that it encourages business efficiency and a better balance between supply and demand, while extending consumer choice (Plantenga and Remery, 2009). The Laing and Buisson annual series of market reports suggests that in the UK there has been a 70 per cent increase in for-profit provision since 1997 and that the for-profit sector is now the major provider of childcare for children aged 3 and under. Approximately 80 per cent of all childcare and 40 per cent of early educa-tion is now provided by for-profit businesses, excluding family day care. Mostly, these for-profit providers are small entrepreneurs owning between one and five nurseries. However, 10 per cent of this market is now provided by corporate companies, some of which are offshore, meaning that the company itself is not based in the UK (Penn, forthcoming).

In view of the fact that official statistics tend to be poor, national and international research into the impact of childcare markets on childcare availability, sustainability, quality and outcomes for children is a particularly important source of information. This chapter focuses on England as far as childcare market policy develop-ments are concerned and reviews some national and international evidence on impact; the statistics quoted, however, will frequently be UK-wide. It concludes that the very concept of a childcare market is problematic.

What is a childcare market?

In a market, buyers and sellers negotiate the exchange of goods or services; typically in neoliberal economies this process is free or largely free of government interven-tion. In some countries, local or central governments may choose to protect buyers by regulating competition between market traders and by ensuring minimum quality standards for the goods being sold. In the UK, the Office for Standards in Education (Ofsted) is the major regulatory body for early years education and care, although it does not deal with competition issues.

In the present global economic climate, childcare markets and the marketisation of other social welfare provision more generally, are a rapidly growing phenomenon (Lloyd and Penn, 2010). In many European countries, market forces are increasingly substituting for the role of public bodies in sectors that traditionally received public funding such as the provision of human services, including childcare. In addition, childcare markets in other English-speaking nations such as the USA, Canada and Australia, in the Netherlands (Lloyd and Penn, 2010), on the African continent

(Penn, 2008; Penn and Maynard, 2010) and in the Asia Pacific region (Yuen and Grieshaber, 2009), are the dominant delivery model for early years provision.

Behind the transition of public to private provision is the expectation that the market will create better incentives for providers to offer consumers more choice and competitive pricing, leading to a better balance between supply and demand. If such a demand-led market is supported by public funding in the form of vouchers, tax credits or other types of consumer (demand-side) subsidies, this is expected to boost the growth and sustainability of the private sector. It can be argued, though, that nationally and internationally, the increasing marketisation of childcare and parallel developments in other areas of education and social welfare, signify a retrenchment in welfare states (Ward and Eden, 2009).

Childcare markets appear to generate different consequences for the quality and sustainability of early years services, depending on the socio-economic conditions where they operate and on the administrative organisation of services. Historically, countries employ differentiated systems of early education and childcare, which embody different traditions, are governed by different administrative and policy systems, and in which responsibility may rest with different government ministries. Very few countries have truly integrated provision (Kaga et al., 2010).

Generally speaking, in those countries where early years provision is education-led provision, at least from the age of 2 or 3 upwards, such as in France or Belgium, the market argument has made few inroads. Where provision has traditionally been more childcare-led, more fragmented and inadequate, the for-profit sector has made more inroads, although the extent of this crucially depends on how funding is offered and regulations applied.

The English childcare market

Before 1997, state-funded early education for 3- and 4-year-old children operated alongside an alternative private early education market, mainly in the form of playgroups (Statham et al., 1990). Free early education in state nursery schools or nursery classes attached to state primary schools was mostly confined to disadvantaged areas, in the absence of a national early childhood education and care policy (Penn, 2009a). However, over half of 4-year-olds were admitted to reception classes (i.e. the first class for children in the maintained primary sector), although 5 was the compulsory school starting age.

In contrast with primaries, nursery schools operated with much better staff/child ratios and different curricular programmes. At that point, all non-education early years provision was administered by social services departments at a local level. This provision included day nurseries, community nurseries and out-of-school clubs, as well as family day care with childminders. The private for-profit sector was very small and in practice choice was limited, as different forms of provision were unequally distributed. Some better-off families, especially in London, used private nannies. Parents paid the full costs, until the pre-1997 Conservative government briefly introduced a nursery voucher system.

Between 1997 and 2010, the Labour government instituted many changes to the early years sector (Cohen et al., 2004). Just over a decade ago, all administrative and policy responsibility for early years services was transferred to the (then) Department for Education and Skills, to try to introduce a more coherent approach. Nevertheless, lines of official responsibility even now remain complex and fractured, and a fully harmonised registration and inspection regime for state-funded and private early education and childcare provision remains elusive (Andreae and Matthews, 2006). Devolution has also made some difference. An overview of early years policy developments in the four countries making up the UK since Devolution in 1998 can be found in Clark and Waller (2007).

The English childcare market since 1997

Though heralded by some as a quiet revolution (Smith, 2007), the Labour government's National Childcare Strategy (DfEE, 1998), actually consolidated the existing mixed economy (Lloyd, 2008).

Working within the parameters of the existing childcare market, the Labour government introduced three policy innovations:

- an entitlement for 3- and 4-year-old children to universal and free part-time early education
- an income-related entitlement for employed parents on low to middle incomes or those in education or training to support with childcare costs via the tax and benefit system, in order to promote mothers and lone parents in employment
- extra support for children and families in disadvantaged areas or circumstances in accessing early education and childcare provision.

Case study 1 describes a successful private for-profit childcare business operating within the post-1997 childcare market.

🗀 Case study 1: Sunrise Day Nursery

Sunrise Day Nursery is located in an attractive and spacious single-story building within large grounds adjacent to an industrial estate just outside a major metropolitan area. It represents the predominant format of private childcare business in England: a small partnership business operating one or two settings. Sunrise is one of two private for-profit day nurseries managed by Rosa Stainton, in partnership with a friend who owns 40 per cent of the business. Rosa is a female entrepreneur passionately committed to high quality childcare provision for the children of working parents. Both settings are registered for 150 children under 5,

(Continued)

(Continued)

have been rated 'outstanding' by Ofsted, are filled to capacity and generate a good profit. This has allowed Rosa to invest in accredited management training for all her room leaders. She is also about to introduce a differentiated pay structure which acknowledges management responsibilities and skills.

The nurseries had their origins in a pre-school playgroup set up by Rosa in response to her own childcare needs after the birth of her son some 30 years ago. But the parent committee-run not-for-profit and part-time pre-school playgroup model did not match Rosa's aspirations for young children and for managing a thriving childcare business. Soon, she and a friend were discussing the possibility of a business start-up loan with their local banks, although locating a bank supportive of a private nursery business plan took a while. So far, the lure of financing from venture capital firms has been resisted, although this might have allowed a faster and more extensive expansion of the business. Rosa considers the risks associated with external shareholders looking for a rapid return on their investment too great, especially in the current economic climate.

While Rosa is appreciative of the staff childcare training support she has received from the local authority over the years, she does not consider its business support suitable for this type and level of operation. To run this childcare business poses essentially the same challenges as any other 'people' business, in her view, especially the need to avoid customers, in this case parents, running up debts. Rightly proud of where she has got to, Rosa believes that managing a high quality childcare business requires a continuous hands-on approach which cannot easily be delegated.

Early education and marketisation

The roll-out of universal part-time early education for 3- and 4-year-olds was completed in 2004. From September 2010, this free entitlement was extended to 15 hours weekly for 38 weeks annually, to be delivered flexibly in response to parental wishes. Funded on a per capita basis, it can be provided by private for-profit and not-for-profit childcare businesses and indeed by childminders forming part of an accredited childminding network. All these providers must meet Ofsted registration requirements by working within the Early Years Foundation Stage curricular framework introduced in the 2006 Childcare Act (DCSF, 2008).

The Labour government argued for this integration of early education with childcare provision on the basis that no sensible distinction could be made between early education and childcare (NAO, 2004). The legal distinction between childcare and nursery education for young children was removed altogether in the Childcare Act 2006; Section 18 sets out how the term 'early years provision' applies to provision of integrated early learning, development and care.

By 2010, over half of 3-year-olds and some 20 per cent of 4-year-olds were receiving early education within private for-profit and not-for-profit settings (DfE, 2010). Childcare for under 3s is now also predominantly delivered within private settings, most of it in the private for-profit sector. Free early education has proved very popular with parents, although uptake among the most disadvantaged families is lower than among better-off families (Speight et al., 2010). The present coalition government is committed to extending access to such part-time early education to targeted groups of 2-year-old children from the most disadvantaged families after a successful pilot (Smith et al., 2009).

England's heavy reliance on private sector businesses to deliver early years provision to children aged 3 and over is virtually unique within Europe (Penn, 2009b). Only the Netherlands shares a similar childcare delivery model, although Dutch early education is delivered in primary schools (Lloyd and Penn, 2010). France and Belgium, for example, offer 28 hours of free education per week in state provision for all children aged over 30 months. Take-up is almost complete, even by disadvantaged families (OECD, 2006).

Promoting the English childcare market: the 2006 Childcare Act

The promotion of the English childcare market was reinforced by the introduction of the 2006 Childcare Act, which explicitly encourages the marketisation of early education and childcare. In this respect, too, England is almost unique in Europe, where only the Netherlands passed similar legislation.

The Act introduced two important innovations: a market facilitation duty for local authorities and a duty to 'close the gap' in attainment between the most and least well-off children through the provision of early years services (see Chapter 3). Section 8(3) allows local authorities to act only as 'provider of last resort', and restricts their ability to establish new services or expand their own provision in competition with existing good quality provision.

Finally, the Childcare Act 2006 also established a means to 'professionalise' the early years workforce by attracting graduates (Lloyd and Hallet, 2010). It introduced the status of Early Years Professional (EYP), a new leadership role with associated publicly funded training open to graduates. Though initially described as equivalent to Qualified Teacher Status, this interpretation of the new status does not reflect the reality in terms of pay and conditions.

The role of an EYP is confined to settings within the private for-profit and not-for-profit sector, as they cannot work in maintained schools unless they also have Qualified Teacher Status (CWDC, 2008). There is a clear link between the profitability and sustainability of the childcare market and the wages of those working in the sector; better qualifications should mean higher rates of pay. English childcare practitioners frequently earn little more than the minimum wage, though the level of qualified staff is steadily rising (Phillips et al., 2010). At the time of writing, the coalition government has decided to continue funding EYP training in 2012–15.

Case study 2 documents the marketisation of childcare via specific legislation in the Netherlands, the only OECD country which has adopted similar childcare legislation to England.

Case study 2: The marketisation of Dutch childcare

Unlike in England, Dutch early education and childcare are provided and funded separately. Schools offer part-time publicly funded nursery education to children from their 4th birthday, before they start compulsory schooling at age 5. Part-time playgroups allow young children to socialise with peers and offer places subsidised by local authorities to children with additional needs, such as having a different first language than Dutch. Registered childcare in private for-profit and not-for-profit day care centres or with childminders is used by some 40 per cent of children under 4, mostly part time. While maternal employment rates are high, more Dutch mothers work part time than in any other OECD member state.

The 2005 Dutch Childcare Act (Wet op de Kinderopvang) radically changed the way in which this system is funded. The Netherlands shares with England the unique distinction of having introduced legislation specifically aimed at encouraging the marketisation of childcare. In order to encourage employment by securing sufficient good-quality childcare for working parents, the Dutch Childcare Act introduced a demand-led childcare market. Under the Act's 'tripartite' method of funding childcare, costs are shared between central government, employers and parents.

Via income-related childcare tax credits and employer childcare contributions, compulsory since 2007, parents receive two-thirds of their total registered childcare costs. While there is an upper limit on the hourly childcare costs funded under the tax credit system, the upper income level beyond which parents no longer qualify for financial support has been raised annually since 2005.

Three of the 2005 Dutch Childcare Act's provisions are particularly interesting:

- For dual-earner families, both employers share the employer contribution.
- Informal carers, such as grandparents, can register as childminders without any obligation to care for children other than those from within their own families.
- Childcare provision was largely deregulated, though compliance with basic quality criteria is required.

The impact of the Act was revolutionary. Parental childcare costs are now demonstrably lower, there has been a huge increase in overall uptake of registered childcare, and registered childminder numbers rose by more than 200 per cent.

(Continued)

(Continued)

The 40 per cent rise in the uptake of childcare tax credits exceeded the Dutch government's predictions and hence its annual childcare budget projections. Childcare waiting lists grew and a rise in maternal employment rates failed to materialise.

The Act's unintended consequences in terms of childcare overspend soon generated amendments designed to rebalance the financial responsibilities for childcare provision and secure the system's long-term viability. A freeze on tax credit levels was introduced in late 2009, while childminding brokerage agencies, which link parents with providers and which played a prominent role in 'formalising' informal care, were phased out. From 2011, grandparents are no longer able to register as childminders, unless they agree to certain conditions. These include a willingness to care for a certain number of children, not all from their own family.

Financial support for the English childcare market

The English National Childcare Strategy also offered supply-side subsidies in the form of start-up and other business support grants to private childcare businesses. Such start-up grants helped support the transformation of playgroups into not-for-profit sessional or full day care businesses and the establishment of out-of-school provision.

Demand-side subsidies in the form of parental tax credits were introduced to help parents buy registered childcare in the growing childcare market. To qualify for income-related tax credits, parents in dual-earner families or lone parents had to work first in excess of 16 hours, now 24 hours, per week. Despite this support, most parents still pay by far the larger share of childcare fees, which have been rising by around 5 per cent annually (Goddard and Knights, 2009).

The choice of tax credits as a policy instrument contradicts the recommendations of an influential OECD survey report which concluded that: 'a public supply-side investment model managed by public authorities brings more uniform quality and superior coverage of childhood populations than parent subsidy models' (OECD, 2006: 114). The Labour government acknowledged that childcare markets may fail in disadvantaged areas and therefore offered additional financial support to ensure equal access for all children (HM Treasury, 2004).

Childcare markets in disadvantaged areas

The very programmes designed to ensure equal access in disadvantaged areas were nevertheless expected to operate within the childcare market. Neighbourhood

Nurseries, introduced in England around 2000, embodied an alternative model of childcare and early education provision in areas where the childcare market operated inefficiently (Neigbourhood Nurseries Initiative Research Team, 2007). But once the government's extra financial support tapered off, the initiative faltered. A longitudinal study of contracting local childcare markets identified the seasonal or intermittent nature of the local jobs available and imperfect workings of the tax credit system as possible factors depressing parental demand (Dickins et al., 2005).

The most visible part of the National Childcare Strategy's support for disadvantaged families with young children was the Sure Start programme, a high-profile area-based initiative (see Chapter 2). Sure Start local programmes offered a range of health and family support services to all children under 4 and their families living in some 500 disadvantaged areas. A requirement for providing full-time early years education and childcare provision was introduced at an advanced stage of the programme's implementation. By 2010, this initiative had been transformed into the much less generously funded Sure Start Children's Centres programme and was rolled out to 3500, mostly disadvantaged, English communities.

The location of Children's Centres often poses a risk to local childcare businesses. They may be reluctant to invest in the most disadvantaged areas as lack of parental demand for more than the free entitlement to early education affects provider profitability. This is evidenced by the fact that in 2009 58 per cent of a sample of local authorities themselves provided full childcare in Children's Centres, while only 10 per cent of centres made a surplus (NAO, 2009). Despite official recognition of the contribution of good early years provision to children's well-being and life chances, outside the statutory entitlement, this is not free at the point of delivery even in Children's Centres. Instead, Children's Centres must adopt a cost-neutral business model, where private for-profit or not-for-profit businesses deliver early education and childcare provision, offering full-time places to many of the most disadvantaged children with the help of local government subsidies. However, the advent of subsidised Children's Centres in some areas may attract parents away from established private-sector provision and undermine their financial viability.

Two National Audit Office reports (NAO, 2006, 2009) suggested that most Children's Centres experienced problems offering sustainable childcare. Where local government itself provides services as 'a last resort', this contradicts the intentions of the 2006 Childcare Act. A House of Commons Select Committee Inquiry into Children's Centres queried the self-financing basis underpinning their early years provision and recommended that Centres' public funding formula should be formalized and increased, though 'with due consideration for the impact on local childcare markets' (House of Commons, 2010: 24). In late 2010, the coalition government abolished the requirement for Children's Centres to deliver full day care in disadvantaged areas.

The impact of childcare marketisation

During the last decade, most of the rapid expansion of childcare provision has been among stand-alone private for-profit childcare businesses and small chains (up to five nurseries), which now make up 75 per cent of the private childcare sector. In contrast, numbers of childminders and sessional childcare providers such as playgroups has steadily decreased. Expansion and consolidation within the UK private childcare market has been documented since 2002 in health and social care market research company Laing and Buisson's annual series of UK nursery market reports.

The recent recession appears to have had an impact. Between 2008 and 2009, numbers of all types of childcare businesses fell, as did the number of children attending. Only full day care, including that offered in Children's Centres, remained at the same level (Phillips et al., 2010). In 2009, almost 40 per cent of private nurseries had seen their economic performance weaken in the previous year, while a third of these nurseries reported a significant worsening (Laing and Buisson, 2009).

Increased corporatisation as part of the growth of private for-profit company involvement has been a distinctive aspect of increasing marketisation of childcare in recent years. The size of this corporate childcare sector grew seven times over a 10-year period, to the point where it accounted for some 46 per cent of all day nursery places in the UK (Penn, 2007).

Some of the large childcare chains are shareholder companies, listed on the stock market, either in their own right or as part of a larger diversified corporation. These shareholder companies provided about 8 per cent of the total UK childcare places in 2009. Illustrative of how this field is characterised by market mobility, is the fact that only one of the corporate childcare chains that were operating in 1998 are still under the same ownership and management (Penn, 2009c).

The impact of this exponential growth has not been properly investigated. Since 2008, Ofsted no longer distinguishes between for-profit and not-for-profit childcare, but instead uses the categories of childcare providers 'on domestic' and on 'non-domestic' premises (Ofsted, 2010). This causes problems in monitoring growth and quality trends for different types of providers.

Despite continuing misgivings about the efficiency of local childcare markets in disadvantaged areas, the then Labour government restated its confidence in their operations in its last review of the childcare strategy (HM Government, 2009). This suggests that the 2006 Childcare Act was not yet fully achieving its intended effects. As a significant proportion of early education is delivered within the childcare market by private providers, lack of provider sustainability may pose a risk not only to wrap-around childcare provision, but also to children's core early learning, development and care entitlement.

Childcare markets and childcare quality

Childcare quality has been strongly linked to beneficial impacts on children's well-being and future life chances, particularly for disadvantaged children (Sylva and Taylor, 2006), amongst whom those from minority ethnic communities are disproportionately represented. Emerging evidence implicates not just location, but also type of provider in childcare quality.

Both national and international research suggests that within childcare markets, for-profit childcare is generally of a lower quality than not-for-profit childcare (Mathers et al., 2007; Sosinsky et al., 2007). Admittedly, there is variation among each type of provider and good quality may be found in top-level private for-profit provision. In England, early education delivered in state-funded settings such as nursery schools and combined centres has consistently achieved higher quality ratings than other forms of early years provision (Roberts et al., 2010).

In the UK, the findings on children's social and educational outcomes from two major longitudinal studies and two large-scale evaluations identify the longer-term adverse impact on children's learning outcomes of lower quality in the private sector as compared to the state sector. These are: the Effective Provision of Pre-school Education (EPPE) project (Sylva et al., 2004), the Millennium Cohort Study (Mathers et al., 2007) and the evaluations of the Neighbourhood Nurseries Initiative (Mathers and Sylva, 2007), and the pilot extension of early education to 2-year-old children (Smith et al., 2009).

Studies from Canada (Cleveland et al., 2008), from the USA (Sosinsky et al., 2007) and from the Netherlands (de Kruif et al., 2009) moreover suggest that for-profit childcare is of a significantly lower standard than not-for-profit or state-funded childcare. Among provisional explanations put forward by the UK and Dutch researchers is that staff qualifications, notably the involvement of trained teachers and in England graduate leadership, make a critical difference to quality and impact.

It is disturbing that the poorest quality childcare continues to be found in the poorest areas of England, despite the presence of Children's Centres (Ofsted, 2008). There appears to be a strong case for considering the impact of type of provider on quality of provision within the childcare market as part of further developing early years policy.

Final thoughts

Increasing marketisation of English early years provision has consolidated two parallel childcare markets, one with fully state-funded or subsidised provision for poor children, and one for the children of better-off employed parents. Also discernible is a trend towards individual rather than collective responsibility for childcare provision. While sustained by a range of government subsidies, this childcare market does not offer parents and children genuine choice.

This chapter has discussed additional evidence that within this market both quality and sustainability of provision are problematic, even where it is aimed at children living in disadvantaged circumstances, as in Children's Centres. It has highlighted contrasts between the English childcare market and the situation in several European countries, where the early years education and childcare system receives considerable and direct public funding, although there is more similarity with English-speaking countries like Canada and Australia. As it is heavily regulated and partly subsidised, this market is 'atypical' compared to the 'pure' markets of classical economic theory.

Not only is the childcare market's sustainability at risk, but evidence of a unifying and integrated concept behind it is lacking. How was this childcare market allowed to develop in this way? Alternative models are feasible in principle, according to Moss (2009), while Apple (2000) characterises the trend towards marketisation of education services in general as internally contradictory and rejecting of the universalist and redistributive ethos of the welfare state.

The rationale for childcare markets is even contested within the field of economics. According to Cleveland and Krashinski (2004), there is a strong economic justification for state support for universal early education and childcare as a 'public good'. This is directly related to young children's well-being and quality of life, as well as to their future life chances. The evidence suggests that the very concept of childcare markets remains problematic.

▢ Summary

- This chapter describes the process of increasing marketisation of early childhood provision in England in recent years, and explores research evidence for its impact on children's well-being and longer-term social and educational outcomes.
- Emerging national and international evidence suggests that such childcare market systems move away from the principle of equity in early years provision, failing to provide equal opportunity for all children within a universal system.
- The questions for discussion and suggested readings aim to encourage debate about the state's role in providing and regulating early years services, as it requires states to strike a proper balance between serving the interests of parents and the wider family, of children and of the state itself.

⚇ Questions for discussion

1 To what extent can childcare markets promote equity in early years education and childcare?
2 Are primary guiding principles of competition and individual choice the appropriate values in this area of provision?
3 What might be seen as feasible alternatives to childcare markets? To what extent are such alternatives compatible with wider government policy objectives in the UK? *(Higher-level question)*

Further reading

Levels 5 and 6

Clark, M.M. and Waller, T. (eds) (2007) *Early Childhood Education & Care: Policy and Practice*. London: Sage.
Recent early years policy development in the four countries making up the UK and in the Republic of Ireland is lucidly explained in the different chapters of this edited volume.

Lloyd, E. and Penn, H. (2010) Why do childcare markets fail? Comparing England and the Netherlands. *Public Policy Research*, 17(1): 42–8.
This article provides succinct descriptions of the Dutch and English childcare markets, forming a good introduction to the concept of childcare markets. Both countries passed legislation promoting childcare markets, setting them apart from the rest of Europe.

Levels 6 and 7

Penn, H. (2007) Childcare market management: how the United Kingdom government has reshaped its role in developing early childhood education and care. *Contemporary Issues in the Early Years,* 8(3): 192–207.
This article presents a transparent overview of increasing childcare marketisation in Britain, as well as clearly setting out the rationale for and against childcare markets.

Scheiwe, K. and Willekens, H. (eds) (2009) *Child Care and Pre-school Development in Europe: Institutional Perspectives.* Basingstoke: Palgrave Macmillan.
This book's historical insights into the pathways by which European childcare systems emerged enable new interpretations of current policy challenges and anomalies, as well as making for fascinating reading.

Websites

http://eppe.ioe.ac.uk
This EPPE (Effective Provision of Pre-school Education) project site contains all reports on the first major European longitudinal study of a national sample of the impact of early years provision on young children's development (intellectual and social/behavioural).

www.ness.bbk.ac.uk
The website of the National Evaluation of Sure Start contains a wealth of material on the challenges of providing integrated childcare, early education, family health and family support services in disadvantaged areas and the methodology required for measuring their effectiveness.

References

Andreae, J. and Matthews, P. (2006) Evaluating quality and standards of early years education and care. In G. Pugh and B. Duffy (eds) *Contemporary Issues in the Early Years*, 3rd edition, 49–62. London: Sage.
Apple, M.W. (2000) *Official Knowledge: Democratic Education in a Conservative Age*, 2nd edition. London and New York: Routledge.

Children's Workforce Development Council (CWDC) (2008) *Induction and Information Guide: Early Years Professionals*. Leeds: CWDC.

Clark, M.M. and Waller, T. (eds) (2007) *Early Childhood Education and Care: Policy and Practice*. London: Sage.

Cleveland, G. and Krashinski, M. (2004) *Financing ECEC Services in OECD Countries*. Paris: OECD.

Cleveland, G., Forer, B., Hyatt D., Japel, C. and Krashinsky, M. (2008) New evidence about childcare in Canada: use patterns, affordability and quality. *Institute for Research in Public Policy: Choices*, 14(12). Available at: www.irpp.org/choices/archive/vol14no12.pdf (accessed 30 September 2010).

Cohen, B., Moss, P., Petrie, P. and Wallace, J. (2004) *A New Deal for Children? Re-forming Education and Care in England, Scotland and Sweden*. Bristol: The Policy Press.

De Kruif, R., Riksen-Walraven, J., Gevers Deynoot-Schaub, M., Helmerhorst, K., Tavecchio, L. and Fukkink, R. (2009) *Pedagogische Kwaliteit van de Nederlandse Kinderopvang in 2008*. Amsterdam: Nederlands Consortium Kinderopvang Onderzoek.

Department for Children, Schools and Families (DCSF) (2008) *Statutory Framework for the Early Years Foundation Stage,* 2nd edition. Nottingham: DCSF.

Department for Education (DfE) (2010) *Statistical First Release: Provision for Children Under Five Years of Age in England. January 2010*. SFR16/2010. London: Department for Education.

Department for Education and Employment (DfEE) (1998) *Meeting the Childcare Challenge*. Green Paper. London: HMSO.

Dickins, S., Taylor, J. and La Valle, I. (2005) *Local Childcare Markets: A Longitudinal Study*. Research Report No. SSU/2005/FR/016. London: HMSO.

Goddard, K. and Knights, E. (2009) *Quality Costs: Paying for Early Childhood Education and Care.* London: Daycare Trust.

HM Government (2009) *Next Steps for Early Learning and Childcare: Building on the 10-Year Strategy.* Nottingham: DCSF.

HM Treasury (2004) *Choice for Parents: The Best Start for Children. A Ten Year Strategy for Childcare.* London: The Stationery Office.

House of Commons (Children, Schools and Families Committee) (2010) *Sure Start Children's Centres: Fifth Report of the Session 2009–10.* Vol. I. London: The Stationery Office.

Kaga, J., Bennett, J. and Moss, P. (2010) *Caring and Learning Together: A Cross-national Study on the Integration of Early Childhood Education within Education*. Paris: UNESCO.

Laing and Buisson (2009) *Children's Nurseries: UK Market Report 2009*. London: Laing & Buisson.

Laing and Buisson (2010) *Children's Nurseries: UK Market Report 2010*. London: Laing & Buisson.

Lloyd, E. (2008) The interface between childcare, family support and child poverty strategies under New Labour: tensions and contradictions. *Social Policy and Society*, 7(4): 479–94.

Lloyd, E. and Hallet, E. (2010) Professionalising the early childhood workforce in England: work in progress or missed opportunity? *Contemporary Issues in the Early Years*, 11(1): 75–88.

Lloyd, E. and Penn, H. (2010) Why do childcare markets fail? Comparing England and the Netherlands. *Public Policy Research*, 17(1): 42–8.

Mathers, S. and Sylva, K. (2007) *National Evaluation of the Neighbourhood Nurseries Initiative: The Relationship between Quality and Children's Behavioural Development*. Research Report No. SSU/2007/FR/022. London: DCSF.

Mathers, S., Sylva, K. and Joshi, H. (2007) *Quality of Childcare Settings in the Millennium Cohort Study.* Research Report No. SSU/2007/FR/022. London: DCSF.

Moss, P. (2009) *There Are Alternatives! Markets and Democratic Experimentalism in Early Childhood Education and Care*. The Hague: Bernard van Leer Foundation.

National Audit Office (NAO) (2004) *Early Years: Progress in Developing High Quality Childcare and Early Education Accessible to All*. Report by the Comptroller and Auditor General. London: The Stationery Office.

National Audit Office (NAO) (2006) *Sure Start Children's Centres.* London: NAO.

National Audit Office (NAO) (2009) *Sure Start Children's Centres: Memorandum for the Children, Schools and Families Committee.* London: NAO.

Neigbourhood Nurseries Initiative Research Team (2007) *National Evaluation of the Neighbourhood Nurseries Initiative: Integrated Report.* Research Report No. SSU/2007/FR/024. London: HMSO.

Organisation for Economic Cooperation and Development (OECD) (2006) *Starting Strong II: Early Childhood Education and Care.* Paris: OECD.

Ofsted (2008) *Early Years: Leading to Excellence 2005–2008.* London: Ofsted.

Ofsted (2010) *Registered Childcare Providers and Places in England at 30 September 2010.* London: Ofsted.

Penn, H. (2007) Childcare market management: how the United Kingdom government has reshaped its role in developing early childhood education and care. *Contemporary Issues in the Early Years,* 8(3): 192–207.

Penn, H. (2008) *Early Childhood Education and Care in Southern Africa: A Perspective Report for CfBT Educational Trust.* Reading: Centre for British Teachers.

Penn, H. (2009a) Public and private: the history of early education and care institutions in the United Kingdom. In K. Schweiwe and H. Willekens (eds) *Child Care and Pre-school Development in Europe: Institutional Perspectives,* 105–25. Basingstoke: Palgrave Macmillan.

Penn, H. (2009b) *Early Childhood Education and Care: Key Lessons from Research for Policy Makers.* Brussels: European Commission. Available at: www.nesse.fr/nesse/nesse_top/tasks/analytical-reports/ecec-report-pdf (accessed 30 September 2010).

Penn, H. (2009c) International perspectives on quality in mixed economies of childcare. *National Institute Economic Review,* 207(1): 83–9.

Penn, H. (forthcoming) Gambling on the market: the role of for-profit provision in early childhood education and care. *Journal of Early Childhood Research.*

Penn, H. and Maynard, T. (2010) *Siyabonana: Building Better Childhoods in South Africa.* Edinburgh: Children in Scotland.

Phillips, R., Norden, O., McGinigal, S. and Oseman, D. with Coleman, N. (2010) *Childcare and Early Years Provider Survey 2009.* Research Report No. DFE RR-012. London: Department for Education.

Plantenga, J. and Remery, C. (2009) *The Provision of Childcare Services: A Comparative Review of 30 European Countries.* Brussels: European Commission.

Roberts, F., Mathers, S., Joshi, H., Sylva, K. and Jones, E. (2010) Childcare in the pre-school years. In K. Hansen, H. Joshi and S. Dex (eds) *Children of the 21st Century: The First Five Years,* 131–51. Bristol: The Policy Press.

Scheiwe, K. and Willekens, H. (eds) (2009) *Child Care and Pre-school Development in Europe: Institutional Perspectives.* Basingstoke: Palgrave Macmillan.

Smith, R., Purdon, P., Schneider, V., La Valle, I., Wollny, Y., Owen, R., Bryson, C. Mathers, S., Sylva, K. and Lloyd, E. (2009) *Evaluation of the Early Education Pilot for Two Year Old Children.* Research Report No. DCSF-RR134. London: DCSF.

Smith, T. (2007) Early years services in Britain 1997–2007: a quiet revolution. *Journal of Children's Services,* 2(2): 26–38.

Sosinsky, L., Lord, H. and Zigler, E. (2007) For-profit/non-profit differences in center-based child care quality: results from the National Institute of Child Health and Human Development Study of Early Child Care and Youth Development. *Journal of Applied Developmental Psychology,* 28(5): 390–410.

Speight, S., Smith, R. and Lloyd, E. with Coshall, C. (2010) *Families Experiencing Multiple Disadvantage: Their Use of and Views on Childcare Provision.* Research Report No. DCSF-RR191. London: DCSF.

Statham, J., Lloyd, E., Moss, P., Melhuish, E. and Owen, C. (1990) *Playgroups in a Changing World.* London: HMSO.

Sylva, K., Melhuish, E.C., Sammons, P., Siraj-Blatchford, I. and Taggart, B. (2004) *The Effective Provision of Pre-School Education (EPPE) Project: Final Report.* London: DfES/Institute of Education, University of London.

Sylva, K. and Taylor, H. (2006) Effective settings: evidence from research. In G. Pugh and B. Duffy (eds) *Contemporary Issues in the Early Years,* 165–77. London: Sage.

Ward, S. and Eden, C. (2009) *Key Issues in Education Policy.* London: Sage.

Yuen, G. and Grieshaber, S. (2009) Parents' choice of early childhood education services in Hong Kong: a pilot study about vouchers. *Contemporary Issues in Early Childhood,* 10(3): 263–79.

CHAPTER 9

SUPPORTING EARLY YEARS PRACTITIONERS' PROFESSIONAL DEVELOPMENT AS A VEHICLE FOR DEMOCRATISATION

Dawn Tankersley, Ulviyya Mikailova and Gerda Sula

Overview

This chapter addresses the work of the International Step by Step Association (ISSA) and its member non-governmental organisations (NGOs) in the area of professional development of in-service practitioners in the former communist bloc region. Since beginning its work in the region more than a decade ago, ISSA has brought new values and principles into the Early Childhood Education (ECE) sector of the region, including: a new image of the child, child-centred teaching, social inclusion and other civic values, building communities of learners, child agency and family/community participation. The *Step by Step Program and Teacher Standards for Pre-school and Primary Grades* (ISSA, 2002) revised in 2005 and again in 2010 as *Principles of Quality Pedagogy*, are an example of a practical tool

(Continued)

(Continued)

for translating principles into practice and promoting sustainable change at the individual, school and societal levels. Examples, as well as challenges, from focus areas outlined in *Competent Educators of the 21st Century: Principles of Quality Pedagogy* (ISSA, 2010) are presented. We discuss how work in these focus areas has influenced some changes in the behaviours of practitioners, as well as the challenges that still exist in introducing a new paradigm of early childhood education in the region. Practitioners in this chapter will refer to early childhood professionals who either have a pre-school education college diploma (two-year degree) or university diploma (four-year degree).

Background

Until the early 1990s, the educational system in the Soviet Union and communist bloc countries of Central/Eastern Europe, Central Asia, and the Caucuses provided for both the care and education of young children in state-supported centres. These centres had the dual purposes of putting women into the workforce and ensuring that children started to develop the values they would be expected to hold as future citizens of their societies. These are common goals in educational systems in most countries throughout the world, including those with democratic governments. However, while in these institutions well-trained professionals (practitioners with two- to four-year degrees) in early childhood development took care of children's physical and cognitive development, the education system did not encourage the development of the habits, skills and knowledge needed to be active members of participatory democracies. Constructivism was not promoted as a way of learning (Wood, 2006). Childhood was seen as preparation for becoming adult workers, rather than a period of time that has its own inherent value, a crucial period in children's life if they are to reach their full potential.

Education (including early childhood education), as in most places in the world, was a very teacher-centred process led by professionals who took care of children both for parents and for the state. The learning process consisted mostly of memorisation and recitation. There was a lack of both the understanding and the skills required to develop in children the abilities to listen and to consider multiple sides of an issue or argument, to use critical thinking and to express differences while respecting others as equals. The educational process followed a 'factory assembly line' philosophy, viewing children as empty vessels to be filled with the required knowledge and skills to be ready for the next factory line of compulsory education.

After the fall of the communist bloc in Europe and Central Asia in the early 1990s, many factors, such as economic crisis, increased unemployment, sharp decrease in public investment and a lack of professional development opportunities for practitioners resulted in a loss of interest in pre-school services and cuts in funding.

The model described above was increasingly seen as woefully inadequate for meeting the educational goals of democratic societies – that call for each child to develop her full potential, to learn how to learn and to be an active citizen. Instead of the factory model, the concepts of child/learner-centred pedagogy based on the concepts of constructivism (Piaget, Vygotsky) and progressive education (Dewey) were introduced and gained popularity in the region (Nutbrown et al., 2008).

In 1994, a cohort of educators from 15 different countries with funding from the Open Society Institute (OSI) introduced the Step by Step program into the existing government teacher-training systems (Klaus, 2004) as a way to use early childhood education opportunities to foster democratic principles and actions in teaching staff, young children, their families and communities (ISSA, 2002) through the implementation of a more child-versus-teacher-centred methodological approach to education. The Step by Step program was the very first, and for many years the only ECE program, which opened a 'window' to the new ideas and promoted revisiting the approaches, policies and practices of how care and education were provided in the early years.

In 1999, the 29 non-governmental organisations that were implementing the program joined together to establish the International Step by Step Association (ISSA), also with assistance from OSI. ISSA is a membership organisation that connects professionals and organisations working in early childhood development and education located in Central/Eastern Europe and Central Asia. Its over-arching goal is to promote inclusive, quality care and education experiences that create the conditions for all children to become active members of democratic knowledge societies (ISSA, 2010). Through a network of progressive professionals in each country, the following concepts were introduced into the region:

- equal access to quality education and care opportunities
- child-centred, individualised teaching and learning, combining high-level instruction with support for the needs of each child
- development of skills and dispositions for lifelong learning and participation in a democracy
- recognition of educators' many roles as facilitators, guides and role models in the learning process and as active members of their communities
- family involvement in children's development and education
- community engagement in public education
- respect for diversity, inclusive practices and culturally appropriate learning environments
- self-improvement and ongoing professional development (ISSA, 2010).

Through ongoing professional development, capacity building, networking and mutual cooperation at the country, regional and international levels, ISSA and its member NGOs contribute to: influencing educational policies; improving the quality of practitioners' performance; creating alternative forms of early childhood development services, including community-based education initiatives; and supporting democratisation in early years services and communities in general to include more voices in deciding and implementing what is in the best interests of each child.

Changes and challenges

Initially, ISSA's member NGOs introduced a new paradigm of democratisation in the form of a child-centred approach to early childhood education in their countries through in-service teacher training. Some changes were incorporated very easily by practitioners, while others still remain on the surface level in many countries. As expected, factors such as cultural and pedagogical traditions, social, political and economic background, the political climate for NGO development and the culture of civil participation all influenced the level of how easily or how deeply changes were affected. However, it was also found that when the ISSA NGOs focused teacher training around the *ISSA Pedagogical Standards/Principles,* influencing individual practice, early childhood centres, schools, communities and educational policy and practice were also more successful (Howard et al., 2010).

Influence on individual practice

Although the use of the *ISSA Standards/Principles* by practitioners was shown to improve teaching skills, increase efficacy and elevate the practitioners' professional status, there were also challenges in applying them to practice (Howard et al., 2010). In this section, we identify both changes that were made at the individual practice level, and those that continue to be challenging, using the seven focus areas identified in the current *Competent Educators of the 21st Century: Principles of Quality Pedagogy* (ISSA, 2010) in terms of practitioners making the move into the paradigm of child-centred democratic teaching.

Interactions: Teaching in a 'factory' model of education is a one-way action in which practitioners tell children what they need to know and then ask the children to regurgitate that information to ensure that they have learned it. In contrast, teaching through interaction is made up of two-way actions between different parties. With the Step by Step program introducing new understandings of early childhood development, practitioners started to consider even very young children as active agents and co-constructors of knowledge, and to develop the skills to engage in interactions with them that incorporate an interchange of ideas and knowledge. This was a major move away from a traditional philosophy of education towards more progressive conceptualisations. Practitioners also needed understanding and skills in how to individualise their interactions to meet each child's needs, as well as how to facilitate children's interactions so that they were also learning from their peers.

A way to help practitioners develop these skills has been to build learning communities of practitioners in which they themselves can interact with and learn from each other. Practitioners for the first time were invited, encouraged, and provisions were made for them, to work as a team, which in itself was a major cultural change. When practitioners are encouraged to engage in co-construction of knowledge with others and when mentors personalise their interactions with practitioners, they can see these skills demonstrated and they have support to practise these kinds of interactions in their own classrooms.

Family and Community: Promoting family partnerships in early childhood centres and schools was one of the major successes of the Step by Step program (Klaus, 2004). Family members quickly became more involved in their children's education by participating in more frequent two-way communication between themselves and practitioners (both formally and informally), by joining their children in classroom activities, and by becoming more involved in decision-making processes about their children. In addition, although school boards were in existence, in reality they had little or no participation in decision making at the school level. The program helped parents and community members find a voice in the education of their children as the case study below illustrates.

Case study 1: Fostering parent involvement in their children's learning

Since Azerbaijan's independence from the Soviet Union, the government has attempted to move towards the creation of a more modern system of education and has initiated a national education sector reform process. According to different stakeholders, the current system does not prepare pupils well enough to continue their education at higher educational institutions, to work and to actively participate in civil activity in society and family life. Some critics attribute these difficulties to the low-level of professionalism and quality of the teachers. The educational attainment of students, according to Crawford (2000), is limited because qualities such as the ability to master knowledge, to engage in logical and critical thinking, to be creative and to demonstrate leadership are not sufficiently developed in schools. The Step by Step program was launched in Azerbaijan to begin to address some of these concerns and to contribute to broader educational reform efforts, including opening the educational system to parents and members of the community.

The program was seeking to promote the development of children's critical thinking, creativity and leadership skills which were perceived to be lacking from the traditional educational approach. Step by Step began in pilot pre-schools in 1998 and was expanded into the primary schools in 1999. In 2002, its fifth implementation year in Azerbaijan, the Step by Step program provided training to more than 500 teachers in 12 regions all over the country, serving more than 10,000 children and their families. At the primary level, the Step by Step program has been implemented in 86 classes of 35 schools in 17 regions throughout the country and covers 1750 children.

(Continued)

(Continued)

Step by Step schools in Azerbaijan develop partnerships with parents and the broader community in order to encourage them to engage in their children's education and the educational process in general. Activities that foster relationships with parents and the community include inviting parents and community members to volunteer as classroom assistants, to participate in school renovation, to create school materials, to organise events and to donate clothing, equipment and books. Step by Step staff offer training courses on parent/community advocacy and encourage the development of parent initiative groups to implement different projects that support schools.

> [Parent involvement] is the strength of the SbS program. We learn how to involve parents. They learn how to work with us and the children. This experience resonates among the education district community. (School principal)

As part of the new relationship between teachers, parents and community, participants reported a strong emphasis on joint working and sharing knowledge about education. As one parent said, there are efforts to 'find a common language between teachers and parents'.

Administrators, trainers, teachers and parents also referred to closer teacher–parent relationships. At least one of each of the stakeholders (administrators, teachers, trainers and parents) referred to the changes in parents' attitudes towards their children's learning, notably in collaborating and helping their children both in school and at home. Interview responses showed that parents now know what happens in the classroom, show interest in the school, feel responsible for their child's learning process and appreciate the program.

Parents and trainers both report teachers' increased knowledge and trust of children's families. This contrasts with the attitude of teachers towards parents in non-Step by Step classrooms and signals a change in the Soviet tradition of education where schools, not parents, are primarily responsible for the education of children (a long-term tradition negatively affecting efforts to involve parents).

Some difficulties noted by teachers and trainers were diverse backgrounds and levels of education in reaching out to parents and the community.

Also, teachers and administrators found that time is needed to effect change in parents' attitudes about classroom learning. One administrator also expressed that the program needs a lot of teacher energy (Kazimzade et al., 2005).

Throughout the ISSA region, family and community involvement occurred more easily in areas where practitioners and families came from the same linguistic, cultural and socio-economic backgrounds. Such involvement remains a challenge in communities where Roma and other socially disadvantaged children live, and affects how well the concept of democratisation in early childhood centres and schools is actually occurring.

Inclusion, Diversity and the Values of Democracy: When ISSA first developed teacher standards in 2002 (ISSA, 2002), it did not include a standard that specifically focused on this area, assuming instead that these were adequately included in the six other standards originally developed. However, as the standards were used and implemented throughout the former communist region, ISSA and its members found that many children of traditionally excluded groups in the region were being denied their right to quality educational experiences (ISSA, 2005). Few practitioners and centres/schools working to meet the standards were adequately focusing on inclusion, diversity and the values of democracy.

In order to address this gap, ISSA added a new standard on social inclusion (ISSA, 2005). The Step by Step NGOs undertook extensive training and mentoring for practitioners in social justice concepts, especially in programs that included Roma children and families. This training helped practitioners and school leaders become aware of their own beliefs, attitudes and experiences around differences, and of how these affect their communication with children and families, as well as their teaching strategies. All Step by Step NGOs later received training for trainers in education for social justice.

However, three major problems continue to emerge in this attempt to incorporate diversity work into educational programs in early childhood centres and schools. First, the tendency to use a 'heroes, holidays and food' approach actually reinforces stereotypes and misconceptions about ethnic groups (such as all Roma travel in wagons and live in the woods). Second, practitioners often focus on singular parts of children's identities, such as belonging to a particular ethnic group or a disability they may have, and fail to acknowledge wider/multiple aspects of identities. Third, many practitioners are still challenged by developing an inclusive environment which allows meaningful participation for children with special educational needs alongside their mainstream peers.

Democratisation cannot occur without recognising and honouring inclusiveness in its widest definition, recognising diversity and using it as a resource, understanding social justice principles in connection with everyday practice, and practising active participation and openness in accommodating the needs of diverse groups of parents and families. The non-profit organisation DECET (Diversity in Early Childhood Education and Training) views early childhood provision as meeting places where people can learn from each other across cultural and other borders, and therefore as public provision that can effectively address prejudices and discrimination. ISSA's next step will be to further support practitioners who are members of professional learning communities to address these issues more rigorously.

Assessment and Planning: In the former Soviet-influenced system of teaching, practitioners followed a highly prescribed curriculum, and assessment and planning were not flexible in meeting the needs of individual children.

As active participation is an essential concept of democracy, assessment and planning processes needed to become more participatory. The Step by Step program introduced several new concepts, including:

- assessment needing to be 'authentic' (gathering evidence of children's growth and learning in ways that resemble 'real life' based on what children do naturally in a variety of contexts)
- the importance of assessing children on their acquisition of new knowledge and skills in multiple ways, including through systematic and continuous observation and children's portfolios
- children and parents being part of the assessment and planning processes
- planning being based upon observation and assessment of what children already know and their interests.

A remaining challenge for ISSA is the lack of assessment around children's involvement in play and learning. According to Laevers (2005), involvement means being intensely engaged in activities and is considered to be a necessary condition for deep-level learning and development. Observing children's level of involvement is a way to measure not just the context and outcome of learning, but also the effectiveness of the process (Bertram and Pascal, 2004).

Also, in supporting young children to engage in the process of self-assessment – enabling them to have a more active role in the learning process – children can therefore learn that assessment is not something apart from learning and done to them, but a collaborative process between child and teacher/practitioner.

Teaching Strategies: Practitioners' use of different teaching strategies can either promote or impede democratic processes in the classroom; a challenge for practitioners has been an eagerness to apply new practices, without analysing underpinning philosophy or considering the implications for children. A reason for this may be that the Step by Step model was designed and introduced by international early childhood education experts and has not been sufficiently 'owned' by practitioners.

For example, a whole-class morning meeting/circle time was introduced in training as an important feature of building community in the classroom, which practitioners embraced without fully understanding its intention. Enthusiasm for incorporating this strategy can be attributed to the familiarity of the more teacher-centred approach of children learning in large groups, rather than through child-led and small group activities.

Similarly, in the introduction of learning centres, many practitioners assigned children to centres and expected them to rotate in a designated time block. Although this was an improvement on whole-group instruction, it defeated the purpose of providing children with real choices and of experiencing the responsibilities that come with freedom of choice.

However, where practitioners were able to reflect on and understand the purpose of new strategies, then internalisation of the philosophy behind the strategy occurred, as the following case from Albania demonstrates.

Case study 2: Classroom management style

During 2006–2007, Neta V., an experienced Albanian pre-school teacher within the Step by Step program, was involved in a longitudinal case study to analyse which characteristic she considered most important in her classroom management style. She was asked to specify which classroom management techniques she had used before receiving any training, and after a year of being supported with training and mentoring.

Initially, she considered it very important to ensure that children followed classroom rules; that she could manage a disruptive child and quieten a noisy child. At the end of the year, she focused much more on helping children to develop supportive structures for themselves so that they could independently solve issues such as learning how to share one toy or take turns on the swing. Children followed rules they themselves had established, thus giving them power and responsibility. Neta V. reported that she learned to apply the '10-second technique', whereby she breathed slowly in and out for at least 10 seconds before intervening to solve a quarrel between children. The change in approach was dramatic, even though her goals were the same – an organised classroom and well-behaved children. She reported that the shift from teacher-centred to child-centred learning and management was organic, and she felt more self-assured to try out the new techniques (Sula, 2007).

Learning Environment: The process of creating an enriching, developmentally appropriate and inclusive learning environment where all children feel that they belong has two aspects: the physical and the social/emotional. In the Step by Step program, immediate improvements were seen in the physical environment where materials were sorted by use into learning centres and were placed at child level for easy access. Also, the environment in general looked more appropriate for children's learning and was more cheerful.

Helping practitioners create appropriate social/emotional learning environments was more of a challenge. They needed to let go of their training around controlling the classroom and allow children to explore and discover, to develop self-control and to develop social skills such as cooperation and negotiation.

Professional Development: The Step by Step program introduced the concept of a practitioner's/teacher's professional development in a very different way from how it had been approached in the past. This concept included:

- decentralised, school-based professional development vs strictly centralised, university-based development
- ongoing vs once every five years

- practical vs theoretical
- delivery by practising master teachers vs theorist faculty
- interactive constructivism vs faculty-centred lecturing.

Practitioners entering the Step by Step program were introduced to its philosophy and goals, as well as practical ideas on how to achieve those goals in a series of training courses. This was later expanded to include the concept of school-based professional development through establishing training centres in which a community of practitioner learners could be established and best practices observed. In 2002, the *ISSA Pedagogical Standards* were introduced (ISSA, 2002) and mentoring systems were initiated to improve practice based on these standards as parameters of best practice.

A challenge has been to empower practitioners to play leadership roles in curriculum development and school reform. Peeters (2008) states that it is essential practitioners make major contributions to the process of professionalising the field, and that they must be co-constructors of continuously evolving professionalism. However, the professionalisation process is not limited to the responsibility of the individual practitioner, but must be seen as a social practice which is the consequence of interaction between social evolution, policy measures, new scientific insights, and between researchers, staff, families and children. Fullan (2007) stresses the importance of collaborative teams in the improvement process. The ability to collaborate – on both a large and small scale – is one of the core requisites of post-modern society. In short, without collaborative skills and relationships, it is not possible for practitioners to be agents for social improvement.

🗀 Case study 3: Mentoring meetings

In a project on Education for Social Justice conducted by the Step by Step Centre Albania, in collaboration with UNICEF, teachers/practitioners embraced the necessity of shorter, more frequent meetings, rather than longer periods of training spaced far apart. These meetings were conducted as group mentoring meetings, using the ISSA Standards as a starting point and guide. The teachers reported that meetings where the group discussed a topic gave them the opportunity to better understand information contained in the standards and encouraged them to apply and support each other in their everyday practices. At the end of the school year, 95 per cent of the teachers reported satisfaction with the new training model compared with previous in-service training. They believed this new approach to professional development allowed time for reflection and further internalisation (Sula, 2009).

The influence on schools and communities

In many cases, individual practitioners' work in their classrooms was able to influence the larger school community and culture. The factor that most influenced the ability to see changes at the school level was the percentage of practitioners in a school/centre working with the *ISSA Pedagogical Standards/Principle*, as this created the opportunity for establishing peer learning communities. These learning communities, built of practitioners, promoted the exchange of ideas and discussion of challenges and tended to create a culture of teamwork and mutual support in individual early childhood centres and schools and across school networks in the same region. Other factors that promoted change at the centre/school level included: supportive school leaders, creating partnerships with teacher training institutes and universities, and getting support from parents and communities through training in order for them to be informed consumers and advocates of quality (Howard et al., 2010).

The influence on education policy and practice

New policy priorities and agendas focused on improving the quality of education are on the rise. This represents a departure from old policy which traditionally focused almost solely on the structural aspects of education systems. Step by Step NGOs have also been involved in collaborative efforts and in moving the national policy agenda towards increased practitioner and programme quality. While it is difficult to attribute policy change directly to the influence of Step by Step, NGO directors and others report anecdotally that in many of their countries the ISSA Standards are highly valued and looked upon as an important resource for creating new education policy. Examples of developing national policy change across the region include new or revised:

- national learning standards
- teacher quality standards
- national curricula
- systems of professional development, teacher preparation and quality assurance
- priorities focused on decentralisation of the education process. (Howard et al., 2010)

For every NGO that reported the development of new systems for teacher preparation or professional development, another reported that there was no national system into which the standards or mentoring and certification could be assimilated, 'both because of lack of stability and changing leadership at the national level and where highly centralised systems of regulations still existed' (Howard et al., 2010: 27). A common recurring issue was a lack, at the national level, of a consistent understanding and definition of quality. Without a clear and specific definition of what quality is and looks like, national efforts to move forward with any improved quality assurance and teacher quality measures will be difficult.

Final thoughts

In this chapter, we have identified the challenges that arise in creating early childhood environments that develop the habits, skills and dispositions that have the potential to build and strengthen democratic participation. The International Step by Step Association and its member NGOs accepted this challenge 15 years ago as communist governments in the former Soviet Union and Central and Eastern Europe fell and began the transition to democratic societies.

The largest struggle, however, has been how to develop not only a few practitioners in a country in best practice, but to start a movement where practitioners would also become agents of change in improving the quality of education for all children by promoting democratic principles in practice. Where professional learning communities promote democratic practices in their centres/schools, practitioners have also begun to influence their societies in general. They can demonstrate how the voices of parents, children and community members who care about them can create the conditions for every child to reach his full potential and develop the skills necessary for being a successful and active member of a democratic knowledge society.

▢ Summary

- To improve the quality of early childhood education and care and promote democratic principles, a multi-faceted approach is required, including: interactions that co-construct knowledge, creating family/community partnerships, inclusive practices that incorporate diversity, inclusion in assessment and planning, and creating learning environments and reflective practice.
- Building learning communities is a highly effective way to incorporate quality and democratic practices in early childhood centres and schools.
- In order to successfully create early childhood centres and schools which prepare children to be active participants in a democratic knowledge society, it is not enough to focus just on practitioners. All members in a community, including children, families and staff must be involved in the process.
- With time and attention, we can create a different society, one where everyone is able to reach their full potential, starting with the youngest members.

Questions for discussion

1 Do practitioners in long-standing democracies also face challenges in making their practice more democratic? How can these challenges be addressed?
2 How can democratic practices in early childhood programs be fostered, while at the same time keeping children's academic outcomes high?
3 How can practitioners become agents of change in improving the quality of education for all children and promoting democratic principles in practice in countries without well-developed democracies? How do you see this process? *(Higher-level question)*

Further reading

Levels 5 and 6

Coughlin, P., Hansen, K., Heller, D., Kaufmann, R., Rothschild Stolberg, J. and Burke Walsh, K. (1997) *Creating Child-centered Classrooms: 3–5 Year Olds*. Washington, DC: Children's Resources International.

This book describes the principles of the Step by Step program in creating child-centred classrooms, as well as giving practical suggestions for different kinds of activities. It shows how to build an integrated curriculum using 10 activity centres – literacy, mathematics/manipulatives, art, blocks, cooking, dramatic play, music, outdoors, sand and water, and science.

Howard, M., Tuna, A., Cincilei, C., Rajabova, T., Vonta, T. and Tankersley, D. (2010) *Study on the Implementation of the ISSA Pedagogical Standards and their Impact on ECDE Policies and Practices in the Region of ISSA's Network and Beyond (2001–2008): Executive Summary*. Budapest: International Step by Step Association.

This document summarises a study on the outcomes of the work undertaken over an eight-year period using the ISSA Pedagogical Standards in relation to learning content and information about and insights into the project.

Levels 6 and 7

Please contact ISSA at www.issa.hu for access to the following documents.

Howard, M., Tuna, A., Cincilei, C., Rajabova, T., Vonta, T. and Tankersley, D. (2010) *Study on the Implementation of the ISSA Pedagogical Standards and their Impact on ECDE Policies and Practices in the Region of ISSA's Network and Beyond (2001–2008): Executive Summary*. Budapest: International Step by Step Association.

This is an account of the full study of the effects of implementing the ISSA Pedagogical Standards, including case studies from the Branch Office of the International Organization of Open Society Institute Assistance Foundation in the Republic of Tajikistan; the Step by Step Educational Program in Moldova; and the Educational Research Institute, Centre for Educational Initiatives – Step by Step in Slovenia.

ISSA (2004) *Educating for Democracy: The Journal of the International Step by Step Association*. 10th anniversary edition, issue 8.

This journal explains the journey of the Step by Step program and the NGOs that implemented it during its first 10 years, looking at its unique accomplishments and looking forward to the challenges and opportunities facing them in the future.

Tankersley, D., Brajkovic, S., Handzar, S., Rimkiene, R., Sabaliauskiene, R., Trikic, Z. and Vonta, T. (2010) *Putting Knowledge into Practice: A Guidebook for Educators to Work with Principles of Quality Pedagogy*. Budapest: ISSA.

This book describes the theory and research used in developing ISSA's definition of quality pedagogy in the publication *Competent Educators of the 21st Century: Principles of Quality Pedagogy*. It describes the 20 principles distributed among the seven focus areas: Interactions; Family and Community; Inclusion, Diversity and Values of Democracy; Assessment and Planning; Teaching Strategies; Learning Environment; and Professional Development, and gives examples of how to meet those principles under each of the 85 indicators of quality.

Websites

www.decet.org
This is the portal website for DECET's publications.

www.issa.nl
This is the portal website for ISSA's publications.

Notes

1   Early Childhood in Azerbaijan has been defined as a period of life between 0 to 6 years of age. According to the new Education Law which was adopted in 2009, free of charge pre-school education is provided to young children aged 3 to 5 and school readiness programs are provided to children aged 5 to 6. The services are mainly provided by centre-based public kindergartens with very few private exceptions. Around 11 per cent of children below 6 years of age are covered with large discrepancies in enrolment between urban and rural areas. Most of the children are from urban areas with a very high concentration of services in the capital of Baku. This low access to pre-school education significantly affects children's success in primary education; 75 per cent of mothers think that pre-school education is either important or very important (Study on Parental Knowledge, Attitudes and Practices for Child Care and Rearing in Azerbaijan (UNICEF/MOE/SSC, 2006)). The major reason for children not attending a kindergarten appears to be lack of public kindergartens rather than financial and/or logistical reasons.

2   It is interesting that in spite of the wide use of the term 'pre-school education', at present pre-school teachers are still called pre-school carers in Azeri.

References

Bertram, T. and Pascal, C. (2004) *A Handbook for Evaluating, Assuring, and Improving Quality in Early Childhood Settings*. Birmingham: Amber Publishing.

Crawford, A. (2000) *A Study on In-service Education and Classroom Practices in Azerbaijan: Into the 21st Century*. Available at: http://dspace.khazar.org/jspui/handle/123456789/234/4/A.%20Crawford. doc (accessed 13 May 2011).

Fullan, M. (2007) *Kuptimi i ndryshimit te ri ne arsim*. Tirana: CDE.

Howard, M., Tuna, A., Cincilei, C., Rajabova, T., Vonta, T. and Tankersley, D. (2010) *Study on the Implementation of the ISSA Pedagogical Standards and their Impact on ECDE Policies and Practices in the Region of ISSA's Network and Beyond (2001–2008): Executive Summary*. Budapest: International Step by Step Association.

International Step by Step Association (ISSA) (2002) *Step by Step Program and Teacher Standards for Pre-school and Primary Grades*. Budapest: International Step by Step Association.

International Step by Step Association (ISSA) (2005) *ISSA Pedagogical Standards for Pre-school and Primary Grades*. Budapest: International Step by Step Association.

International Step by Step Association (ISSA) (2010) *Competent Educators of the 21st Century: Principles of Quality Pedagogy*. Budapest: International Step by Step Association.

Kazimzade, E., Mikailova, U., Neuman, M. and Valdiviezo, L. (2005) Evaluation of the Step by Step program in Azerbaijan. *Educating Children for Democracy*, 5, summer/fall: 25–32.

Klaus, S. (2004) Stepping into the future: a history of the Step by Step program. *Educating Children for Democracy: The Journal of the International Step by Step Association*. 10th anniversary edition, issue 8: 3–13.

Laevers, F. (2005) *Well-being and Involvement in Care Settings: A Process-oriented Self-evaluation Instrument*. Leuven: Kind & Gezin and Research Centre for Experiential Education. Available at: www.kindengezin.be/Images/ZikohandleidingENG_tcm149-50761.pdf (accessed 2 May 2011).

Nutbrown, C., Clough, P. and Selbie, P. (2008) *Early Childhood Education: History, Philosophy and Experience*. London: Sage.

Peeters, J. (2008) *The Construction of a New Profession: A European Perspective on Professionalism in Early Childhood Education and Care*. Amsterdam: SWP Publishers.

Sula, G. (2007) Reformat e edukimi parashkollor ne Shqiperi. *Revista Pedagogjike*, 7(2): 77–92.

Sula, G. (2009) *Final Report on 'Education for Social Justice'*. Tirana: UNICEF/Step by Step Centre.

UNICEF/MOE/SSC (2006) *Study on Parental Knowledge, Attitudes and Practices for Child Care and Rearing in Azerbaijan*. UNICEF/MOE/SSC.

Wood, F. (2006) *Addendum to National Education Strategy for Albania*. Tirana: UNICEF.

PART 4

FRAMEWORKS, REGULATIONS AND GUIDELINES

CHAPTER 10

THE RHETORIC AND REALITY OF A NATIONAL STRATEGY FOR EARLY EDUCATION AND ASSESSMENT

Lesley Staggs

Overview

This chapter considers how, as direct public funding for early years education increased in England from 1997 under the then Labour government, so too did the government's desire to direct and control both the curriculum content and pedagogy of early years settings. At times, this process has united the early years sector, while at others it has been divided by it. In this chapter, I explore how the Early Learning Goals (QCA, 1999) and Curriculum Guidance for the Foundation Stage (QCA, 2000) were developed to replace the Desirable Learning Outcomes (SCAA, 1996). I discuss the tensions between implementing early years policy

(Continued)

(Continued)

that is driven by research and practice, which places play at the heart of young children's learning, and the more formal approach to learning which was effectively promoted by key national players such as the schools inspection body (Ofsted) and those responsible for the National Literacy Strategy (NLS) (DfEE, 1998), in ensuring that *their* priorities, based on this more formal approach, were not undermined. I also reflect on how, in the following decade, government increased its control over the work of early years practitioners through a national strategy and a specific stage for the learning and development of children from birth to age 5, the Early Years Foundation Stage.

The beginning of a national strategy for the early years

Before 1996, the availability of free nursery education was dependent on local government decisions. Maintained (i.e. public) nursery schools and classes, providing places for 3- and 4-year-olds, were more widely available in urban areas with high levels of poverty and deprivation. These were staffed by qualified graduate-trained teachers, and supported by two-year-trained nursery nurses. Premises were either purpose built or adapted to meet the needs of young children and were well resourced. The gap in provision was filled by the voluntary and private sector, with parents required to pay for these places. These forms of provision were often held in shared premises such as village halls, with staff normally less well qualified, or unqualified, and with low levels of pay. Unpaid volunteers were widely used and parent funding was supplemented sometimes by public grants and often by fundraising. Education became compulsory the term after a child's 5th birthday, but in many areas children went to school before that date, often to compensate for the lack of nursery places.

The Labour governments of 1997–2010 are rightly credited with the considerable focus on, and investment in, the early years. However, it was the previous Conservative government that in 1996 introduced nursery vouchers for 4-year-olds, allowing parents to choose a free part-time nursery education place for children for the three terms following their 4th birthday. These places could be in the private, independent, voluntary or maintained sector and the setting then reclaimed the funding from government. At that stage, it was already becoming apparent that there would be a price to pay for the increased focus and funding on early education – accountability. In particular, there was a concern that there should be evidence that this money was making a difference to children's outcomes. This was always going to be problematic with such young children and the demand for evidence became an ever-growing area of controversy during the following decade.

The Desirable Learning Outcomes

The Desirable Outcomes for Children's Learning on Entering Compulsory Education (DfEE/SCAA, 1996), normally referred to as the Desirable Learning Outcomes (DLOs), were developed by the School Curriculum and Assessment Authority, later to become the Qualifications and Curriculum Authority (QCA) in 1996, to accompany the introduction of nursery vouchers. A slim document set out the DLOs, organised in six areas of learning, which were similar to those already used in many early years settings. These areas were:

- Personal and social development
- Language and literacy
- Mathematical development
- Knowledge and understanding of the world
- Physical development
- Creative development.

It was at this stage that concerns began to be articulated about there being, for the first time, a single, national set of educational expectations for young children (see David, 1998). During events organised by local authorities to introduce the DLOs, many practitioners welcomed a document that reflected the importance of children's personal, social and physical development but were concerned that there was an assumption that all children should be at the same stage of learning and development at the same point in their lives. There was unease about the assumption that the same expectations could be made of maintained, private and voluntary providers, given the differences in staff training, qualifications and resources (Hevey and Curtis, 1996).

A change of government, a change of strategy

The election of a Labour government in May 1997 saw an almost immediate change in early years provision. Nursery vouchers became nursery grants and local authorities were given the responsibility for managing nursery places, supporting partnership between the range of providers and working with them to ensure all were of good quality. QCA was remitted both to review the DLOs and to take forward the introduction of a statutory national system for assessing children when they entered primary school, i.e. baseline assessment. A senior officer was appointed at QCA to bring together and lead what it then described as its 'under-fives responsibilities'. For the first time, the national curriculum and assessment agency was entering the area of early years, where children attended settings for differing periods of time or not at all, and where the provision might or might not be in a school with a qualified teacher.

At the same time, the controversy that was to be the context for the next decade and beyond was growing. On the back of the then prime minister's pledge that the new government's priority would be 'education, education, education', raising standards in literacy and numeracy became the focus of both funding and policy, led by the National Literacy Strategy (NLS) (DfEE, 1998) and National Numeracy Strategy (NNS) (DfEE, 1999). Detailed and prescriptive programmes, huge amounts of training, dedicated school professional training days and funding for school and local authority staff to drive forward these programmes meant that although they had no statutory basis, they were regarded by most schools as quasi-statutory. Subsequently, these became the aspects of the curriculum on which schools focused their time and effort. Teacher education was revised to ensure that all new teachers were thoroughly versed in teaching these programmes. Very significantly, local authorities were monitored and challenged by the Strategies' teams. Ofsted inspection focused on these areas, with the then Chief Inspector strongly supporting this approach.

The pedagogical debate: play versus formal learning

From the beginning, the early years sector was anxious about the effect this new regime would have on young children (David, 1996). Nursery vouchers, and then the nursery grant, had resulted in more and more primary schools moving to a single intake (i.e. at one specific point in the year) into their reception classes for 4- and 5-year-olds, resulting in young 4-year-olds being taken into classes which often did not change their organisation and practice to reflect the needs of these younger children. With the introduction of the Strategies, these children were expected to participate in a literacy hour and a numeracy hour (of 45 minutes' duration) from the beginning of the reception year, with expectations that went far beyond those set out in the DLOs. Early years experts and practitioners challenged the inclusion of the youngest children in primary schools, and pointed to the lack of evidence that beginning formal teaching earlier has any long-term benefit for children. In a review of school starting age in Europe, Sharp (2002) concluded that in most European countries children remain in pre-schools and kindergartens until they begin school at age 6 and that available evidence suggested any academic benefit of early entry to school is not sustained in the longer term; also that early introduction to a formal curriculum could have a negative impact on children's self-esteem and motivation to learn.

Developing the Early Learning Goals

In 1998, QCA was remitted by the government to review the DLOs. It soon became apparent that, in order to do this, polarised views would need to be brought together as everyone with an interest in early years wanted to have their voice heard. Officers at QCA responsible for national curriculum subjects wanted to ensure that there would be progression into those subjects as they began to be taught in Key Stage 1 in primary schools (at age 5). There was pressure to start with a curriculum for children older than 5 and work backwards in the name of continuity and progression. The NLS framework, including teaching expectations for children as young as 4 in the reception year, was already published and being vigorously promoted by the government.

A set of teaching objectives was identified which teachers were expected to teach from the beginning of the reception year in a structured hour-long session. Those responsible for this development, including both NLS staff and government officials, wanted to ensure that the revised DLOs reflected this initiative. The NNS framework (DfEE, 1999), following a format similar to the NLS framework, was in draft format leading to similar pressure to ensure that the revised DLOs reflected the same expectations. Ofsted actively promoted the approaches of both Strategies with its early evaluations of the NLS, including the Literacy Hour, reporting on how young children in reception classes responded positively to the lessons and adapted easily to their structure (Ofsted, 1999).

There were however equally vociferous voices who wanted the revised DLOs to be driven by the play-based learning that research and experience demonstrated best meets the needs of young children. Early years academics, experts and organisations also demanded to be involved as decisions were made and drafts developed. Concerns were widely expressed about the increasing formalisation of the reception year and diminishing opportunities for children to explore their own interests and learn at their own pace. Opportunities for play were felt to be diminishing and pressure on young children increasing. There was also concern that not enough attention was being given to children's emotional development and well-being and their communication and language development (see, for example, David, 1996, 1998). From these academics and experts there emerged a group, the Curriculum Guidance Working Group (CGWG), which worked with QCA to develop the Early Learning Goals (QCA, 1999), the Curriculum Guidance for the Foundation Stage (QCA, 2000) and the Foundation Stage Profile Handbook (QCA, 2003). Their role was formalised by the then Minister for Children, and the group was given a remit to advise ministers and officials on early education matters – a role they retained until the election of the coalition government in 2010.

As QCA's lead early years officer at this time, a major part of my role was talking to early years practitioners, experts and academics across England. Discussions with groups of practitioners around the country, as part of QCA's informal consultation process, echoed the anxieties of the academics and experts referred to above. These groups were passionate about the importance of children's personal and social development, questioning the view of those who believed this happened 'incidentally' and without effort and planning on the part of practitioners. In the same way, they raised concerns about an over-emphasis on literacy and mathematics with little emphasis on language development. The overwhelming view of such practitioners, whatever their work context, was that unless they were given the time and opportunity to focus on and prioritise children's personal, social and language development, the foundations on which other more formal learning was built would be very unsound. During these discussions, it became apparent that the 'what' of young children's learning was very difficult to detach from the 'how,' and it gradually became clear that more than a set of revised learning outcomes would be needed. Many practitioners reported fewer opportunities for what they described as 'real' play where children initiated and developed their interests and adults supported as appropriate. Whilst this was a particular issue for those working in reception classes with the youngest children, it was seen as an increasing issue for many practitioners who worked with even younger children, where parental pressure for formal education was often cited as an explanation for using didactic teaching methods with 3- or indeed 2-year-olds. Some practitioners were able to resist these pressures. However, others reported that they felt they had neither the confidence nor the theoretical understanding to challenge what their experience, and the reactions of the children they were working with, told them was a wrong approach. For example, when presented with an outcome meant for a 5-year-old, such as being able to hold a pencil, not all practitioners had the knowledge and understanding to know what that meant for the young 3-year-olds in their setting. This is not surprising, given that many had little formal training and qualifications, as discussed above. These issues were not confined to the private and voluntary sector as many teachers working in the maintained early years sector had had little or no training in working with children under 5 (see Abbot and Pugh, 1998).

The Early Learning Goals

To fulfil its remit to publish a set of revised learning outcomes, QCA published the Early Learning Goals (ELGs) in October 1999 (QCA, 1999) and immediately attracted widespread criticism, particularly from the early years sector, as learning goals for young children had not been formally consulted on; the idea of 'goals' for learning was widely condemned, and in particular some of the goals for literacy were felt to be inappropriate.

The DLOs had set a precedent for a set of national outcomes which all funded settings for 3- and 4-year-old children were required to work towards. The initial remit had been to review these and, at a time when targets and centrally determined expectations were being increasingly promoted as the way of improving standards, removing rather than changing them was never an option.

Practitioners had become used to the six areas of learning embedded in the DLOs and many were using them as the basis for their planning. To avoid unnecessary change, they were therefore retained as a way of organising the ELGs but with two important additions in response to the sector views described above: the addition of emotional development to the area of personal and social development, and the addition of communication to the area of language and literacy. However, the new goals were very different to the DLOs in that they were no longer to be achieved when children reached compulsory school age (the term after they reached the age of 5), but at the end of the reception year when children's ages would range from almost 5 to almost 6 years. The final ELGs reflected the requirement to accommodate the agreed expectations of the Numeracy and Literacy Strategies, and also the Ofsted view that these were perfectly achievable by the end of the reception year. This led to some goals, particularly in the area of literacy, being set at a level that most children continue to struggle to achieve, despite unprecedented emphasis, guidance and training in literacy for practitioners. Early Years Foundation Stage Profile national data for 2009/2010 shows that less children (65 per cent) achieved a 'good level' (i.e. in terms of achieving most of the ELGs in full) in Communication, Language and Literacy than in any other area of learning (DfE, 2009).

Establishing a play-based Foundation Stage

During the period of consultation described above, government had heard the strong messages from the early years sector for the need to link the early learning goals to an understanding that the period of children's learning and development, from age 3 to 5 years, is a distinct stage that has value and merit in its own right and is not simply a preparation for later schooling. Also, that during this early stage of learning and development the key role of play needed to be recognised. QCA was remitted to develop curriculum guidance which set out the learning and teaching appropriate for children during what was to be described as the Foundation Stage. It was to include all 3- and 4-year-old children in publically funded early years education and the whole of the reception year of primary school; QCA consultations both before and after the establishment of the Foundation Stage showed widespread support for this development.

Developing the Curriculum Guidance for the Foundation Stage

The argument had been made and accepted by QCA, DfES and ministers that additional guidance for implementing the ELGs was needed. The early years experts and academics who were members of the newly established Curriculum Guidance for the Foundation Stage Working Group (CGWG) had been active both in winning this argument and in contributing to the development of the guidance. However, it was not possible to produce this more substantial piece of work within the agreed time frame for the publication of the ELGs in October 1999.

The concerns set out above, and the reaction of officials and minsters, did much to ensure that the subsequent guidance promoted a distinct phase where play was seen as pivotally important. It meant that the new guidance was developed in a much more open and transparent way than would otherwise have been possible, with members of the CGWG playing an active role not only in its development, but also in mediating its messages with officials and ministers.

The Curriculum Guidance for the Foundation Stage

In contrast to the publication of the ELGs, there was a warm welcome for the Curriculum Guidance for the Foundation Stage (CGFS) (QCA, 2000) following its launch in March 2000. When *Nursery World* magazine published its review of the year, Blytham (2000) described the CGFS as being enthusiastically received. Media coverage and direct feedback received in my role as QCA's lead early years officer at meetings, conferences and training events, showed that the establishment of the Foundation Stage was widely welcomed by the early years sector. For the first time, the curriculum for children aged 3 to 5 was given the same legal status as other stages of the National Curriculum, for children older than 5. Many nursery and reception teachers were pleased to have their own 'national curriculum' which they could use to defend their early years practice. Local authority early years advisers welcomed the status and support it gave to their work.

The introductory sections of the guidance, taken from the Early Learning Goals booklet, set out the aims and principles on which the CGFS is based and affirmed the importance of play throughout the Foundation Stage. The remainder of the guidance was organised around the six areas of learning of the EYFS referred to earlier (see p. 144).

For each area, key messages about learning and teaching were set out, followed by guidance on how practitioners could support the learning of 3-, 4- and 5-year-olds to give them the best opportunity to achieve each of the ELGs for that area by the end of the reception year. Alongside these goals, 'steps' to achievement were set out as an example of what progress towards the goals might look like. These 'stepping stones' were intended to ensure that practitioners without a strong understanding of how children develop and learn, did not make simplistic links between the ELGs and the curriculum for children aged 3 and 4. There was pressure from DfEE officials to make the guidance age-related with sections for 3-, 4- and 5-year-olds. However, after much debate, the compromise was that the stepping stones and goals should be colour-coded into three bands: yellow, blue and green, to help practitioners focus on the stage of development that was most likely to be appropriate for the children they were working with. They were additionally guided that although, for example, it was likely that 3-year-old children would be assessed as being within the yellow band, and 5-year-old children within the green band, practitioners should use their observations to plan what was appropriate for individual and groups of children, thus recognising that children develop and learn in different ways and that whilst age may be a guide to ability and achievement, practitioners needed to make their own, observation-based assessments of the stage of development of individual children.

In an attempt to ensure that practitioners did not feel that they had to juggle con-flicting guidance, the CGFS made clear the synergy between the ELGs and the objec-tives of the National Literacy and Numeracy Strategies. Practitioners were advised that these did not need to be brought together into formal literacy and numeracy hours until the end of the reception year. However, many members of the CGWG felt that this unhelpfully gave recognition to the more formal approach to learning in the non-statutory NLS and NNS frameworks, as part of a guidance that was to become a statu-tory requirement from September 2000, and part of the National Curriculum in September 2002, and were critical of the decision to promote the importance of these frameworks within the CGFS.

Aligning assessment to the curriculum: the Foundation Stage Profile

The implementation of the Foundation Stage with its ELGs and guidance meant that the existing baseline assessment needed to be reviewed and aligned with these revised expectations. The 90 accredited schemes already in existence reflected the expectations of the DLOs and focused on entry to school at age 4 or 5, which for almost all children was part way through the Foundation Stage. Both the content of the assessment schemes and the fact that assessment did not take place at the end of the Foundation Stage, were inappropriate. There was also an increasing desire from ministers and the DfES to have assessment data that was nationally comparable.

The decision was made to move to a single, national assessment to take place at the end of the Foundation Stage which would reflect the expectations of the ELGs. This immediately changed the main purpose of the ELGs in that they ceased to be primarily goals which set out aspirations for most children at age 5 (i.e. the end rather than the beginning of the primary school reception year) and which guided practice in early years settings. Instead, the ELGs became an assessment instrument through which all children's achievement across England could be judged and by which, in turn, the effectiveness of early years settings and local authorities could also ultimately be assessed. Unlike the CGFS, the development of what became the Foundation Stage Profile (FSP) (QCA, 2003) was contracted to an external agency, but the processes by which it was developed and implemented were similar, in that the CGWG and practitioners contributed to its development throughout. Its development was also subject to the same pressures to ensure alignment with other policies, in particular the NLS and NNS. In line with the principles and approaches of the CGFS, the FSP did not require any additional assessments or testing, but was to draw on practitioners' existing knowledge of children based on their ongoing observations within their practice. It was to be a 'snapshot' of children at the end of the Foundation Stage which would provide information for parents and Year 1 teachers (i.e. the first year of the national curriculum in primary schools). Critically, it covered all six areas of learning which was especially important in maintaining the principles and aims of the Foundation Stage.

From its publication (QCA, 2003), letters to the media, debates at teacher union conferences and letters to DfES officials and ministers, raised issues about the manageability of the FSP. It required practitioners, mostly reception teachers, to assess how many of the nine items (scale points) each child had achieved in each of the 13 scales that covered the six areas of learning. The content of these items should have been familiar to practitioners as the first three reflected the 'stepping stones' already issued as part of the Curriculum Guidance, and the next five embodied the ELGs which practitioners had been expected to work with since the introduction of the Foundation Stage in September 2000. The final point on the scale was designed to describe children whose achievement went beyond the ELGs. In large measure, the controversy was directly attributable to the limited training that had accompanied the initial introduction of the Foundation Stage. Many reception and Year 1 teachers were trained for the primary (5–11), rather than the nursery (3–5) age range and did not have a secure understanding of the CGFS and its play-based approach. Also, more critically, they had little experience of ongoing observation-based assessment of individual children as a strategy to support individualised planning. Typically, Year 1 teachers had no training about the Foundation Stage and therefore struggled with the information given as a starting point for planning for children as they moved into Key

Stage 1. In subsequent years, this problem was addressed by national and local author-ity guidance and training, but it meant that from the beginning, the DfES and minis-ters were constantly questioning whether the FSP was unnecessarily burdensome. However, one undoubted benefit of the FSP was that it ensured that reception teach-ers developed their practice in line with all six areas of the CGFS and did not focus solely on literacy and numeracy.

Beyond the Foundation Stage: the Early Years Foundation Stage

Alongside the developments in early education for 3- and 4-year-olds described above, there had been rapid developments in childcare driven by a policy of helping parents of young children to work in order to lift children out of poverty (see Chapter 2). Concerns about the quality of provision in many early years settings providing for the youngest children had led to the development and publication of *Birth to Three Matters* (BTTM) (DfES, 2002), which consisted of guidance for those working with babies and toddlers up to the age of 3. The Government's Ten Year Childcare Strategy launched in 2004 (DfES, 2004a) included a decision to bring together guidance for children under 3 (BTTM) and the CGFS, to produce a single guidance framework for those working with children from birth to 5 that would incorporate statutory national standards for health and safety, minimum staffing ratios and wider aspects of care.

Previously, in 2003, the National Literacy and Numeracy Strategies had been brought together to form the Primary National Strategy (PNS) (DfES, 2004b) covering ages 5 to 11. This was then expanded to include a dedicated team of Foundation Stage advisers led by a National Director for the Foundation Stage. By placing this team within the PNS, it was expected that the real and perceived differences of approach between the NLS, NNS and CGFS could be resolved. However, the growing lobbying about standards in reading was, as so often in the past, looking to the early years as the problem. Literacy, and in particular phonics, took on a disproportionate impor-tance within the Foundation Stage focus of the PNS following the review of early read-ing led by Jim Rose (known as the Rose [2009] review), which recommended a single approach to teaching reading using 'synthetic phonics', despite the very limited research evidence supporting this narrow approach.

At the same time, the Foundation Stage team within the PNS was leading the devel-opment of the single integrated guidance framework for children from birth to 5, which was to become the Early Years Foundation Stage (EYFS) framework (DfES, 2007). This needed to reflect significant changes in early years provision since the publication of the CGFS. Every Child Matters (DfES, 2003), with its focus on an inte-grated approach to providing services for children and their families, now provided an overarching context for all policies relating to children. Free part-time funded nurs-ery education places now included all 3-year-olds and there had been a significant growth in childcare, including for children younger than 3. Government policy focused on bringing together all aspects of early education and childcare under the umbrella of the EYFS. The effective abolition of the distinction between education and care for very young children was enshrined in the Childcare Act 2006 (Owen and Haynes, 2008). However, practitioners were understandably anxious about more change as they felt they were just getting to grips with both the CGFS and BTTM.

The EYFS framework emerged amidst all of this policy development and demonstrated the continued tensions between a play-based approach and one which promoted a more formal approach to teaching and learning. Media coverage showed that the strengthened principles and commitments in the EYFS to a play-based approach to young children's learning were widely welcomed by early years practitioners. However, there was significant criticism of other sections of the document which reflected a more formal approach characteristic of schooling (Goouch, 2008). For example, the learning and development grids which broke down the stages of development from birth to 5 in each of the six areas of learning into small steps, were used as a tool for assessment and data collection, rather than as primarily a guide to practitioners on how best to support children's learning and development, whilst those for literacy and mathematics reflected the prescriptive approach previously promoted by the PNS. Despite one of the EYFS commitments being that 'all areas of learning and development are equally important and inter-connected' (DfES *Practice Guidance*, 2007: 5) the focus of government, through the national strategy, continued to be on literacy and numeracy within the EYFS with a focus on the same unrealistic ELGs that had led to so much criticism 10 years previously. The 2010 coalition government's proposal for an early review of the EYFS under Dame Claire Tickell (2011) has been largely driven by this opposition. Tickell's remit was to conduct an evidence-led review, building on what worked well in the EYFS and improving on those aspects which were problematic (DfE, 2010).

Final thoughts

This chapter has offered an overview of curriculum developments in the early years in England, over the last 14 years. In the chapter, I have outlined the tensions and challenges involved in developing a curriculum framework and an assessment strategy that embody early years principles and practice, within a government policy framework that focuses on preparation for, and raising standards in, primary schooling. The struggle to make play more visible within national early years curriculum and assessment frameworks continues (Goouch, 2010). However, I have argued that making the case for a play-based curriculum was always going to be difficult where settings were required to demonstrate measurable outcomes related to school readiness in terms of literacy and numeracy. Those who advocated more formal approaches to teaching and learning could often show the short-term progress in children's learning that government was seeking. The appetite for taking a long-term view was never strong enough amongst policy makers and politicians, concerned with a quick impact and their next election prospects, to give play to the key role argued for by the early years sector through to the end of the Early Years Foundation Stage. It remains to be seen whether the recommendations from the Tickell (2011) review, referred to above, will mean that the progress made can be sustained, or if formal learning will have an ever-increasing role in early education.

 Summary

- The period between 1997 and 2010 saw an unprecedented focus on the early years. For the first time, children aged 3–5 had their own curriculum and assessment framework, which aimed to reflect their specific needs.
- The Foundation Stage, with its linked guidance and assessment, was not created in a vacuum. External and competing policies influenced its development and implementation. This influence has grown in the latter part of the decade with a growing focus on phonics and reading.
- The Foundation Stage guidance and assessment emphasised play as a key way of learning in the early years, but the continued focus on literacy and numeracy skills has meant that many children continue to experience a more formal approach to teaching, especially in reception classes.

 Questions for discussion

1 How can practitioners promote the value of play for children in their setting?
2 What are the advantages and disadvantages of including babies, toddlers and children up to the age of 5 in a single curriculum framework?
3 The review of the EYFS recommends a significantly slimmer and less prescriptive framework. What do you think could be the advantages and disadvantages of such change? *(Higher-level question)*

Further reading

Levels 5 and 6

Miller, L., Cable, C. and Goodliff, G. (eds) (2010) *Supporting Children's Learning in the Early Years*, 2nd edition. London: Routledge.
This is a collection of chapters covering children's learning and development in a broad range of areas.

Pugh, G. (2010) The policy agenda for early childhood services, in *Contemporary Issues in the Early Years: Working Collaboratively for Children,* 5th edition. London: Sage.
Gillian Pugh considers developments in England in relation to the availability and organisation of early childhood services and thus provides a broad policy background for this chapter.

Levels 6 and 7

Brooker, L., Rogers, S., Ellis, D., Hallet, E. and Roberts-Holmes, G. (2010) *Practitioners' Experiences of the Early Years Foundation Stage*. Research Report No. RB-029. London: Department for Education.
This research report describes the context, design, conduct and findings of an inquiry into practitioners' experiences of the Early Years Foundation Stage.

Goouch, K. (2008) Understanding playful pedagogies, play narratives and play spaces. *Early Years: An International Journal of Research and Development*, 28(1): 93–102.
This paper considers an aspect of playful practice, 'storying events', in the context of political dominance of curriculum content and teaching methods.

Tickell, C. (2011) *The Early Years: Foundations for Life, Health and Learning*. Available at: http://media.education.gov.uk/MediaFiles/B/1/5/%7BB15EFF0D-A4DF-4294-93A1-1E1B88C13F68%7DTickell%20review.pdf (accessed 30 May 2011).
This is Dame Claire Tickell's review of the EYFS and subsequent recommendations for change in relation to the statutory current early years curriculum and assessment framework.

Websites

www.education.gov.uk
This is the official website for the UK Department of Education and reflects current government policy. Search under 'early years' for the latest initiatives and reports.

www.foundationyears.org.uk
This is a government-supported website, operated by 4Children, providing information for families and practitioners about care, curriculum, support and advice from pregnancy to age 5.

References

Abbot, L. and Pugh, G. (1998) *Training to Work in the Early Years*. Buckingham: Open University Press.
Blytham, J. (2000) The year ahead. *Nursery World,* 20 December, p. 5.
David, T. (1996) Curriculum in the early years. In G. Pugh (ed.) *Contemporary Issues in the Early Years: Working Collaboratively for Children,* 2nd edition. London: Paul Chapman Publishing/National Children's Bureau, Early Childhood Unit.
David, T. (1998) Learning properly? Young children and desirable outcomes. *Early Years*, 18(2): 61–5.
Department for Education (DfE) (2009) *National Early Years Foundation Stage Data 2009*. Available at: www.education.gov.uk/rsgateway/DB/SFR/s000961 (accessed 28 April 2011).
Department for Education (DfE) (2010) *Review of the Early Years Foundation Stage*. Available at: www.direct.gov.uk/en/Nl1/Newsroom/DG_189908 (accessed 17 January 2011).
Department for Education and Employment (DfEE) (1998) *The National Literacy Strategy: A Framework for Teaching*. London: DfEE.
Department for Education and Employment (DfEE) (1999) *The National Numeracy Strategy*. London: DfEE.
Department for Education and Employment/School Curriculum and Assessment Authority (DfEE/SCAA) (1996) *Desirable Outcomes for Children's Learning on Entering Compulsory Education*. London: DfEE/SCAA.

Department for Education and Skills (DfES) (2002) *Birth to Three Matters: A Framework to Support Children in their Earliest Years*. London: DfES.

Department for Education and Skills (DfES) (2003) *Every Child Matters: Change for Children*. London: HMSO.

Department for Education and Skills DfES (2004a) *Choice for Parents: The Best Start for Children: A Ten Year Childcare Strategy*. London: DfES.

Department for Education and Skills (DfES) (2004b) *Primary National Strategy: Excellence and Enjoyment*. London: DfES.

Department for Education and Skills (DfES) (2007) *Statutory Framework for the Early Years Foundation Stage*. Nottingham: DCSF.

Goouch, K. (2008) Understanding playful pedagogies, play narratives and play spaces. *Early Years: An International Journal of Research and Development*, 28(1): 93–102.

Goouch, K. (2010) *Towards Excellence in Early Years Education*. London and New York: Routledge.

Hevey, D. and Curtis, A. (1996) Training to work in the early years. In G. Pugh (ed.) *Contemporary Issues in the Early Years: Working Collaboratively for Children*, 2nd edition. London: Paul Chapman Publishing/National Children's Bureau, Early Childhood Unit.

Ofsted (1999) *An Interim HMI Evaluation of the Literacy Strategy*. London: Ofsted.

Owen, S. and Haynes, G. (2008) Developing professionalism in the early years: from policy to practice. In L. Miller and C. Cable (eds) *Professionalism in the Early Years*. London: Hodder Education.

Qualifications and Curriculum Authority (QCA) (1999) *Early Learning Goals*. London: QCA.

Qualifications and Curriculum Authority (QCA) (2000) *Curriculum Guidance for the Foundation Stage*. London: QCA.

Qualifications and Curriculum Authority (QCA) (2003) *Foundation Stage Profile Handbook*. London: QCA.

Rose, J. (2009) *Independent Review of the Primary Curriculum: Final Report*. Available at: www.education.gov.uk/publications//eOrderingDownload/Primary_curriculum_Report.pdf (accessed 18 February 2011).

SCAA (1996) *Desirable Outcomes for Children's Learning on Entering Compulsory Education*. London: SCAA.

Sharp, C. (2002) School starting age: European policy and recent research. Paper presented at the Local Government Association (LGA) Seminar, National Foundation for Educational Research, London, 1 November.

Tickell, C. (2011) *The Early Years: Foundations for Life, Health and Learning. An Independent Report on the Early Years Foundation Stage for Her Majesty's Government*. Available at: www.education.gov.uk (accessed 26 May 2011).

CHAPTER 11

INCORPORATING SAFEGUARDING AND WELL-BEING IN UNIVERSAL SERVICES: DEVELOPMENTS IN EARLY YEARS MULTI-AGENCY PRACTICE IN SCOTLAND

Wendy Rose

Overview

In this chapter, I explore how Scotland has been developing and implementing a new approach to early years multi-agency practice for children and families. This is part of a national programme to improve outcomes for all children and young people, *Getting it Right for Every Child*, and an important mechanism for delivering Scotland's vision outlined in its *Early Years Framework*. The approach is described, showing how it is built on common principles and values and core components, supported by a set of national practice tools. The emphasis in *Getting it Right for Every Child* is on whole system change that can only be achieved by a positive shift in culture, systems and practice from all those working with children and families. The chapter concludes with some of the early evidence of the benefits of the new way of working for organisations as well as for young children and their families.

Scotland has been pursuing a rather different direction from the other countries of the UK with its overarching policy to improve outcomes for all its children and young people, *Getting it Right for Every Child* (*GIRFEC*). This approach, now being implemented, requires whole system change. It is about the way in which the needs of each and every child are identified and met, and puts children's well-being at the heart of all that is done with and for them (Aldgate, 2008). It sets out a framework for all agencies and practitioners working with children and young people with the aim of delivering coordinated support and services, and is underpinned by common principles and values, and a set of core components governing work with children. The child is placed firmly at the centre of the work of each agency with the intention that children, young people and their families get the help they need when they need it (Scottish Government, 2008).

This chapter describes how the *GIRFEC* approach has been applied in early years' multi-agency practice and how the key role of a *named person* for each child is being introduced. It reflects the priorities for action of Scotland's *Early Years Framework* by strengthening universal services to improve early identification and intervention, and supporting parents when they need it with integrated services developed in line with *GIRFEC* principles (Scottish Government and COSLA, 2011). The chapter concludes with some of the messages about the benefits and challenges emerging from the development and early implementation of the new approach by the pathfinder project in one Scottish authority, Highland.

Scotland in the wider UK policy context

> The Government is committed to 'A Scotland in which every child matters, where every child regardless of their family background, has the best possible start in life'. (Scottish Executive, 2001: 7)

Over the last decade, the four nations of the UK have been committed to improving outcomes for all their children and young people. This commitment involves both promoting their well-being now as well as ensuring their well-becoming in the future (Ben-Arieh, 2001), with the intention that children can become 'successful learners, confident individuals, effective contributors and responsible citizens' (Scottish Government, 2008: 5). Such aspirations immediately raise issues about those children who are going to have difficulty in doing well. If all children are to be able to fulfil their full potential, it follows that the children who face particular adversities in their lives are likely to require additional support to overcome them (HM Government, 2004).

Increasingly, governments have acknowledged that, if there is to be any chance of narrowing the gap in outcomes between those who do well and those who do not, special attention has to be paid to children's early experiences and the impact of adverse circumstances on children's development and well-being at an early stage. Evidence is now compelling that children's early experiences have a significant effect on how well they do as they make the transition from childhood through adolescence and into adulthood (Scottish Government and COSLA, 2008; Marmot, 2010). As the review, *Fair Society, Healthy Lives* says (Marmot, 2010: 16):

> Giving every child the best start in life is crucial to reducing health inequalities across the life course. The foundations for virtually every aspect of human development – physical, intellectual and emotional – are laid in early childhood.

However, Marmot argues that:

> Focusing solely on the most disadvantaged will not reduce health inequalities sufficiently. To reduce the steepness of the social gradient in health, actions must be universal, but with a scale and intensity that is proportionate to the level of disadvantage. We call this proportionate universalism. (Marmot, 2010: 9)

The implication is clearly that to give all children the best possible start in life requires a range of universal policies and services provided within a coherent framework within which additional support can be planned and delivered for those children and their families who are likely to have difficulty in doing well. In Scotland, the need for effective multi-agency services to be in place from pre-birth which deliver a unified and coordinated approach to prevention, early identification of concerns and structured interventions is a priority of the national early years' policy framework (Scottish Government and COSLA, 2008).

The big challenge is translating such policy aspirations into practical and positive action by practitioners and their managers across all the agencies which are likely to have contact with families who have very young children. For families with children, from pre-birth onwards, there will be a plethora of potential professionals involved, from midwives, obstetricians, general practitioners and health visitors to staff of playgroups, nurseries and other early years services. If the family is also experiencing problems of health, disability, unemployment, housing, poverty, domestic violence and/or substance misuse, the number of professionals with different agency responsibilities can then multiply.

The difficulties of achieving effective collaboration where more than one agency is involved in working with a family have been well documented (see, for example, Gardner, 2003; Allnock et al., 2006; Rose, 2011). Families' experience in this respect varies – some report receiving excellent, well coordinated help, while others experience services as fragmented and unpredictable, undergoing multiple assessments according to each agency's protocols, telling their stories many times over, and feeling alienated and excluded from developing and managing a plan of services to help them (as reported, for example, in Department of Health, 2001; Scottish Executive, 2001; Rose, 2011). Working in silos, failure to communicate and share information appropriately, absence of well planned, resourced and coordinated services, and uncertainty about individual agencies' roles and tasks have all featured as criticisms of multi-agency collaboration in child inquiry reports, case reviews and inspections (Rose and Barnes, 2008).

Recent government policies have sought to address some of these persistent and enduring problems. In England under the New Labour government, a 'Duty to Co-operate' was incorporated into legislation, in the Children Act 2004, which requires local action to improve information sharing and to address some of the systemic and cultural barriers to effective working together between agencies. A number of projects have also been tried to support local cooperation. One example was the short-lived development in England of *ContactPoint* (first known as the *Information Sharing Index)* which would have been an online directory available to authorised staff to find out who else was working with the same child and to be able to share information (HM Government, 2010: 44) – a change of government resulted in its demise.

Another example is the Common Assessment Framework (CAF), developed as a national consent-based tool to enable early and effective assessment of children who need additional services or support from more than one agency, recording 'in a single place and in a structured and consistent way, every aspect of a child's life, family and environment' (HM Government, 2010: 44).

Scotland has diverged from its neighbouring countries with its approach of *Getting it Right for Every Child* that requires whole system change at the level of culture, systems and practice. The approach starts in the universal services of health and education, these being the core services with which almost all children and families are likely to have a significant level of contact from pre-birth onwards. The universal services provide important opportunities for early identification of difficulties and for early intervention. As a consequence, there is strong commitment by the government to using the strength of universal services to deliver prevention and early intervention:

> Too much of recent investment has gone into small scale projects bolted on to universal services rather than building the capacity of the core services that children and families come into contact with on a regular basis. This has to change. (Scottish Government and COSLA, 2008: 17)

Furthermore, although its aim is transformational change, the approach builds on existing organisational structures in the firm view that the emphasis on continued restructuring is misplaced and can impede improvements in service delivery being achieved, as concluded by Baginsky (2008) and other commentators.

Influences on the development of *Getting it Right for Every Child*

Achieving better integrated children's services

The foundation for *GIRFEC* was laid down in a key policy report, *For Scotland's Children* (Scottish Executive, 2001). This report reviewed the journey of a million children in Scotland from birth to adulthood and noted the uneven journey for many, especially those who began in poverty and deprivation. The report set out the policy framework to give every child in Scotland the best possible start in life and identified what had to change to improve services. It emphasised the importance of achieving integrated working between services and introduced the idea that every child should have a *named individual* in the universal services of health or education. This individual would be the main point of information/reference for the child and family and would coordinate arrangements for considering whether other, more specialist services might be required (Scottish Executive, 2001: 90).

It's everyone's job to keep children safe

At the same time, there was political and professional concern, as elsewhere in the UK, about how well children were being protected from harm. Following an inquiry into the death of a 3-year-old child in 2000 (Kennedy McFarlane), an audit and review of child protection in Scotland was undertaken, '*It's Everyone's Job to Make Sure I'm Alright*' (Scottish Executive, 2002). The review identified areas of good practice but also highlighted weaknesses in the child protection system (Vincent and Morgan-Klein, 2008). It revealed that agencies such as education and health, which had the most contact with children, often failed to see child protection as their responsibility, despite the growing emphasis since the 1970s on the importance of inter-agency working. Rather, they viewed it as an activity undertaken by social workers and the police. As Vincent and Morgan-Klein (2008: 56) explain:

> When health and education agencies referred to another agency they often felt they had also referred on responsibility for the child's well-being. A consequence of this was that many children were in need because they were not receiving the services they needed from health and education.

These concerns were not peculiar to Scotland but were being noted elsewhere in the UK. Lord Laming in his report on progress in child protection in England in 2009 believed it was important to reinforce the point that:

> Colleagues in education, early years, health and police are vital partners in protecting children and they need to be willing and proactive in discharging their statutory duty to cooperate on child safeguarding. (Laming, 2009: 36)

The review in Scotland argued strongly that everyone was responsible and accountable for children's safety and stressed the importance of relevant information being shared between agencies. As a result, it recommended that all providers of universal services first asked 'what can I or my agency do to help this child?' before considering whether they needed any information or help from other agencies to protect the child (Vincent and Morgan-Klein, 2008: 56). Once they had done this, they should consider whether the information they had should be shared with the social work department or the police (Scottish Executive, 2002). The intentions behind the recommendation were not about reducing unnecessary referrals to social work services but about ensuring proactive and appropriate involvement by universal services, and working together with other targeted or specialist services as needed. The recommendations of this review were reinforced in *Protecting Children: Framework for Standards* (Scottish Executive, 2004) and were another important building block in the development of the *GIRFEC* approach.

Indicators of children's well-being

Across the UK at this time, with the emphasis on improving outcomes, increasing interest was being shown by governments in finding a language to express their policy aspirations for all children which would mark a departure from past practices of framing policy in terms of 'child care' and 'child welfare' (Rose and Rowlands, 2010: 67). The concept of well-being had been in use by children's campaigners, academics and others for decades but new governments at the turn of the century adopted it as a unifying idea for their more broadly based policies. Scotland translated the concept of well-being into a set of *Well-being Indicators* which could be used in several different ways: in practice to understand more specifically what was happening in the lives of individual children and to plan what needed to change, to provide coherence in local service planning and to permit aggregation in order to assess more generally how well children in the population were doing (Rose and Rowlands, 2010: 85).

Eight well-being indicators were identified as the basic requirements for all children and young people to grow and develop and reach their full potential: they were that children should be 'safe, healthy, active, nurtured, achieving, respected, responsible and included' (Scottish Government, 2008: 12). As Aldgate points out, the indicators have much in common with UNICEF's broad definition of well-being (Aldgate, 2010: 34):

> The true measure of a nation's standing is how well it attends to its children – their health and safety, their material security, their education and socialization, and their sense of being loved, valued, and included in the families and societies into which they are born. (UNICEF, 2007: 4)

The well-being indicators are at the heart of the *GIRFEC* practice model and provide a common language for agencies, families and practitioners to discuss and record a child's strengths and areas of difficulty, and to plan and review the effect of support and services on that child's progress.

The core components of *GIRFEC*

A set of 10 core components are provided as a benchmark to help practitioners apply the *GIRFEC* approach in their areas of work. These are drawn from the strong evidence base of theory, knowledge and research which has informed the overall development of the approach (Scottish Government, 2008: 14):

1 a focus on improving outcomes for children, young people and their families based on a shared understanding of well-being
2 a common approach to gaining consent and to sharing information where appropriate
3 an integral role for children, young people and families, in assessment, planning and intervention
4 a coordinated and unified approach to identifying concerns, assessing needs, agreeing actions and outcomes, based on the Well-being Indicators
5 streamlined planning, assessment and decision-making processes that lead to the right help at the right time
6 consistent high standards of cooperation, joint working and communication where more than one agency needs to be involved, locally and across Scotland
7 a lead professional to coordinate and monitor multi-agency activity where necessary
8 maximising the skilled workforce within universal services to address needs and risks at the earliest possible time
9 a confident and competent workforce across all services for children, young people and their families
10 the capacity to share demographic, assessment and planning information electronically within and across agency boundaries through the national eCare programme where appropriate.[1]

GIRFEC values and principles

The *GIRFEC* framework itself is underpinned by common values and principles which apply across all aspects of working with children and families. They reflect legislation, standards, procedures and professional expertise, and provide a common platform for promoting the well-being of children and young people (Scottish Government, 2008: 15–17):

- Promoting the well-being of individual children and young people
- Keeping children and young people safe
- Putting the child at the centre
- Taking a whole child approach
- Building on strengths and promoting resilience
- Promoting opportunities and valuing diversity
- Providing additional help that is appropriate, proportionate and timely
- Supporting informed choice
- Working in partnership with families
- Respecting confidentiality and sharing information
- Promoting the same values across all working relationships

- Making the most of bringing together each worker's expertise
- Coordinating help
- Building a competent workforce to promote children and young people's well-being.

As part of progressing the *Early Years Framework*, the values and principles are being used to form the basis of a common values statement for the early years workforce, to be launched alongside a common core of skills, currently in development (Scottish Government and COSLA, 2011: 12).

Stradling and colleagues observe (2009: 6) that the core components and the values and principles combine the aspirational aims and objectives of *GIRFEC* with statements about the mechanisms for delivering *GIRFEC*, including the critical importance of a skilled workforce within universal services, the new role of *lead professional* and streamlined planning processes.

The *GIRFEC* approach in practice

A third and important piece of the jigsaw puzzle which makes up the *GIRFEC* approach is the national practice model which was developed for use by all practitioners, either on a single agency or multi-agency basis, to assess, plan, take action and review a child's progress (Scottish Government, 2008). The practice model (Figure 11.1) has three main components. First, it is based around the eight areas of well-being, described earlier in the chapter. As Aldgate underlines, the *Well-being Indicators* can be used for several purposes at different stages of work with families: they can act as an *aide-memoire* in identifying concerns, help to formulate a child's plan and be used to measure outcomes at the end of the period of treatment or intervention (Aldgate, 2010: 36). Second, if further information is needed to understand what is happening to a child, there is an ecological assessment tool, the *My World Triangle*, providing a mental map to help practitioners and families explore a child's world and gather information about a child's experiences, looking at the strengths and pressures, and the needs and risks in their lives. A third tool, the *Resilience Matrix* (adapted from the work of Daniel and Wassell, 2002) can be used to make sense of large amounts of information that may have been gathered. Information can be grouped around the four headings of *resilience*, *vulnerability*, *protective environment* and *adversity* 'so that the balance of strengths and needs can be judged' (Scottish Government, 2008: 29).

The practice model promotes the participation of children, young people and their families in gathering information and making decisions, as well as ensuring that information about children and young people is gathered and recorded in a consistent way by all agencies. In this way, a greater level of shared understanding between all those involved can be achieved right from the beginning, even in the most difficult and complex circumstances.

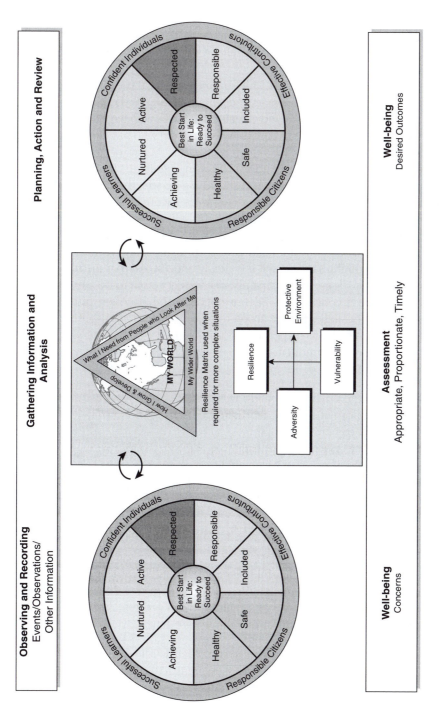

Figure 11.1   The National Practice Model

Source: Scottish Government (2010a: 49) published by kind permission of the Scottish Government

The *named person* in early years services

A significant feature of *GIRFEC* has been recognition that at various times in their lives many children and their families would benefit from some extra help and that this would be best provided by universal services within their neighbourhoods and communities (Scottish Government, 2010b). Children and families, therefore, need to know where to turn as their first point of contact and who they can talk to about any worries or problems affecting them. Similarly, individuals or agencies who have concerns about a child's well-being need to be able to contact a professional who has knowledge of the family and will either take action or help them take action. As part of the development of the *GIRFEC* approach in the pathfinder project in Highland, the concept of the *named person* was introduced for each child and young person, thereby implementing the earlier recommendation in *For Scotland's Children* (Scottish Executive, 2001).

The *named person* is always a practitioner in the statutory services. During pregnancy and the early period following the birth, a child's *named person* is the midwife and then the health visitor until the child goes to primary school where the role is assigned to a member of the school staff. It is clearly understood that the role is about good practice – in most cases, the *named person* does not have to do any more than usual. However, when a concern has been brought to the attention of the *named person*, it is *their* responsibility to take action to provide help or arrange for the right help to be provided. In order to respond proportionately, the *named person* asks the same five questions any practitioner should ask when faced with a concern about a child (Scottish Government, 2010b: 2):

- What is getting in the way of this child's well-being?
- Do I have all the information I need to help the child?
- What can I do now to help this child?
- What can my agency do to help this child?
- What additional help, if any, may be needed from others?

Should there be concerns that a child may not be safe, then it is expected that the *named person* or other practitioners involved will need to consider four further critical questions (Scottish Government, 2010b: 4):

- Why do I think this child is not safe?
- What is getting in the way of this child being safe?
- What have I observed, heard or identified from the child's history that causes concern?
- Are there factors that indicate risk of significant harm present, and, in my view, is the severity of factors enough to warrant immediate action?

At this point, if the child is considered to be at risk of harm, relevant information *must* be shared between agencies to enable an assessment to be undertaken to decide whether actions are required to protect the child, in accordance with local child protection procedures. These actions may result in a single agency or multi-agency plan, according to the needs of the child.

Where the *GIRFEC* plan is multi-agency, a *lead professional* is agreed as the first point of contact with the child and family and to coordinate the actions set out in the *Child's Plan*. They also liaise regularly with all the partners to the plan (Scottish Government and COSLA, 2011: 25). The *named person* may take on this role so long as it is compatible with their core responsibilities and area of expertise. However, if the *named person* is not the *lead professional*, they will still 'continue to have an important role for the child and family working within their core role, and will work with the *lead professional* to help bring about improved outcomes in the child's well-being' (Scottish Government, 2010b: 7).

The case study below about Ben illustrates how, in practice, a health visitor as the *named person* can play a critical role in identifying potentially serious and complex difficulties, and, working with the family, draw in a range of specialist professionals within a multi-agency plan to help the child and family.

📁 Case study: Ben

When Ben was aged 3, he was taken to Accident and Emergency because he had fallen through a glass door. Two weeks later, he was back. This time he had inserted something up his nose and his parent couldn't remove it. The health visitor made a follow-up visit. It was apparent that Ben's mum, who had three other children to care for, was struggling to manage him. Ben was noticeably overweight for his age, he was still in nappies and not toilet trained, his sleep patterns were erratic, he was prone to mood swings, he had speech difficulties and he seemed to have no sense of danger. He was always getting minor bumps and scrapes and didn't seem to recognise the potential dangers in everyday places around the home and outside. He needed to be constantly watched. The health visitor decided that a multi-agency referral was necessary and referred Ben to the community paediatrician, the speech and language therapist, the dietician and the community occupational therapist.

A child's plan was drawn up by the health visitor, the community paediatrician, the dietician, the learning disabilities nurse, the speech and language therapist, an educational psychologist, an early years worker, a nursery worker and the mother. Ben had significant problems including global developmental delay (i.e. in all developmental areas); he was also diagnosed with ADHD and had sensory problems.

A package of support was put in place including attendance at the child development centre, overnight respite and access to the Webster-Stratton programme for the parents, one-to-one-nursery support and extended nursery hours, speech and language therapy and occupational therapy and a diet that included fish oils and which was dairy-free.

(Continued)

(Continued)

Intermediate outcomes

Whilst recognising that this multi-agency package will need to be in place for some years and adjusted as Ben grows, there has already been a significant shift in his behaviour and mood swings since he went on the new diet.

Source: Stradling et al., 2009: 119, published by kind permission of the Scottish Government

Final thoughts

Messages from implementation:

> Every child and young person in Scotland is on a journey through life ... As they progress, some may have temporary difficulties, some may live with challenges that distract them on their journey and some may experience more complex issues. No matter where they live or whatever their needs, children and families should know where they can find help, what support might be available and whether that help is right for them. (Scottish Government, 2008: 5)

An evaluation of implementation in Highland of *GIRFEC* by Stradling et al. (2009) shows transformational change has taken place in the first year of implementation (Aldgate, 2010: 37). Even in a relatively short time, green shoots of change are being identified. There are, for example, fewer children on the child protection register, fewer inappropriate referrals to the children's hearings, and evidence of more stream-lined processes with fewer meetings taking place. Significantly, there is an increase in plans for individual children in the community, which Aldgate sees as suggesting 'early intervention is beginning to have an effect and that help is more targeted' (Aldgate, 2010: 38).

There is positive support for the new way of working from practitioners across all agencies and evidence of change following the introduction of *named persons*. Children's needs are being identified at an earlier stage, and children are being sup-ported within the universal services for longer while receiving targeted help for shorter periods of time. There is evidence that the *named person* is playing a key role in sup-porting the transition from single- to multi-agency help. Similarly, the working relation-ship between the *named person* and the *lead professional* is proving critically important to the effective assessment and planning of multi-agency support. As dis-cussed earlier in the chapter, effective multi-agency work is notoriously difficult to achieve but the findings of the evaluation suggest 'the key factors here appear to be continuity, trust and mutual respect for each other's areas of expertise and contribution' (Scottish Government, 2010b: 10). Even more importantly, children and families are able to identify positive differences and report that they feel more equal and included.

In reporting on Scotland's *Early Years Framework: Progress So Far* (Scottish Government and COSLA, 2011), there is clear affirmation of the commitment by the government and local authorities to the importance *GIRFEC*'s contribution can make to the delivery of improvements in early years services:

- *GIRFEC* delivers a stronger and co-ordinated teamwork approach for children, especially for those with complex needs, and identifies and involves all agencies who can meet the assessed need. (2011: 22)
- The common values required by the Early Years Framework are enshrined within the *GIRFEC* values and principles. These values and principles are currently being embedded across Scotland, particularly in the *GIRFEC* pathfinder areas where the values have influenced areas such as multi-agency training and service cultures. (2011: 12)
- The *GIRFEC* approach facilitates and supports local reviews of partnership arrangements, including private and third sector partners, intended to lead to improved outcomes for all children and young people. (2011: 17)
- In meeting the priority of simplifying and streamlining delivery, the *GIRFEC* approach makes clear the need for a lead professional to co-ordinate the services and support for individual children. (2011: 30)

GIRFEC is not statutory but it is a key part of the Scottish Government's policy for children, described by the Minister for Children and Early Years in 2010 as 'the golden thread that knits together our policy objectives for children and young people' (Scottish Government, 2010a: 3). The Scottish Government is actively engaged in supporting and promoting *GIRFEC* implementation, so, although it does not apply to the whole of Scotland yet, local authorities are certainly all well on the way to implementing it, and NHS Chief Executives have all appointed *GIRFEC* change managers. As implementation progresses, it will be interesting to see if an approach which ambitiously sets out to change culture, systems and practice for all children can contribute to the desired improvements in Scotland in the well-being of children in their early years.

▢ Summary

- In this chapter, I have described an ambitious programme of transformational change taking place in Scotland, *Getting it Right for Every Child*, and the way this new approach to multi-agency practice for all children is being implemented as part of Scotland's early years policy.
- Key differences to policy in England have been identified.
- The core objectives for *GIRFEC* include improving child protection, taking a broader view of children's well-being and achieving better integrated children's

(Continued)

(Continued)

services. These have been incorporated into the *GIRFEC* Values and Principles, Core Components, the National Practice Model and the introduction of key roles, the *Named Person* and the *Lead Professional*.

- Early findings from evaluating *GIRFEC* in practice in the early years suggest that practitioners and children and their families perceive positive benefits in the new approach, with evidence of earlier identification of difficulties and more appropriate and inclusive intervention.

 Questions for discussion

1 In what ways does the GIRFEC approach differ from the system for supporting families in your own experience/location?
2 GIRFEC is described as requiring changes in systems and culture. What does this mean to you and why do you think that it might be necessary?
3 Take the five questions that the named person must ask themselves and apply them to a child in your care/setting about whom you might have some concerns. To what extent are these questions helpful in clarifying the concerns and helping to identify possible action?
4 What critique can you offer of the GIRFEC approach and what do you consider would be the main problems and issues in trying to implement such a systems change? *(Higher-level question)*

Further reading

Levels 5 and 6

Aldgate, J. (2008) *Why Getting it Right for Every Child Makes Sense in Promoting the Well-being of all Children in Scotland*. Edinburgh: Scottish Government. Available from www.scotland. gov.uk/gettingitright
This report provides further explanation, rationale and justification of the GIRFEC approach in Scotland.

Frost, N. and Parton, N. (2009) *Understanding Children's Social Care: Politics, Policy and Practice*. London: Sage.
Chapter 4 of this book, 'Safeguarding, child protection and children in need', gives a clear description and analysis of the children's safeguarding system in England and of the policy transition from a narrow definition of child protection to the broader concept of safeguarding.

Levels 6 and 7

Aubrey, C. (2010) Leading and working in multi-agency teams. In: G. Pugh and B. Duffy (eds) *Contemporary Issues in the Early Years*, 5th edition. London: Sage.
In Chapter 15 of this book, Carol Aubrey critiques the concept of partnership working in multi-agency contexts.

Munro, E. (2011) *The Munro Review of Child Protection: Final Report – A Child-centred System*. CM062. London: HMSO. Available at: www.education.gov.uk/publications
This report is based on a major review of the child protection system in England with criticisms and recommendations for future changes. Here, you will also find links to the interim report and extensive evidence review.

Websites

www.scotland.gov.uk/publications
This website contains Scottish Government policy documents relevant to this chapter.

www.scotland.gov.uk/gettingitright
This is the website for *Getting it Right for Every Child* related publications.

Note

1   eCare is the name given to the Scottish Government's multi-agency information sharing framework which covers, amongst other aspects, consent, standards, security, procurement, organisational development and technical issues relating to the electronic sharing of personal data (see www.scotland.gov.uk/DataSharingAndeCare).

References

Aldgate, J. (2008) *Why Getting it Right for Every Child Makes Sense in Promoting the Well-being of all Children in Scotland*. Edinburgh: Scottish Government. Available at: www.scotland.gov.uk/gettingitright

Aldgate, J. (2010) Child well-being, child development and family life. In: C. McAuley and W. Rose (eds) *Child Well-Being: Understanding Children's Lives*. London: Jessica Kingsley.

Allnock, D., Akhurst, S., Tunstill, J. and NESS Research Team (2006) Constructing and sustaining Sure Start Local Programme partnerships: lessons for future inter-agency collaboration. *Journal of Children's Services*, 1(3): 29–39.

Baginsky, M. (ed.) (2008) *Safeguarding Children and Schools*. London: Jessica Kingsley.

Ben-Arieh, A. (2001) Evaluating the outcomes of programs versus monitoring well-being. In: T. Vecchiato, A.N. Maluccio and C. Canali (eds) *Evaluation in Child and Family Services*. New York: Aldine de Gruyter.

Daniel, B. and Wassell, S. (2002) *Assessing and Promoting Resilience in Vulnerable Children,* vols 1, 2 and 3. London: Jessica Kingsley.

Department of Health (DoH) (2001) *The Children Act Now: Messages from Research*. London: The Stationery Office.

Gardner, R. (2003) Working together to improve children's life chances: the challenge of inter-agency collaboration. In: J. Winstein, C. Whittington and T. Leiba (eds) *Collaboration in Social Work Practice.* London: Jessica Kingsley.

HM Government (2004) *Every Child Matters: Change for Children.* London: Department for Education and Skills.

HM Government (2010) *Working Together to Safeguard Children: A Guide to Inter-agency Working to Safeguard and Promote the Welfare of Children.* London: Department for Children, Schools and Families.

Laming, Lord (2009) *The Protection of Children in England: A Progress Report.* London: The Stationery Office.

Marmot, M. (2010) *Fair Society, Healthy Lives. The Marmot Review: Executive Summary.* London: The Marmot Review.

Rose, W. (2011) Effective multi-agency work in children's services. In: J.P. Seden, S. Matthews, M. McCormick and A. Morgan (eds) *Professional Development in Social Work: Complex Issues in Practice.* London: Routledge.

Rose, W. and Barnes, J. (2008) *Improving Safeguarding Practice: Study of Serious Case Reviews 2001–2003.* London: Department for Children, Schools and Families.

Rose, W. and Rowlands, J. (2010) Introducing the concept of child well-being into government policy. In: C. McAuley and W. Rose (eds) *Child Well-Being: Understanding Children's Lives.* London: Jessica Kingsley.

Scottish Executive (2001) *For Scotland's Children: Better Integrated Children's Services.* Edinburgh: Scottish Executive.

Scottish Executive (2002) *'It's Everyone's Job to Make Sure I'm Alright': Report of the Child Protection Audit and Review.* Edinburgh: Scottish Executive.

Scottish Executive (2004) *Protecting Children: Framework for Standards.* Edinburgh: Scottish Executive.

Scottish Government (2008) *A Guide to Getting it Right for Every Child.* Edinburgh: Scottish Government.

Scottish Government (2010a) *A Guide to Implementing Getting it Right for Every Child: Messages from Pathfinders and Learning Partners.* Edinburgh: Scottish Government.

Scottish Government (2010b) *Practice Briefing 1: The Role of the Named Person.* Available at: www.scotland.gov.uk/gettingright/publications/practicebriefings

Scottish Government and COSLA (2008) *The Early Years Framework: A Joint Scottish Government and COSLA Policy Statement.* Edinburgh: Scottish Government.

Scottish Government and COSLA (2011) *Early Years Framework: Progress So Far.* Edinburgh: Scottish Government.

Stradling, B., MacNeil, M. and Berry, H. (2009) *Changing Professional Practice and Culture to Get it Right for Every Child: An Evaluation of the Development and Early Implementation Phases of Getting it Right for Every Child in Highland: 2006–2009.* Edinburgh: Scottish Government.

UNICEF (2007) *Child Poverty in Perspective: An Overview of Child Well-Being in Rich Countries. Innocenti Report Card 7.* Florence: UNICEF.

Vincent, S. and Morgan-Klein, N. (2008) From 2000: a period of significant reform. In: A. Stafford and S. Vincent (eds) *Safeguarding and Protecting Children and Young People.* Edinburgh: Dunedin Academic Press.

CHAPTER 12

RECONCEPTUALISING POLICY MAKING IN THE EARLY YEARS

Denise Hevey and Linda Miller

Overview

In the final chapter of this book, we draw together and discuss some of the key themes and critical issues emerging from the preceding chapters and reflect on the implications for policy making and implementation. In doing so, we consider how policy making in the early years might be reconceptualised.

Living with constant change

'Liquid life' is a kind of life that tends to be lived in a liquid modern society. 'Liquid modern' is a society in which the conditions under which its members act change faster than it takes the ways of acting to consolidate into habits and routines. (Bauman, 2007: 1)

Many practitioners will find that this quote resonates with their experience of the current pace of policy innovation and change made even more pronounced by a change of government in the UK in 2010. It could be argued that the children's policy agenda is too important to leave to the whims of politicians and that a core programme or policy framework for the long term should be drawn up and agreed on a cross-party basis. However, this would be difficult to achieve given the contentious nature of policy making and the continuing backdrop of fast-paced social and technological change. As Lesley Staggs notes in Chapter 10, policy makers' and politicians' appetite for taking a long-term view was never strong enough, as their concerns lay with quick impact and their next election prospects.

Evidence-based policy revisited

In a number of chapters in this book (see, for example, Chapters 2, 3 and 5), the trend towards evidence-based policy (i.e. using evidence from research and evaluation to help formulate policies and select appropriate interventions) is documented – a position we supported in Chapter 1. As we discussed, this approach has been restated and reinforced by the commissioning of a number of government-sponsored reviews relating to the areas of health (Marmot, 2010); poverty and life chances (Field, 2010); early intervention (Allen, 2011); the Early Years Foundation Stage curriculum framework (Tickell, 2011) and most recently child protection (Munro, 2011). These reviews have all sought to evaluate the evidence from research as a basis for shaping future policy; however, there are a number of caveats that need to be applied.

First, when evaluating evidence, primacy has normally been given to research in the scientific/positivist tradition, which values randomised controlled trials as the 'gold standard' and gives much less weighting to evidence from other forms of evaluation research (see, for example, evaluation methodology adopted in Field, 2010 and Allen, 2011). While well established in relation to medical treatments, the relevance of scientific method to the complexities and subtleties of social and educational research is more questionable. In addition, most of these sorts of studies have been carried out in the USA rather than in the UK, and cross-cultural translation cannot be assumed since social and educational practices are culturally embedded.

In contrast, Professor Chris Pascal has made an eloquent case for in-depth, authentic, qualitative, practitioner-based research (Pascal, 2011). She reinforces the view that practice should be 'evidenced' but that large-scale, tightly controlled but superficial studies are not necessarily the best way of doing this. History is littered with attempts to uproot and transplant apparently effective innovations into different ecological contexts while missing the key factors – the subtlety of effective practice, the complexity of context and the drive of an original 'charismatic innovator', such as Malaguzzi's visionary work in the nurseries of Reggio Emilia (Malaguzzi, 1996).

Second, the move from evidence base to policy implications requires an effort of interpretation as well as a political and moral decision making (Frost, 2011).

Thirdly, unfettered evidence-based policy suffers from what Moss, in Chapter 7, has described as 'a democratic deficit'. It involves attempting to reduce essentially political and moral decisions to technical ones based on 'what works'. It ignores the central importance of developing a shared vision, purpose and mode of operation for services through democratic participation at all levels from early years settings to government.

Reconceptualising early years policy

The evidence for early intervention and investment in high quality services for young children and their families is consistent and irrefutable as we see from a number of chapters in this book. This is well illustrated by the government reviews referred to earlier in this chapter and from longitudinal studies. These include the impact of different pre-school experiences on children's development (e.g. Sylva et al., 2010); economists' assessments of the costs and benefits of family support and interventions (e.g. Waldfogel, 2006) and European reviews of messages from research for policy makers (Penn, 2009). However, bearing in mind the caveats discussed above about evidence-based policy making, it is clear that the evidence does not speak for itself – there are always alternative interpretations, as well as a range of possible solutions.

In addition, for evidence to inform policy making, the political will must be present and the issue seen as sufficiently high amongst competing priorities; otherwise evidence can be ignored or down-played. Stuart Shanker and Roger Downer in Chapter 5 recognise the importance of timing and of a receptive ear in the government of Ontario, in order for the evidence from the EPIC project to be enacted in policy, leading to the roll-out of pre-schools based on EPIC principles.

In turn, policy pronouncements do not easily translate into universal, consistent implementation in practice. Ball (2006) introduced the notion of a 'policy to practice trajectory' through which policy formulation and implementation, he argued, could be subject to a variety of influences and obstacles. A key factor in this argument is that practitioners at local level are not simply rational technicians implementing policy and guidelines but reflective practitioners and thinking, feeling and moral beings.

Drawing on the chapters in this book, we propose four over-arching and enduring principles which we believe should underpin any current or future policy for early years. We hope these principles might support practitioners in their reflections on policy. We discuss each of these principles in turn below and the implications for policy making and implementation.

Principle 1: Child-centredness

Putting the child at the centre of all policies for young children and families begins with valuing children for who they are now, not who they will become and whether or not they will make a positive contribution to the economy. To use Qvortrup's

(2005) term, children should be treated as human beings not human becomings. Children have rights, and parents, carers and the state have responsibilities to support them through to adulthood.

In 1991, the UK became a signatory to the United Nations Convention on the Rights of the Child (UNICEF, 1989) including the rights to education, protection from harm, access to health, enough money to support good development, the right to rest, play and leisure, and for their voice to be heard in matters affecting them. Yet in 2008 the UK Children's Commissioners' commented on the lack of statutory protection for children's rights in Northern Ireland and the fact that:

> The UNCRC has not been fully brought into legislative and policy processes in England. (UK Children's Commissioners' Report to the UN Committee on the Rights of the Child, 2008: 5, cited in Jones and Walker, 2011: 19)

Valuing young children for who they are now implies providing services and opportunities that enhance their experience and enjoyment of this unique stage of childhood. This might lead to questioning, for example, education policies that emphasise school readiness as the primary purpose of pre-school education, as suggested by Lesley Staggs in Chapter 10.

Similarly child-centredness in family policy implies that services and support for parents are seen primarily as a means of supporting children rather than an end in themselves. One of the lessons learned from Sure Start (Chapter 2) and reinforced by the EPPE project (Sylva et al., 2010) was that the quality of the Home Learning Environment (HLE) is critical to young children developing their full potential. Outreach and parent support activities need to help parents improve the HLE, rather than just cope better with their own problems; though this may be a necessary first step. The evident success and popularity of parent education programmes, as Mary Crowley documents in Chapter 6, demonstrates that interest is not confined to the minority of parents who are labelled as having difficulty in coping. The majority of parents are positively motivated by the desire to help their children and can benefit from support and advice at appropriate points in the life cycle. Also, as discussed in Chapter 3, we know that what parents do with their children is more important than who they are.

Principle 2: Democracy

Democracy, interpreted in its widest sense, is based on a fundamental belief that all human beings – children as well as adults – have a right to participate in shaping their worlds. For Stuart Shanker and Roger Downer in Chapter 5, developing the educational potential of every child is linked overtly to their commitment to participatory democracy. Peter Moss, in Chapter 7, explored the wider meaning of participatory democracy at the level of day-to-day involvement of children and practitioners in making choices. In Chapter 9, Dawn Tankersley and colleagues describe the transformative power of professional development, based on child-centred and democratic principles, in empowering practitioners from previously oppressive regimes to develop curricula, practice and choice in ways that involve and impact on families and community 'to create a different society'.

Listening to children and representing the child's voice in the organisation and practice of institutions reflects the UNCRC (UNICEF, 1989) and is well established as good practice with school-aged children. More recently, the same principle has been extended to work with very young children through methods such as the Mosaic approach (Clarke, 2010) and through the practice of pedagogical documentation originating in the nurseries of Reggio Emilia (Malaguzzi, 1996), with their commitment to participatory democracy. This is a style of democracy that works from 'the bottom up' (see also Moss in Chapter 7).

There is, however, a need to exercise caution in relation to top-down policy making, in that it is easy for the language of democratic participation to be used by governments for their own ends:

> [P]articipatory efforts can remain tokenistic, or even manipulative ... Public engagement activities enhance the credibility of commissioning organisations without devolving decision-making power to users. (Simpson and Connor, 2011: 42)

Democratic participation alone may not guarantee that services are provided equitably, especially in relation to marginalised and disadvantaged groups. For example, the early evaluation of Sure Start Local Programmes (see Chapter 2) found that within the disadvantaged areas that were targeted, the better-off, more articulate families took most advantage of services, thus actively discouraging the participation of those most in need.

Principle 3: Equality and equity

Without sufficient income for essentials, children in poor families have an unequal start in life and suffer from reduced life chances in terms of their current and future health, development and well-being (Marmot, 2010). *Doing Better for Families* (OECD, 2011) states that, although considerable progress towards eradicating child poverty was made in the UK in the last decade, progress has now stalled. The Institute for Fiscal Studies (Joyce, 2011) argues that this is due to regressive taxation changes, introduced by the new coalition government in 2010 and 2011, having a particularly negative impact on families with children.

However, the message of the Field review (2010) suggests that further universal reductions in poverty would have marginal effects on children's well-being and that spending on universal services and benefits should be reassessed in favour of targeting more resources towards those most in need. The approach, discussed by Sue Owen, Caroline Sharp and Jenny Spratt in Chapter 3, clearly illustrates how individual local authorities can adapt and amend their services in order to meet the twin objectives of narrowing the gap in attainment between the least and most disadvantaged children (targeted) whilst continuing to promote improvement for all children (universal).

'Targeted universalism' is ideologically distinct from the previous Labour government's approach of 'progressive universalism', as discussed by Angela Underdown and Jane Barlow in relation to health priorities in Chapter 4. Whilst prioritising services to those most in need is presented as uncontestable in England, targeted universalism is far from a benign concept as it carries within it the seeds of progressive decommitment from universal services and a reduced requirement for multiagency cooperation. This is in sharp contrast to the policy approach in Scotland, described by Wendy Rose in Chapter 11, which emphasises the centrality of universal services to all children's well-being and safeguarding in its broadest sense. As services and support become increasingly targeted at those most in need, there is a danger of reverting to a blaming culture where the poor, workless and homeless are considered responsible for their plight. However, as Simpson and Connor (2011: 161) state:

> [Thus] consciousness remains partial if we focus our analysis on a personal/local level and fail to notice the ways in which these are social trends that are linked to structural injustices.

Having argued in favour of a strong base of universal services, a fair and equitable chance for every child does not mean treating all children the same, but necessitates responding to their individual needs. Some children and families need more help to access early years services alongside their peers. Other children and particularly those with disabilities, whether psychological or physical, may need intensive specialist support to benefit fully from the services they can access. This is clearly demonstrated by the case study in Chapter 5 of the child whose chronic hyper-arousal distorted his behaviour and made him appear almost un-teachable.

The government's policy of 'targeted universalism' is situated within a mixed economy of care and an ideological commitment to minimising the role of the state and maximising the use of the market. In Chapter 8, Eva Lloyd has garnered evidence to offer a damning critique of marketisation as a mechanism for ensuring equal access to high quality early years services. She concludes that a pure childcare market system moves away from the principle of equity and questions whether market solutions are the best way to provide equal access to early years services.

Respecting diversity and valuing the different ethnic and cultural heritages of children and families is an essential aspect of the principle of equality and equity that has been enshrined within curriculum and regulatory frameworks (DfES, 2007). Yet with the best intentions, policy seems to be inexorably moving towards 'normalisation', both in terms of expected developmental outcomes for all children (see Lesley Staggs' account in Chapter 10), and in terms of expectations of 'normal' family life.

> By normalizing we mean that a dominant 'way of being' emerges and governments want their citizens to aspire to these norms. (Frost, 2011: 49)

Our adoption of equity as a principle should lead to questioning policies that emphasise the primacy of English, Christian traditions as opposed to developing tolerance and mutual respect of different cultures and heritage. The principle of equality and equity should lead us to question every policy in terms of: Whose interest does this serve? Who does this benefit? And how can we support the most disadvantaged and those with additional needs?

Principle 4: Professionalism

The professionalisation of the early years workforce has been on an upward trajectory for at least the last decade, both nationally and internationally (see, for example, Miller and Cable, 2011) and professionalism is a principle which underpins all the chapters in this book. In particular, in Chapter 9, we see the transformative power of professional development.

All of the policy reviews referred to earlier in this chapter have made the connection between high quality services and a highly qualified workforce. For example, the Tickell review (2011: 42–3) states that:

> The evidence is clear on how a well-qualified and appropriately skilled early years workforce makes a real difference to the quality of provision and outcomes for young children and it calls on government to ... retain a focus on the need to upskill the workforce, to commit to promoting a minimum level 3 qualification and to maintain the ambitions for a graduate-led sector.

One criticism of workforce development policy in England has been around the monitoring and evaluation of practice through a highly regulated and externally imposed system and an exclusive focus on competencies (Cameron and Moss, 2007; Miller, 2008). It is therefore encouraging to see that the Tickell review (2011) proposes a move away from prescription and places greater emphasis on professional judgement, thus recognising the complex contexts in which early years practitioners work.

In our discussion below, we use the term professionalism to capture a range of meanings and implications at *individual, workplace* and *government policy* levels.

At an *individual level*, professionalism means a personal commitment to continuing professional development (CPD) and to upholding ethical principles and values and, where relevant, a professional code of conduct. It involves practitioners taking responsibility for their actions and the quality of their work – striving for excellence rather than just to be 'good enough'. The work of Dahlberg and Moss (2005) has been influential in reinstating ethics and emotional labour as key and valid concepts in the work of early years practitioners and central to developing democratic practices. Professionalism also implies interrogating policies and practices in relation to the principles held and in the context of dominant discourses.

At a *workplace/organisational level*, professionalism implies a commitment to high standards of training and CPD. It means valuing staff through appropriate remuneration and working conditions. It also requires, through shared dialogue, agreement about the principles, values and approaches that underpin the ethos of a setting or service, and careful consideration and evaluation of new policies and initiatives in the light of these.

At *government level*, developing professionalism in the early years needs to go beyond the rhetoric of valuing the high level of skills and knowledge essential for effective practice, and especially for leadership of practice. Whilst acknowledging the need for minimum standards within a diverse workforce, to ensure common expectations and entitlements for children and families, there is a need to understand that the complexity of early years services cannot be fully encapsulated in external frameworks, guidance and regulation, but requires space for the professional judgement and creativity of well-qualified practitioners (see Tickell, 2011).

Final thoughts

At the time of writing, the future of early years policy in England is uncertain. The coalition government has stated a commitment to early years as central to government strategy and the outcomes of five major reviews are now available. However, although the direction of travel in terms of 'targeted universalism' and a reduced role for the state has been announced, the extent to which evidence and recommendations from reviews will inform policy making is less clear. What *is* clear is the critical role that informed and reflective practitioners have in establishing the ethos of their settings through promoting professionalism and continuous improvement in practice and in evaluating and translating government policy initiatives into day-to-day practice with children and families. We hope that this book has contributed to an understanding of the nature and importance of early years policy and an ability to analyse, question and evaluate policies so that practitioners are empowered to decide the extent to which they can embrace, comply with or actively resist policy initiatives in their future practice.

Summary

In this chapter, we have argued that:

- the evidence in favour of early intervention and investment in high quality early years services is now irrefutable
- early years services in England have experienced unprecedented rates of change
- evidence-based policy making is not a simple translation from facts to policy but requires evaluation, interpretation and political and moral judgements
- policy can be influenced and amended at various points along the trajectory between formulation and implementation, including by reflective practitioners deciding whether and how to apply in practice

(Continued)

(Continued)

- early years practitioners can be powerful rather than powerless in the face of policy changes
- reconceptualising early years policy involves identifying the enduring principles on which policy should be based and evaluated. These include:
  - o Child-centredness
  - o Democracy
  - o Equality and Equity
  - o Professionalism.

Questions for discussion

1 How helpful do you find the term 'liquid life' in relation to your professional working life and the impact of recent and current policy changes?
2 In what ways are the four principles of child-centredness, democracy, equality and equity and professionalism reflected in your work setting or a setting that you are familiar with?
3 In reconceptualising early years policy, what would be your main priority area for change? *(Higher-level question)*

Further reading

Levels 5 and 6

Miller, L. and Cable C. (eds) (2011) *Professionalization, Leadership and Management in the Early Years*. London: Sage.
This is a collection of chapters which charts the growth of professionalisation in the early years and critiques some key issues such as professional identity and gender.

Paige-Smith, A. and Craft, A. (eds) (2011) *Developing Reflective Practice in the Early Years*, 2nd edition. Maidenhead: Open University Press/McGraw-Hill.
This book aims to support early years practitioners to explore ways in which they can reflect on their practice, and includes chapters on policy, safeguarding and multi-agency working.

Levels 6 and 7

Ball, S.J. (2006) *Education, Policy and Social Class: The Selected Work of Stephen J. Ball*. Abingdon: Routledge.
This book brings together an edited collection of chapters and articles spanning some 20 years by one of the foremost academic analysts of education policy. It includes sections on policy theory and research, policy technologies and analysis, and social class and education policy.

Maloney, M. (2010) Unreasonable expectations: the dilemma for pedagogues in delivering policy objectives. *European Early Childhood Education Research Journal*, 18(2): 181–99.
In this journal article, the author questions the feasibility of expecting early childhood practitioners (pedagogues) to deliver upon ambitious policy objectives when measured against what she considers to be inadequate training in, and staffing and management of, pre-school services in the Republic of Ireland.

Simpson, G. and Connor, S. (2011) *Social Policy for Social Welfare Professionals: Tools for Understanding, Analysis and Engagement*. Bristol: The Policy Press.
This is an introduction to policy analysis aimed at all those who work with children and families. The book starts with a brief history of social policy in the UK before introducing key economic and political theories that inform different perspectives in policy making, as well as discussing the role of social welfare professionals in analysing and working with policies.

Websites

www.education.gov.uk
The Department for Education website is a source of information for education and children's services in the UK.

www.marmotreview.org.uk
This website has up-to-date information on health inequalities across England, with the facility to identify results for specific regions/locations.

References

Allen, G. (2011) *Early Intervention: The Next Steps*. Available at: http://media.education.gov.uk/assets/files/pdf/g/graham%20allens%20review%20of%20early%20intervention.pdf (accessed 26 May 2011).
Ball, S.J. (2006) *Education, Policy and Social Class: The Selected Work of Stephen J. Ball*. Abingdon: Routledge.
Bauman, Z. (2007) *Liquid Life*. Cambridge: Polity Press.
Cameron, C. and Moss, P. (2007) *Care Work in Europe: Current Understandings and Future Directions*. Abingdon: Routledge.
Clarke, A. (2010) Listening to children. In L. Miller, C. Cable and G. Goodliff (eds) *Supporting Children's Learning in the Early Years*, 2nd edition. London: Routledge.
Dahlberg, G. and Moss, P. (2005) *Ethics and Politics in Early Childhood Education*. Abingdon: Routledge and Falmer.
Department for Education and Skills (DfES) (2007) *The Early Years Foundation Stage*. London: DfES.
Field, F. (2010) *The Foundation Years: Preventing Poor Children Becoming Poor Adults*. Available at: http://webarchive.nationalarchives.gov.uk/20110120090128/http://povertyreview.independent.gov.uk/news/101203-review-poverty-life-chances.aspx (accessed 30 May 2011).
Frost, N. (2011) *Rethinking Children and Families: The Relationship between Childhood, Families and the State*. London: Continuum International.
Jones, P. and Walker, G. (eds) (2011) *Children's Rights in Practice*. London: Sage.
Joyce, R. (2011) *Poverty Projections between 2010–11 and 2013–14: A Post-budget 2011 Update*. London: Institute for Fiscal Studies. Available at: www.ifs.org.uk/publications
Malaguzzi, L. (1996) *The Hundred Languages of Children*. Reggio Emilia, Italy: Reggio Children.

Marmot, M. (2010) *Fair Society, Healthy Lives. The Marmot Review: Strategic Review of Health Inequalities in England Post-2010*. Available at: www.marmotreview.org.uk

Miller, L. (2008) Developing professionalism within a regulatory framework in England: challenges and possibilities. *European Early Childhood Education Research Journal*, 16(2): 255–68.

Miller, L. and Cable, C. (eds) (2011) *Professionalization, Leadership and Management in the Early Years*. London: Sage.

Munro, E. (2011) *The Munro Review of Child Protection: Final Report – A Child-centred System*. CM062. London: HMSO. Available at: www.education.gov.uk/publications

Organisation for Economic Cooperation and Development (OECD) (2011) *Doing Better for Families*. Paris: OECD. Available at: www.oecd.org/document/49/0,3746,en_2649_34819_47654961_1_1_1_1,00.html (accessed 30 May 2011).

Pascal, C. (2011) Practitioner research: an intellectual and adventurous narrative at a tipping point. Key note address to the Inaugural Meeting of the British Early Childhood Research Association, 23–24 February.

Penn, H. (2009) *Early Childhood Education and Care: Key Lessons from Research for Policy Makers*. Brussels: NESSE/European Commission.

Qvortrup, J. (2005) *Studies in Modern Childhood*. London: Palgrave.

Simpson, G. and Connor, S. (2011) *Social Policy for Social Welfare Professionals: Tools for Understanding, Analysis and Engagement*. Bristol: The Policy Press.

Sylva, K., Melhuish, E., Sammons, P., Siraj-Blatchford, I. and Taggart, B. (2010) *Early Childhood Matters: Evidence from the Effective Pre-School and Primary Education Project*. London: Routledge.

Tickell, C. (2011) *The Early Years: Foundations for Life, Health and Learning. An Independent Report on the Early Years Foundation Stage for Her Majesty's Government*. Available at: http://media.education.gov.uk/MediaFiles/B/1/5/%7BB15EFF0D-A4DF-4294-93A1-1E1B88C13F68%7DTickell%20review.pdf (accessed 26 May 2011).

UNICEF (1989) *United Nations Convention on the Rights of the Child*. Available at: www.unicef.org.uk (accessed 30 May 2011).

Waldfogel, J. (2006) *What Children Need*. Cambridge, MA: Harvard University Press.

INDEX

PROFESSIONALIZATION, LEADERSHIP AND MANAGEMENT IN THE EARLY YEARS

Edited by **Linda Miller** and **Carrie Cable** *both at The Open University*

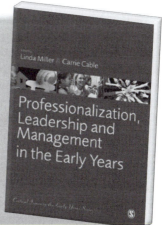

With the rapid change experienced by the Early Years Workforce over recent times, this book considers what constitutes professionalization in the sector, and what this means in practice. Bringing a critical perspective to the developing knowledge and understanding of early years practitioners at various stages of their professional development, it draws attention to key themes and issues.

Chapters are written by leading authorities, and provide case studies, question and discussion points to facilitate critical thinking.

Topics covered include:

- leading and managing in the early years
- reflective journeys
- constructions of professional identities
- men in the early years
- multi-disciplinary working in the early years
- professionalization in the nursery
- child care practitioners and professionalization
- early childhood leadership and policy

Written in an accessible style and relevant to all levels of early years courses, from Foundation Degree to Masters, the book is highly relevant to those studying for the National Professional Qualification in Integrated Centre Leadership (NPQICL) and working towards Early Years Professional Status (EYPS).

CRITICAL ISSUES IN THE EARLY YEARS

November 2010 • 192 pages
Cloth (978-1-84920-553-5) • £72.00
Paper (978-1-84920-554-2) • £23.99
Electronic (978-1-4462-4789-1) • £23.99

NEW FROM SAGE!

THEORIES AND APPROACHES TO LEARNING IN THE EARLY YEARS

Edited by **Linda Miller** *The Open University* and **Linda Pound** *Education Consultant*

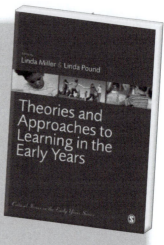

By focusing on key figures in early years education and care, this book considers the influential thinkers and ground-breaking approaches that have revolutionized practice. With contributions from leading authorities in the field, chapters provide an explanation of the approach, an analysis of the theoretical background, case studies, questions and discussion points to facilitate critical thinking.

Included are chapters on:

- Froebel
- Psychoanalytical theories
- Maria Montessori
- Steiner Waldorf education
- High/Scope
- Post-modern and post-structuralist perspectives
- Forest Schools
- Vivian Gussin Paley
- Te Whariki

Written in an accessible style and relevant to all levels of early years courses, the book has staggered levels of Further Reading that encourage reflection and promotes progression.

CRITICAL ISSUES IN THE EARLY YEARS

2010 • 192 pages
Cloth (978-1-84920-577-1) • £72.00
Paper (978-1-84920-578-8) • £23.99
Electronic (978-1-4462-1023-9) • £23.99